THE CITY-STATE

OF THE GREEKS AND ROMANS

THE CITY-STATE

OF THE

GREEKS AND ROMANS

BY

W. WARDE FOWLER, M.A.

FELLOW AND SUB-RECTOR OF LINCOLN COLLEGE, OXFORD

University Press of the Pacific
Honolulu, Hawaii

The City-State of the Greeks and Romans

by
W. Warde Fowler

ISBN: 1-4102-0416-2

Reprinted from the 1893 edition

University Press of the Pacific
Honolulu, Hawaii
http://www.unlversitypressofthepacific.com

S. T. IRWIN

*Hic multum valuit cum vetus amicitia, tum humanitas ejus
et liberalitas, et litteris et officiis perspecta nobis et cognita."*

CICERO. Ad Familiares. i. 9.

PREFACE

THE object of this book is, I hope, sufficiently explained in the introductory chapter. It may, however, be as well to add here that it is an expansion of a short series of lectures given for several successive years to men just beginning the study of ancient history in the school of *Literæ Humaniores* at Oxford. Few of these men were likely to become *specialists*, and as the object of my course was therefore purely educational, I saw an opportunity of stimulating their interest, and of widening their historical horizon, by treating the subject as a whole, instead of plunging at once into the examination of a particular period or author. It occurred to me that I might construct in outline a biography, as it were, of that form of State in which both Greeks and Romans lived and made their most valuable contributions to our modern civilisation, tracing it from its birth in prehistoric times to its dissolution under the Roman Empire.

Such a biography had indeed already been written, and by a man of genius, the late Fustel de Coulanges ; but *La Cité Antique*, brilliant as it is, is a book of one idea, and did not exactly answer the purpose I proposed to myself. I wished simply to sketch the history of the City-State, without reference to any particular view of the origin of its institutions.

In writing out these lectures from the notes I used I have expanded them considerably, especially the last two. They will probably, however, betray their origin as lectures, but I hope they may not be found less readable on that account. In adding notes and references it has been my aim to acquaint the beginner with the names of a few books of the best repute, both English and foreign, as well as with the most important original authorities for the events touched upon. It will probably be found that there are more citations of the *Politics* of Aristotle than of any one other work ; for it was one of my chief objects to connect the history of the City-State as closely as possible with the reasonings of its best philosophical exponent. In order to make sure that every reader, whether he understands Greek or not, shall be able to find the passage to which I am referring without any real difficulty, I have quoted the *Politics* by the paging of the Berlin edition, which will be found on the margin in all important editions of later date, and also in Professor Jowett's translation. Only in quoting the first three books, which in all editions stand in the same order, I have given the number of the book as well as the page. In no case have I given the number of any particular line in the page quoted, for my references are in almost all cases to chapters rather than to sentences, and indeed, if a passage be sought out at all, it is far better that it should be read and weighed in connection with its whole context.

I have to thank several friends for much valuable help in the revision of the proofs. To my colleague, Mr. J. A. R. Munro, I am greatly indebted for the correction of several serious errors, and for many other useful suggestions in the chapters dealing with Athenian history. Professor Gardner has given me most valuable help in the tenth chapter, and Mr. Peters of University College and Mr. Matheson of New College have been kind enough to read other parts of the proofs, and have enabled me to correct many minor shortcomings. In spite of all this friendly aid, however, the book is by no means what I could have wished it to be, and no one is more fully aware of its defects than its author. There is absolutely nothing new in it, and its only justification is that it is an attempt to supply a defect in our educational literature. As an introduction to Greek and Roman history it may, I hope, be of some use; but it can only be so if it is used as an introduction, and not as a means of saving time and trouble in more elaborate studies. The views, for example, which I have expressed as to the tone of the Athenian Demos and the capacity of the Roman oligarchs must be criticised and corrected as the student's knowledge of those periods increases; but the purpose of the book will have been fulfilled if in all such detailed studies he brings to bear upon his work not only a special acquaintance with the facts of one period, but a conviction of the bearing of the whole history of classical antiquity on the interpretation of any one portion of it. I owe this conviction myself chicfly to the late Rector of my college, Mark Pattison. Rarely as his advice was given, it was always of unique value; and I only wish that I had been ready and able to act upon it with greater profit to myself and others.

CONTENTS

CHAPTER I

INTRODUCTORY

CHAPTER II

THE GENESIS OF THE CITY-STATE

CHAPTER III

NATURE OF THE CITY-STATE AND ITS FIRST FORM OF GOVERNMENT

CHAPTER IV

THE RISE OF ARISTOCRATIC GOVERNMENT

CHAPTER V

CHAPTER VI

CHAPTER VII

THE PERIOD OF TRANSITION AT ROME

CHAPTER VIII

CHAPTER IX

CHAPTER X

EXTERNAL CAUSES OF DECAY—IMPERIAL AND FEDERATIVE STATES

CHAPTER XI

Dissolution of the City-State : The Roman Empire

CHAPTER I

As a subject of study, whether in schools or universities, ancient history is almost always separated from modern history; and it cannot very well be otherwise. It takes the learning of a lifetime fully to appreciate what is meant by that unity of history, of which Professor Freeman was never tired of reminding us. No one can really grasp the inter-connection of a long series of events, or see how states and empires crumble and fall, only to rise again in new forms, unless his mind is sufficiently well stored with the detail which must be the material for his thinking powers to work on. Most of us must take it on trust that there is no region of utter desolation lying between ancient and modern civilisation, and dividing them from each other; most of us must be content to choose the one or the other as the field of our investigation.

But we do not only separate modern history from that of the Greeks and Romans: we also

B

separate the histories of these two peoples. Or
rather, even where they are studied at the same
time, little effort is made to look at them as one
great whole. Here, again, want of time to master
the necessary detail is the cause, and the legitimate
excuse. Yet so close is the connection between
these two civilisations, that they may be in some
respects considered as one and the same; and at
the outset of a detailed study of either, it is as well
to see whether they cannot be brought together in
some way which will make it impossible for an
intelligent learner ever to think of them again as
wholly distinct.

Let us consider for a moment the nature of this
close relation between Greek and Roman civilisation.
It is indeed no great matter that the two races were
not far distant from each other in ethnological
descent. They were perhaps not so near of kin
as we once thought, and it seems to be now made
probable that the Romans were more closely allied
to the Celtic race than they were to the Greek.
But they were at least near enough to each other
to feel a certain mutual attraction even early in
their history. There is no trace of any such re-
pulsion between them, as Greek and Phœnician
seem always to have felt for each other, in spite
of constant intercourse; their languages were both
really and obviously related, while the Semitic
speech of the Phœnician and Carthaginian was
a sealed book to both. The veneration shown in
the earliest Roman traditions for the superior gifts
of the Hellenic race finds its counterpart in the

admiring curiosity with which Hellenes of a later age—a Polybius or a Posidonius—could study the manners and institutions of the Romans.

In their religious ideas, too, or at least in the religious practices on which our knowledge of those ideas is chiefly based, there is a close resemblance between the two races. It was easy to identify Greek and Italian deities, when anything was to be gained by doing so; it was by an easy though a gradual process that Roman ritual was so far superseded by Greek, that it is now a hard task to excavate the genuine Italian practice by removing the foreign strata beneath which it lies buried. It is indeed true enough that most races have been much readier than we should at first suppose to adopt the religious customs of their neighbours, or even of peoples far removed from them in kinship or geographical position. But there is hardly a case to be found in which this adoption is so complete as it was at Rome. The Romans believed the Greek forms to have superior efficacy, and they took them over, except on rare occasions, without misgiving. They found nothing in them essentially antagonistic to their own notions of their relations to the gods. In spite of much diversity there was a basis both of conception and practice which was common to both peoples. There were at least two special points of agreement : each believed in certain great deities whom they associated with their history and their fortunes ; and each looked on these deities as *localised* in their cities, as belonging to none but themselves, and as incapable of deserting them except as a consequence of their own short-comings.

In regard to character, it was just the very unlikeness of the two peoples that served to attract them to each other. What the Roman lacked the Greek could supply,—poetry and the plastic arts, and the mythological fancy in which these were so deeply rooted; the power of thinking, too, and the precious gift of curiosity which spurs men to ask questions and to seek for answers to them. Thus the Romans borrowed the finer elements in their civilisation from the Greeks; but they were not without something to give in exchange. They possessed what Matthew Arnold called "the power of conduct" in a far higher degree than the Greeks—the self-restraint, the discipline, the "courage never to submit or yield," which at last placed the dominion of the world in their hands. These qualities were regarded almost with awe by the Greek thinkers who came to know the Romans as conquerors. These, too, and the rare power of governing which the Romans developed out of them, made it possible for Greek culture to survive long after the Greeks had lost their freedom. The Roman dominion became a legal framework on which Greek intelligence could be fitted. And though Greek and Roman never became wholly amalgamated, and East and West always remained in many ways distinct, yet the two great currents poured into a single channel, and ran side by side, like Rhône and Saône after their junction, distinguishable from each other at a glance, yet forming one great stream.

But what is of the greatest moment for our purpose at present is that these two peoples developed *the same kind of polity*. They carried it out with different aims and with very different results ; but the form of political union in which they lived was essentially one and the same, and passed through the same stages of growth. Living as they did in adjacent peninsulas, in the same latitude and in much the same climate, within easy reach of the sea, and in fertile valleys or plains surrounded by mountainous tracts, it was natural that they should develop socially and politically on much the same lines. Like conditions produce like growths, modified only by the inherent differences of stock, and by the forwarding or retarding influences which may be brought to bear on them as they grow. The Greek and Latin States experienced very different fortunes, and their differing characteristics caused them to float in different directions, some going straight onward in a natural order of progress, some being swept into backwaters, and retarded for many generations ; but their State was in all cases *of the same species*, and this species was almost peculiar to themselves among the peoples of antiquity.

This unique form of State was what the Greeks called the πόλις ; a word which, like the Latin *urbs*, may probably have originally meant no more than a fortified position on a hill, to which the inhabitants of the surrounding country could fly for refuge on the approach of an enemy. But the Greek of a more civilised age came to give this word a much wider and deeper meaning, which it is the object of the following chapters to explain and trace out. By this word and its derivatives he sought to express the whole life, and the whole duty, of man ; that union of human beings for a common end, which could alone produce and exercise all the best instincts and abilities of every free individual. The Latin race had no word which was an exact equivalent to this ; for " urbs " never attained to a meaning so profound, and " civitas," which comes nearest to it, is less explicit. The Latin race, indeed, never realised the Greek conception of a πόλις in quite the same degree ; but this was rather owing to their less vivid mental powers than to the absence of the phenomenon among them. Their form of State was of the same kind, their idea of their relation to it was not less definite ; but they had not the instinct to reflect on it or inquire into its nature, and had eventually to fall back on the Greeks themselves for their philosophy of it.

What, then, was this πόλις, this form of political union in which both these races developed their best faculties, and made their lasting contributions to European civilisation ? Our modern notions of a State hamper us much in our efforts to realise what the πόλις was ; nor is it possible to do so completely until we have gained some knowledge of the conditions under which it arose, of its constituent elements, of its life in its best days, and of the causes which sapped its vitality and finally let it be

swallowed up in a vast political union of a totally
different kind. In subsequent chapters some attempt will be made to sketch its history, and to
show where this necessary knowledge may be looked
for. At present we must be content to point out
the most obvious difference between the modern
State and that of the Greeks and Latins, and the
one which will best serve to show the reader that
the study of Greek and Roman history is a very
different task from the study of the growth of
modern European States—a task, too, which, in
some respects at least, is more fruitful and more
suggestive.

By a modern State we mean a country or territory
with a central government and a capital town ; or
a group of such territories, each with its government
and its capital, bound together in a federal league,
like the United States or the cantons of the Swiss
Republic. In this form of State the capital city is
a convenient place for carrying on the central
government, but does not in and by itself constitute
the heart and life of the State. The history of
modern States shows that, while the State is growing, the question is an open one as to where the acts
of government may best be performed. In England
this in the middle ages was just where the king
happened to be, at Winchester, at Marlborough, at
the now obscure Clarendon, as well as in London or
at Windsor. Even in much later times, after the
complete consolidation of a State, it has been found
perfectly possible to transfer the government to
other centres besides the capital city ; as the King's

government in the Civil War was carried on at
Oxford, and the French government at Bordeaux in
1870-71. It is plain, then, that in a modern State
the so-called capital city is not an essential part of
the State's life, and has only grown in course of
time, and from reasons of convenience or tradition,
to occupy the first place in the minds of the people
among all the other towns, as the seat of their
central government. It is plain, for example, that
by the State called France we mean the whole
French people living on French territory, and having
their political existence, not as Parisians but as
Frenchmen, with a convenient centre, Paris.

But the Greeks and Romans conceived of their
State as something very different from this. Athens,
Sparta, Miletus, Syracuse, Rome, *were themselves
cities*, with a greater or less amount of territory from
which they drew their means of subsistence. This
territory was indeed an essential, but it was not the
heart and life of the State. It was in the city that
the heart and life were centred, and the territory
was only an adjunct. The Athenian State comprised all the free people living in Athens, and also
those who lived in the Attic territory ; but these
last had their political existence, not as inhabitants
of Attica, but as Athenians, as citizens of the πόλις
of Athens. So, too, the Roman State, even when it
had extended its territory over the whole Italian
peninsula, was still conceived of as having its heart
and life in the city of Rome, with a tenacity which
led to much trouble and disaster, and ultimately to
the destruction of this peculiar form of State. It

is, then, a City-State that we have to deal with in Greek and Roman history; a State in which the whole life and energy of the people, political, intellectual, religious, is focussed at one point, and that point a city. To understand the life and work of these two peoples, it is indispensable to get a firm grasp of this fact; for their development from first to last was profoundly affected by it, and almost all their contributions to civilisation may be traced to it directly or indirectly.[1]

Now it will not need much reflection to see that a form of State whose most striking feature is *city life*, where the social, political, and intellectual forces at work in it are concentrated at a single point, will be a simpler problem to handle historically than a State in which these forces are spread over a wide area, and over populations differing from each other in many ways. The πόλις was in fact, in most respects though not in all, a more perfect form of social union than the modern State, and its history, if we were more exactly informed about it, would be relatively easier to understand. The difficulties of Greek and Roman history do not lie in the nature of the Greek and Roman form of State, but in the fragmentary character of our knowledge, and in the consequent need of a peculiarly skilful interpretation. And even as it is, it may be doubted whether the study of a comparatively simple organism, even with such drawbacks as these, is not a better introduction to the science

---

[1] Bluntschli, *Theory of the State* (Eng. trans.), p. 34 foll. ; Sidgwick, *Elements of Politics*, p. 211 foll.

of political history than the study of an organism
which is highly complex. We need but call to
mind the most striking institutions which the modern
State has developed, such as Representative Government, Federation, or Local Self-government, to show
how complicated a problem political science has
become.   Or if we look at the earlier history of the
modern State, we again find its difficulties increased
not only by the imperfect cohesion of the States
themselves, but by the presence of two influences
outside them which cannot be left out of account,
viz. the Papacy and the Holy Roman Empire.
The life-history of any one Greek State, or of the
Roman State in its earlier stages, would be, if we
had it complete, a much more exact and instructive
study.

Let us look into this a little more closely ; for
at a time when classical study is in some danger of
losing its prestige and of being left stranded for the
learned few to deal with as wreckage, it is as well
to be sure of our ground in claiming an educational
superiority for it, even on the historical side only.
If it can be shown that the history of the most
perfect State is the best history, and that the πόλις
was a more perfect State than the modern one,
something at least will have been done to prove the
point in question.

What is a State, and what constitutes its excellence as such ?   A State is an aggregation of free
human beings, bound together by common ties, some
of which may be called natural ties, some artificial.
The chief natural ties are community of race, of

language, of religion, of sentiment or historical association, and lastly of land, *i.e.* of the territory which
the State occupies. The most important artificial
ties are law, custom, executive government; these
are common bonds which the people have gradually developed for themselves, and are not, in the
same degree as the natural ties, original factors in
their cohesion. There are also other ties which do
not fall exactly under either of these divisions, such
as the common interests of commerce and of self-
defence.

Now it is obvious that a State, in order to
deserve the name, need not be held together by all
these ties at once. Very few, if any, States have
realised them all. But every State must have what
we call the artificial ties, in some tolerably obvious
form; that is, every State must have at least some
laws which bind the whole community, and a common government to enforce obedience to those laws.
Without these the word State cannot be applied to
it, but only some such vague expression as "nation,"
or "race," or "people," words which in our language
do not usually connote governmental cohesion. We
speak, for example, of the Celtic race, of the Irish,
or even of the Welsh, nation, of the people of the
Jews; and we never use the word "State" of these,
because they have no constitution or secular government of their own. Nor can any community be
properly called a State which is not wholly independent of every other community. India, for example, is not a State, though it has a government and
a law of its own, because that law and government

depend for their ultimate sanction on the will of the Government of Great Britain and Ireland. So, too, the United States of America are only States by courtesy, as it were, while the whole Federation is a State in the true sense of the word.

While, then, every State must be held together by the artificial ties, it may, so long as it is independent, exist as a true State without any of the natural ties, except perhaps that of the land on which its members are settled. But it will be seen at once that it will be a stronger and more securely united State if it be bound together not only by the artificial ties, but also by those which we call natural, or at least by some of them. The greater the number of ties operating to hold a State together, the stronger will that State be. To see this we have only to compare modern France with modern Austria. Of modern States, France has long been the happiest instance of an almost complete union of ties both natural and artificial; hence in great measure her marvellous vitality and power of cohesion, which in this century alone has enabled her to survive two conquests, and to maintain her influence as a great power after disasters which would have utterly crushed a people less firmly knit together. Austria, on the other hand, is weak in all the ties, and especially in those of race, language, religion, and sentiment; and it is a commonplace with politicians that the Austrian empire may easily break up under severe pressure, or only survive by the help of allies whose interests it at present serves. The law which this example illustrates will be found to hold good of States in general, and to serve as a rough, though useful, test of their power of resistance, as well as of their power of cohesion.

It may be doubted, however, whether any modern State has realised the force of these various ties in the same degree as did the City-States of ancient Greece and Italy. The city, in which was their heart and life, could exert over the citizens a more powerful influence than a modern country, for it was capable of being taken in at a glance both by eye and mind, like Rome from the Janiculan Hill:

"Unde totam licet æstimare Romam."

The delight of the Greek poets in the cities they celebrate, whether they are their own homes, or those of their patrons, arises from this feeling of civic patriotism much more than from the enjoyment of natural beauty in and for itself. In regard to the tie of race, the citizens, though not always the whole number of inhabitants, were homogeneous and spoke the same language; and this meant more than it does now. It meant not only a binding connection by descent, but one by religion also; for to believe that you and your fellow-citizens were descended from the same stock implied necessarily that you shared the same worship. The unifying power of religion too, as has often been shown, was itself so strong and irresistible as to be almost beyond the comprehension of a modern unfamiliar with the life of the ancient world. The gods of the city were not only its patrons and protectors; they were looked on as actually inhabitants of it, who could not, and would not, desert it except under conditions too terrible to be contemplated, and who were indissolubly connected with all its history and fortunes. No wonder, then, that besides race, language, and religion, that other tie of common *sentiment*, or, as the Greeks called it, ἦθος, which in modern times is a powerful factor in nationality, should have been doubly strong in the ancient world. It was far less vague, far more distinctly conceivable, then than now; for as the city was itself the State, and all the citizens were brought up on the same plan, and for a common end within a limited space, it was natural that they should look on themselves and their city, on their duties and delights as citizens, with a common pride and exclusiveness which we of the modern world can hardly realise. And if we add to all this the unifying power of the artificial ties, of law and custom and government, which in the πόλις were at least as strong as in the modern State, and in some cases even stronger, we get a picture of a Statehood—if the term may be used—as perfect, it would seem, as man can ever expect to live in. That there were indeed weak points in this form of State is true enough, as we shall see later on; every organism is liable to its own special diseases or parasites. The very intensity of the State-life within the πόλις led in many cases to intense bitterness of faction when faction had once broken out, and to a corresponding weakness in the relations of the State to other States, or to the less civilised peoples beyond the Græco-Italian world.

Yet on the whole it must be allowed that the idea of the State, with all its fruitful civilising results, has never again been so fully realised since the πόλις was swallowed up in the Roman Empire; the ties that hold a State together have never been seen working together with such strength and vitality.

Does it not follow, then, that the life-history of this small but highly-organised form of State must be in some respects peculiarly valuable? If the history of France is a more instructive study than that of less perfect modern States, the history of a πόλις must be more instructive still; as the biography of a man of strong character and original genius, even if his life be passed in a comparatively limited sphere of activity, has often more to teach us than the life of a man of coarser fibre, whose interests and influence reach over a much wider area. If the best history—history in the truest sense of a word of wide meaning—is that of the life of the State which most fully expresses the needs and aspirations of men bound together in social union, then the history of the πόλις is so far more valuable than that of any modern State.

It may indeed be argued, in criticism of this view, that we have no adequate and complete account of the life of any one πόλις from its birth; and that even in tracing the history of Athens and of Rome, we continually find ourselves beset with doubts and difficulties which arise from the scantiness of our information. Here and there a sudden light is flashed on the scene we are exploring, and the next moment all is again in darkness. The ancient historians are often blind guides, and did not regard truth and fact with the same reverence which science has taught our own generation. The monuments and inscriptions which have come down to us, invaluable as they often are, are mostly fragmentary or isolated, and themselves need skilful interpretation before they can be brought to bear on the interpretation of history. Again, the avidity with which every newly discovered scrap of an ancient author is seized upon and made the most of,—often, indeed, made more of than it will bear, —is itself a melancholy proof of the hunger for facts from which all students of antiquity must suffer. The recent discovery of the Aristotelian treatise on the Athenian constitution has, it may be said, only reminded us of our own ignorance of the subject. And in Roman history what would we not give to recover the lost books of Livy, or the *Histories* of Sallust, or the original works from which Plutarch drew his *Roman Lives*, or —better in some ways than all these—the complete texts of any dozen of the great laws passed during the last century of the Republic ? As it is, we are climbing after knowledge in a misty region where endless tracks cross each other, which often come to an end suddenly, or lead us out of our true direction.

All this is indeed unfortunately true. But let us remember certain facts, which may too easily be forgotten.

First, we have an outline knowledge of the whole

history of the ancient City-State, from its birth to its death. We know something of the way in which it came into existence, something of its earlier stages. We know a great deal about its life when it had grown to its full size and strength, and we can trace its gradual decay, until it lost its true nature and became material for a wholly new political system. This is not so with the history of the modern State, which is still comparatively young. We can follow its growth up to a certain point; but there we pass into the region of conjecture, for that growth is in many cases hardly yet finished, and even in the most highly-developed States there is fortunately no sure sign that decay is as yet setting in.

Secondly, we have large portions of the history of the two most famous City-States conveyed to us in the form of priceless literature. Thucydides and Demosthenes, and in a less degree Livy and Cicero, are among the most valuable treasures the world possesses. Even if we consider Livy alone,—the one among these four about whom it is most difficult to be enthusiastic,—apart from a perfection of style which is apt perhaps to become too monotonously perfect, it is impossible not to be sincerely grateful for the preservation of every one of the thirty-five books which remain to us. Now that history has become scientific, Livy does indeed appear to us full of sad shortcomings; yet through him we possess not only a sufficient knowledge of the working of the Roman constitution in its best days, but also a wealth of information about

C

the ideas of the earlier Romans in relation to their
state and their religion. No such literary record
exists of the growth and life of any modern State.
Of Greek literature there is no need to speak here.
From Homer to Herodotus, from Herodotus to
Aristotle, and from Aristotle to Plutarch, we have
the life of the Greeks, both in their πόλις and
in their external relations, mirrored in the most
exquisite of languages, or made the subject of
profound thought.

And this brings us to a third point. We have
not only the history of the πόλις, but also its
philosophy. Its small and compact form, and the
very close relation in which the individual stood to
it, prompted the inquisitive Greek mind to inquire
into its nature. Plato and Aristotle saw that it
was impossible to search out and analyse the
nature of man, without reference to the form of
community in which he lived, and from which he
could not free himself. The State was the chief
agent in making man's life worth living, and he
could not therefore be philosophically treated apart
from the State. The study of the πόλις thus holds
out for us an inducement which the modern State
can hardly be said to offer. We have in the
Republic and *Laws* of Plato, and in the *Politics* of
Aristotle, the thoughts of two of the profoundest of
all thinkers on the nature of the State they lived
in ; and we have also at least something of the
same kind, though of far less value, in Polybius
and Cicero, on the nature and government of the
Roman State.

Lastly, we live in an age in which great store of material has been added to the treasures we already possess. For three centuries after the revival of learning scholars were chiefly busied in recovering the literature of antiquity, and in purifying it from the corruption with which the ignorance or carelessness of fifteen centuries had overlaid it. The process is still going on ; but the work of the nineteenth century has been mainly of another kind. It has lain partly in the interpretation of this literature, with the object of getting at the real life and thought of the Greeks and Romans ; partly in the collection of thousands upon thousands of inscriptions, whether already published or newly found, and in the ordering of them in such a way as to make them easily available for use. And though in the following chapters it will not often be necessary to refer to these vast collections, it may be here pointed out that of all material for the details of the history of the πόλις inscriptions are the most valuable. They are the work of the very men whose customs, laws, or virtues they commemorate, and they have not passed through the perilous process of being worked up into book-history. And if to all this be added the results of the excavation of the buildings and monuments of antiquity, and the light thrown on much that was once obscure by the modern sciences of Comparative Philology and Anthropology, we must allow that never, since the revival of learning, has such a fair field been open to the student of Greek and Roman life.

The vast amount of detail is, in fact, apt to overwhelm us. The division of labour has become so complex that it is rare to find any scholar who has a wide knowledge of antiquity, or can gather it up in his mind and reason on it as a whole. We live in an age of specialisation, and it is inevitable that it should be so. But for that very reason an outline of the history of that peculiar form of State which was developed both by Greeks and Romans may possibly be neither unwelcome nor unprofitable. If those who are beginning to read Greek and Roman history with some serious purpose can have their attention once directed to the unity of the whole story, it is possible that they may never altogether lose themselves in detail, or forget the true relation of the whole to its various parts. And there is perhaps no better way of thus widening their powers of vision, and saving them from that short-sightedness which is the bane of all workers in minute detail, than by selecting one thread, and that the strongest and most easy to follow, and tracing it steadily throughout what we call ancient history. For as we follow the fortunes of the πόλις, we shall be following also the development and the decay of the thought and the social life of the peoples whose political instincts it expressed. We shall be following the safest clue, because in the life of the πόλις was gathered up all that was best and most fruitful in the civilisation of two wonderful peoples. As it grew to perfection, their social instincts and their power of thought grew with it ; as it slowly decayed, their literature, art, and philosophy decayed too.

I shall attempt, then, on these grounds, educational and other, to give some account, however meagre, of each phase of the history of this form of State, from its first appearance to its absorption in the Roman Empire, passing in view the several forms it assumed, pointing out the chief causes of its disintegration, and finally touching on the vast new political system which was built not only on its ruins, but out of them, and was thus the agent in preserving for modern civilisation a great part, at least, of the fruits of ancient experience.

CHAPTER II

WE saw in the last chapter what is the essential difference between the City-State of Greek and Roman antiquity, and the territorial State of modern times. Neither Greek nor Roman could think of his State as having an existence apart from the city in which its business was carried on; while we moderns can perfectly well picture to ourselves a France of which Paris should be no longer the capital, or an Italy where the centre of government should be once more shifted from Rome to Florence or Milan. Once, indeed, in the history of Athens the Athenian people were forced to leave their city, and to take refuge in their ships and in the island of Salamis; yet their State continued to exist, and to exist at Athens. Never at any moment of their history did they show more clearly their conviction of the identity of State and city. The sacred olive-tree in the Erechtheum put forth a fresh sprout, as they believed, but two days after the Persians had burnt the temple. The solemn procession of celebrants passed from the city to Eleusis as usual, and the dust it raised was seen from Salamis, though no living Athenian trod the sacred road that day.[1] Though the citizens could not fulfil their duties to the State and its gods, those duties were mysteriously performed for them, in the proper place and at the proper time. Of all the beautiful myths to which Greek fancy gave birth, none was ever more deeply rooted than this in a solid conviction,—the conviction that the city, with its population, divine and human, was the one essential fact in the life of civilised men.[2]

Now it is plain that the City-State and the modern State, differing in this essential point, must have come into existence in different ways ; that the conditions, the primary factors, out of which they grew, must have been different. And in order to understand the nature and the history of either form of State, it is necessary to begin at the beginning, and find out what those conditions were, and how the State grew out of them. To understand English political history, it is little use beginning with the Great Charter, or even at the Norman Conquest ; we must go back to the first fashioning of English institutions out of elements present before any real State was there.[3] This is no new doctrine or method ; it is as old as

---

[1] Herodotus, viii. 65.

[2] Cf. the pathetic speech of Camillus, at the end of Livy's fifth book, in opposition to the proposal to transfer the city of Rome to Veii, where the claims of the divine population as well as of the human are brought out with all Livy's rhetorical skill.

[3] Freeman, *Growth of the English Constitution*, ch. i. Those

Aristotle. He began his treatise on the State by investigating the elements out of which he believed it to have grown; and he was right in his method and his facts. The search for origins is now so favourite an occupation of the learned as to be occasionally laughed at; but it only shows that we live, like Aristotle, in a scientific age, which is not content with getting to know facts, but seeks to obtain a better knowledge of them by accounting for them. The student of the life of plants or animals must in these days also learn their *morphology*, *i.e.* the beginning and growth of the various forms which they have taken as species. And the principle is the same in all sciences, including the science of the State. The reason for this is very simple. The conditions present at the beginning and during the early stages of a State, as of any species of plant or animal, have deeply influenced the whole life and nature of the organism. " Back to Aristotle " has to be said in these days in many departments of knowledge ;[1] for it was he who first taught that the object of your study is better understood if you can discover how it was born and how it grows.

The origin of the modern State is a complicated study, and of course each individual State has had its own peculiar experiences in its early days, and

who start at a later date are either lawyers like Professor Dicey (*Law of the Constitution*, p. 14), or historians who post-date the origin of modern States, like M. Boutmy, who considers that in the seventeenth century " the French nation was still in embryo " (*English Constitution*, p. 19).

[1] Sir F. Pollock, *History of the Science of Politics*, p. 124.

has gradually developed in its own way. This is more particularly the case with England, which has in many ways been kept as much apart from others in historical experience as in geographical position. But the conditions out of which modern States have arisen have been, in the main, alike in Western Europe, though the various factors have had very different force and weight in different instances. Apart from geographical influences, and the inherent peculiarities of race, they have been chiefly three. First, the raw material, *i.e.* the barbarian people who overran Europe under the later Roman Empire, and dissolved that great political fabric : these peoples had their own primitive institutions,—germs from some of which, in England at least, there has been an abundant growth and excellent fruit. Secondly, the fabric of the Roman Empire, on which these germs were engrafted, the idea of which continued to exist as an object of reverence long after the reality had vanished, and was brought before men's minds once more in visible form by the Holy Roman Empire of Charles the Great and his successors. Thirdly, we have to take into account the civilising power of Christianity in two ways : first, as a moral force, bettering rude institutions ; and secondly, as a great spiritual organism, not indeed directly aiding the development of States,—on the contrary, rather retarding it, yet acting from time to time as a salutary unifying influence for civilisation, in ages when States were struggling into existence amid great perplexities and perils.

This may be just sufficient to show how, in investigating the history of a modern State, the conditions out of which it grew must be ascertained to begin with. But how are we to discover the conditions out of which the ancient City-State was formed? How can we know anything of Athens and Rome before Athens or Rome came into existence? We have here no Gildas, no Anglo-Saxon chronicle, nothing to answer to the monkish records of mediæval Europe. We have no contemporary literature, no inscriptions, hardly anything but traditions and survivals, as will be seen in the course of this chapter. What we can make out is meagre enough, and is arrived at by no direct road of inquiry. But this unknown country has been explored in the course of the last thirty years or so by three distinct routes, and if we follow these we shall find that the efforts of the explorers have not been altogether fruitless. Taking the route of the comparative method, as it is called, we can first compare the institutions of various peoples who have not yet developed a true State, and so gain some general idea of the way in which such peoples live, and of the conditions out of which a State may grow. Then we may go on to compare our results with what little we actually know about the Greeks and Italians before they reached the State; and thirdly, we may verify these results, by seeing whether the elements out of which we suppose the City-State to have originated continued to survive in any shape after the State was formed. Then we shall be in a position to discover how the formation of the State was actually brought about.

In each of these three steps we are dealing with questions of extreme difficulty, which are still but partially investigated. But only the leading results of the comparative method can be indicated here in outline, so far as we have them at present; and on these we can depend with some confidence, leaving details to be corrected as our knowledge advances.

Peoples who have not yet reached the stage of civilisation at which the State begins are never found to be without some kind of organisation. For example, they have a leader or chief, and they reckon their descent, and their relationship to each other, on some sort of principle. We are not here concerned with the various stages through which man has passed before reaching the State, nor with the changes in the idea of relationship which he gradually developed in the course of ages. That is the work of the anthropologist, not of the historian. All we need to ascertain is the nature of the organisation which, in most cases at least, immediately preceded that of the State, and served therefore as a basis for it to grow from.

No true State can come into existence except when the people composing it have been for some time settled down on a definite territory. No wandering or nomad people can make a State in our sense of the word; they must have reached a stage in which they can live comfortably by certain fixed occupations, of which the most important, for the supply of daily food, is agriculture. At some time or other, then, the people, tribe, or stock will have taken possession of a district, either driving out an older population, or amalgamating with them in some way after conquest ; and having thus settled down, will cease for a while to undergo further important changes, tending rather to fix and solidify the organisation, which was as it were only in solution, so long as they were constantly changing the conditions under which they lived. The Greek and Latin stocks, for example, when they wandered into the peninsulas which we know them as inhabiting, must have settled down on the land in some form of organisation, which grew more and more fixed and definite the longer they remained without further migration. We wish to know what this form was.

A vast amount of research has of late years been made and published on this subject; and the chief result of it which concerns us here has been to show (1) that before the final settlement on the land takes place, the main stock is always found to consist of groups or cells, held together by the tie of *Kinship*; (2) that after the settlement has taken place, these groups or cells are still found, but now fixed upon the land in forms which may roughly be described as *village communities*, consisting of a number of families united together.[1]

---

[1] The family, as Aristotle saw, was the ultimate basis of civilised society. But as the subject of this chapter is the Genesis of the ancient State, any inquiry into the origin of the family in pre-existing social forms, or its subsequent development into the

It is true that they were not always *villages*, in our sense of that word. The ancient Celts of Britain, for example, did not live in village groups, —a fact which any one may prove for himself by travelling in Wales at the present day. Various forms of the group are in fact found, and the variation may be due to inherent characteristics of race, or to the stage which civilisation has reached in each case, or to other circumstances, such as the influence of a pre-existing civilisation on the invading people. But the most perfect form of the group seems to be that of the village of kinsmen, and for want of a more comprehensive term we may speak of the group in general as the Village Community.[1]

An excellent picture of the way in which these local groups may be supposed to have come into existence is supplied by Sir Henry Maine in one of his most valuable lectures on these subjects. He quotes the words of an Indian poetess, describing the immigration of a people called the Vellalee into that part of India which was once famous as Arcot. "The poetess compares the invasion to the flowing of the juice of the sugar-cane over a flat surface. *The juice crystallises, and the crystals are the various village communities.* In the middle is one lump of particularly fine sugar, the place where is the temple of the god. Homely as the image is, it seems in one respect peculiarly felicitous. It

group which became the village community, is not here directly called for.

[1] See Maine, *Early History of Institutions*, p. 78 foll.

represents the tribe, though moving in a fused mass
of men, as containing within itself a principle of
coalescence which began to work as soon as the
movement was over." [1]   We cannot, of course, be sure
that such an image as this would exactly represent
the way in which Greeks and Latins, or Celts and
Teutons, settled down on the land which they conquered; for the history of man, as of plants and
animals, presents local variation everywhere.   But
I know of no better way of getting a general idea
of what we suppose to have happened at this
momentous era in the progress of a people, than
by laying to heart this singularly happy illustration.

What, then, were the characteristics of the
Village Community, using the word in the general
sense given above ?   We may recognise four, each
of which is of importance in its bearing on the
development of institutions in later stages of civilisation.   They are gathered from examples of these
groups which have been studied in the life in India,
Russia, and Slavonia; and also from survivals,
in which some one at least of the original features
can be traced, in England, Ireland, Switzerland,
Germany, and other countries.

First, as is implied in what has been said above,
the families of which the community consisted were
originally all akin to one another.   Kinship was
the foundation-stone of the society.   That this
was so in England can still be proved, as is well
known, from the names of many of our villages,

[1] Maine, *op. cit.* p. 71.

such as Wellington (the settlement of the Wellings), Watlington, Wallingford, etc. It was probably the same in India.[1] And though this leading idea of kinship tends ever to become fainter the longer the group remains fixed on the land, and thus loses much of its original binding force, it still may survive as a fiction firmly believed in, or at least as a bond of *brotherhood*, creating a sense of mutual obligation between the members of the group. Even if it passes, as it has passed in Russia and India, from a sense of common descent to a sense of common interest only, it has left a legacy of feeling behind it which could never have been gained, so far as we can see, from any other mode of union.

Secondly, the *government* of the group was in the hands of a council consisting of the heads of the families constituting the group, sometimes with a headman to preside over it. The evidence does not seem to show clearly at present whether the council or the headman is the original form of government, or whether they both worked together from the beginning. Sir H. Maine tells us [2] that in the most perfect village communities in India, *i.e.* in those which have preserved best their original form, it is the council which rules; and in these cases the other institution is either not to be found, or only survives in some form which easily escapes recognition. But it is difficult to imagine a

[1] Green, *Making of England*, p. 183 ; Maine, *Village Communities*, p. 175.
[2] *Ib.* p. 123. Cf. Gomme, *The Village Community*, p. 26.

council without some one to call it together ; and we may perhaps assume that the headman was an original institution of the group, which in some cases grew steadily more important as time went on, or even came to supersede the council altogether. This simple government doubtless exercised a customary judicial power, as it does in Russia at the present day, and regulated the property of the community.[1]

Thirdly, the land from which the group drew its subsistence, and the cultivation of which was the chief employment of its members, was held in common by all the families of which the group consisted. The correspondence in this particular between village communities in various parts of the world is most striking. It might be indeed, and in all probability was most often the case, that the land thus held by the community was held *under a lord*, *i.e.* from a large owner of land, and that some kind of rent was paid to him. The occupiers may even have been in a condition for which we can find no other word but serfdom, though it was perhaps in reality much more favourable than any to which that word can now be applied.[2] But whether they held it from another or not, their tenure of it was a common tenure, and they used it for the advantage, not of individuals, but of the community. In most existing village communities the land, apart from that on which the village stands, is divided into two parts—

[1] Wallace, *Russia*, vol. i. p. 198.
[2] Fustel de Coulanges, *Origin of Property in Land* (translated by Mrs. Ashley), *passim*.

the waste land, or pasturage, which is entirely common to the families, each having the right of feeding so many head of cattle on it ; and the arable land, which is divided up into parcels or strips, and is either redistributed to the various families at regular intervals of time, or has become by degrees apportioned to them permanently. Traces of this system of common pasturage and divided arable land may still be seen in the records and maps of a very large number of English parishes.[1]

Fourthly, the ancient village community had, we may be quite sure, a common worship. Where Christianity has supervened, as in existing European village communities, of course very few traces of this can be found. But the Indian poetess quoted by Sir H. Maine was no doubt representing a general fact when she spoke of the larger crystal in the middle of the group which represented the temple of the god. Whether that god was in all cases the divine ancestor from whom the whole group believed itself to be descended, it is not possible to determine ; but the universal prevalence in early society of the worship of ancestors by groups of kin—a feature which must be passed over here—makes it probable that this was so. Whatever the worship was, we may be certain that, as an essential part of the life of the community, it was shared by all its members.[2]

The four chief characteristics of the early village community are thus—kinship of all the members ;

[1] Seebohm, *English Village Community*, chaps. i. and iv. For other examples see Laveleye, *Primitive Property* (Eng. trans.), *passim*.

[2] Fustel de Coulanges, *La Cité antique*, bk. i.

D

government by a council and a headman ; community of land ; and common worship. It is obvious that a stage of social life which could realise these characteristics must be considerably advanced ; we seem already to see the possibility of a further advance into a higher level of association. But what evidence have we, in the next place, that the Greek and Latin races had attained to this stage before the City-State arose among them ?

There can be no doubt that the Greeks believed themselves to have lived in villages before they advanced to city life ; and it is equally certain that in the less highly civilised parts of Greece, village life predominated even in historical times.

For the first of these facts we have the evidence both of Thucydides and Aristotle, representing the highest point, in two successive centuries, at which Greek political thought had arrived. At the outset of his history, Thucydides gives us a picture of life in Greece as he believed it to have been " in early times " (Thucydides, i. 2, 5 and 6) ; it is no doubt a fancy picture, but contains some elements of truth, and is at least a record of what the inquiring Greek thought. He conceived of the Greeks as living without union or unifying influences, without enterprise in commerce or agriculture, without any object in life beyond that of obtaining the means of subsistence. Had he told us nothing more, we might fairly have guessed that this was a description of the life of men living in some kind of village communities ; for it accords precisely with what we read of those which are still in existence, save that in these agriculture has in most cases become the all-absorbing occupation.[1]   But Thucydides has told us more than this.   Speaking of the prevalence of piracy in those early times, and the comparative respect in which it was held, as an adventurous and honourable trade, he says that the pirates' victims lived in communities which were unfortified, and consisted of one or more villages.   And this is borne out by Aristotle, who, reasoning as usual not on fancy but on facts, describes the village as a union of families, and the city as a union of villages ; thus placing the village midway between family and city in the growth of society.[2]

For the second fact, that village life was prevalent in the less forward parts of Greece in historical times, we have abundant and explicit evidence. Thucydides describes it as existing in Ætolia in his own day ; the skilful Athenian general Demosthenes founded his hopes of conquering Ætolia on the weakness and disunion of a people still living κατὰ κώμας ἀτειχίστους.[3]   The same is implied of the Ozolian Locrians, a few chapters farther on ; and from a later authority[4] we learn that the Acarnanians lived in villages, until at the end of the fourth century B.C. they began to develop something of the nature of a town.   In the Peloponnese the Arcadians had not grown beyond this stage of social life when Epaminondas concentrated a number of

[1] Maine, *Village Communities*, p. 175 ; Mackenzie Wallace, *Russia*, vol. i. ch. viii.   For these characteristics of the village stage of society see also below, ch. iii. p. 60.

[2] *Politics*, i. 2 ; 1252 B.   [3] Thuc. iii. 94, 97 ; cf. 101.

[4] Diodorus, 19, 67.

villages into his new Great City (Megalopolis), destined to overawe Sparta. And lastly, Sparta itself
was a city made up of villages, and so were Elis,
Mantinea, Tegea, and many others ; in the case of
Sparta, owing to the distance from the sea, and the
military strength of the situation, the constituent
villages were never even fortified by an enclosing
ring-wall.

Turning to Italy, we find village settlements
there also, and we have little doubt that they formed,
in some cases at least, among which that of Rome
must be reckoned, the constituent elements of towns.
The Latin words for this kind of community are *vicus*
and *pagus* ; and though we do not know precisely
what their original meaning was, the words were
always used to denote a smaller social unit than a
civitas or state. The word *pagus* fell out of use in
Italy, but was used by Cæsar for the subdivisions
of Gallic *civitates*, *i.e.* the Celtic sept ; *vicus* continued to be used for a hamlet in the country,
together with other words (*fora, conciliabula*) which
probably denote growths of a later time.

There is yet another set of facts to be mentioned,
which will go some way towards strengthening our
argument that the City-State was formed out of an
association of village communities. It is as well,
however, to point out that we shall here be using a
method to which we are frequently driven in ancient
history for want of a better—the method, as we may
call it, of *survivals,* by which we argue back from
the nature of institutions in later times, of which we
know something, to their probable originals or early

history, of which we know nothing directly. For example, if we can discover survivals of the life of village communities in the completed City-State of later times, we may argue back from what we know of these to the features of the original village life before the city arose. From this method we cannot expect more than an approximation to the truth, and it needs skilful handling ; but the same may be said, with even greater force, of reasoning based only on the statements of ancient authors.

It would be indeed strange, on the supposition of which we have already obtained some proof— that cities were formed in most cases out of village settlements—if those settlements did not continue to exist in some form after the city was full-grown ; just as the constituent parts of the caterpillar continue in other forms in the chrysalis and even in the fully developed insect. And, in fact, the early City-State, wherever we have anything like a full knowledge of it, invariably appears as subdivided into smaller groups, which look as if they had some historical relation to the original settlements out of which the city was formed. These are the γένη of Athens, the *gentes* of Rome ; all of them being, like the village community, groups consisting of a certain number of families. We have strong *a priori* reasons for believing these to be the lineal descendants of the original village communities, just as our English parishes of to-day are directly descended from the " hams " and " tuns " (*i.e.* village settlements) of our immigrant forefathers. We have also reason to believe that Aristotle thought these subdivisions of the city to be the same in origin with the village community; for he speaks of the inhabitants of a κώμη as being ὁμογάλακτες,[1] a word which we know was later applied to the members proper of an Athenian γένος; and in another passage he uses the words in almost the same sense, or with a distinction which is not obvious to us. "A city," he says, "is a union of γένη and κῶμαι for a perfect and sufficient life."[2]

What was the nature of these *gentes* and γένη as subdivisions of the population of a city? How far do they show any of those characteristics which we find in the village community? Let us notice to begin with that they were not *political* divisions, either at Athens or Rome; and if we knew anything of them as they existed in other States, we should probably find the same to hold good everywhere. And this means, that they were not associations which had been created after the City-State came into existence, with the object of helping it to perform its work as a political corporation, in matters of taxation or administration; they were strictly *private* associations within the State, and we can conceive of no reason why they should have grown up after the beginning of the State, nor have we any historical trace of such an origin for them.[3] With

[1] *Pol.* i. 2, 6; 1252 B. The meaning of this word is open to doubt. It may be taken as "suckled with the same milk," or "offering a common libation." Mr. Newman does not notice the latter interpretation.

[2] *Politics*, iii. 10, 14; cf. sec. 12; 1280 B and 1281 A.

[3] Both Greeks and Romans attributed them to a legislator, after the birth of the State; but this was simply because they could not account for them in any other way.

the true political divisions of the State, the Trittyes
and Naukraries of Athens (and later the Demes),
and the local tribes and *centuriæ* of Rome, the
gentes and γένη stand in most marked contrast.
We can have little doubt that they were survivals
from the forms of social life which preceded the
State ;[1] and we find in them traces of the same
characteristics which we found in the village community.   On these we can only touch very briefly.

Nothing can be more certain than that the
members of both γένη and *gentes* believed themselves
to be descended from a common ancestor, and therefore to be of one blood.   The very names make this
at once obvious, for both are derived from a root sig
nifying birth, and are related to our own word Kin.
In Rome all members of a gens bore the same name
(Claudii, Cornelii, etc.) ; and both at Rome and
Athens they had their common religious worship,
and also in many cases the exclusive right to fill
the priesthood of some important deity.   Thus at
Athens the gens of the Butadæ held the two great
priesthoods of Athene Polias and of Poseidon
Erectheus ; and we may remember the Roman
story of Fabius Cunctator, who left his command
—with great peril, as it turned out, to the army—
in the hands of his Master of the Horse, in order
to return to Rome and celebrate the rites of his

[1] See Schol. on Hesiod, *Works and Days*, v. 495 (quoted by
Kuhn, *Entstehung*, p. 163), where 360 λέσχαι are spoken of in
Athens, which may have been the original form of the later 360
γένη.   Such conjectures are, however, quite uncertain, and add
little or nothing to the argument.

gens. At Athens, again, we may see a trace of the government of the village community surviving in the ἄρχων τοῦ γένους, or head of the gens, who was at the same time its chief priest. And as regards the common tenure of land, though we have no evidence from Athens, we have strong reason to believe that even this characteristic of the village community survived for a considerable time in the Roman gens; but the evidence for this view, which has been brought together by Mommsen, is too complicated to be inserted here.[1]

We see then that the two leading ideas of the village community, those of kinship by blood (real or assumed) and of a common worship, are also found in the *gentes* of Rome and Athens; and further, that there is some ground for believing that the form of government and the method of land-tenure were originally the same both in gens and village. And as we can discover no other origin for the *gentes* and γένη, we are justified in concluding that they are really survivals of associations which existed before the State came into existence, *i.e.* of some form of village community. They survived into the life of the State, and even to the very end of it, because the ties of kinship and religion could not be dissolved among them, and were strong enough to hold them firmly

[1] For the ἄρχων τοῦ γένους see the new edition of Smith's *Dictionary of Antiquities*, i. 906; and for the common cultivation of land by Roman *gentes*, Mommsen, *Hist. of Rome*, i. 193; Laveleye, *Primitive Property*, p. 164 foll., criticised by F. de Coulanges, *op. cit.* p. 100 foll.

together under the new order of things; and
they remain, as we shall see, as a powerful conservative influence, holding back the State from a
too rapid development as a new organism, and, as it
were, keeping it continually in mind of the rock
from which it had been hewn.[1]

We have been following three lines of reasoning,
and have arrived at the results of three kinds of
evidence,—the nature of village communities in
general; the existence of village communities in
Greece and Italy, both in the earliest times and
after the State arose; and the apparent remains of
such communities, surviving in the State itself long
after it had reached maturity; and the conclusion is
irresistible that the State itself was formed out of
material the original units of which were communities of this kind. The rest of this chapter must be
occupied with some attempt to answer the other
question proposed at the outset, how the State
came to be built up out of this material. How
could these little groups, so sharply separated from
each other in all the interests of human life, come
to be united into one corporation, owning, as we
saw that a State must, one government, one law,
one worship, capable of united action, and suscept-
ible to the impulses of a common patriotic feeling? The problem was a more difficult one than

[1] In the above account of the *gentes* and γένη, nothing has been
said of the larger groups in which these were distributed—the
Phratries and tribes of Athens, and the Curiæ and original tribes
of Rome. The origin of these is far more obscure, and bears less
directly on the subject of this chapter.

we can well realise, and the process was doubtless a much longer one than historians have represented it. We can only see a bare outline of the truth; in no single case of real antiquity can the details be recovered.

Let us first consider what motives or circumstances may have suggested such a union of these small groups into larger ones.

I have said that before a wandering people settles down on a particular territory, it already contains a number of *cells* held together by the tie of kinship. After the settlement, this tie continues to act as a bond; but from that time onwards a new binding principle begins to make itself felt, and by slow degrees takes the place of kinship. This new tie is·the influence of the land on which the community is settled. Kinship is a bond which must sooner or later be relaxed and fail; it can only be kept up by ingenious fictions, and in most existing village communities it has long ago disappeared. But when once a permanent settlement has been made on a tract of land, the land becomes a *home*; it is taken to the heart of the people who live on it and by it, and they hold together for love of it, long after the idea of actual kinship has grown weak or utterly vanished. History teems with examples of this change. We can see it in many of our own English villages, which once were the *hams* or *tuns* of invading Teutonic kinsfolk, and now, though still bearing their kin name, have entirely lost the binding power of kinship, yet exercise over their inhabitants a certain unifying spell, as the places where they and their forefathers have lived and toiled.[1]

But this influence of the land is never so powerful as that of kinship, and it acts in a different way. The tie of blood is strong in small groups, but it cannot create large ones or hold them together; the larger the group of kin becomes, the fainter and more fictitious will be the bond of relationship. But here comes in the influence of the land, and carries on the work which the other had begun. There are not likely to be natural geographical boundaries between the lands of adjacent villages, —no such stern natural limits as between the kin by blood of one set of villagers and another. When once the blood-tie has grown fainter, there is no serious obstacle to the union of villages and their lands in a larger whole, if there be obvious advantage to be gained by it, or if a strong hand urges or forces on the process. And this process may go on, gradually or by leaps, until some natural boundary is reached, such as the sea and the mountain barriers which enclose Attica or Latium, or the Rhine and the Alps, beyond which the Swiss have hardly, and at their peril, succeeded in extending their confederation. Then the land may eventually become a *fatherland*, and acquire a marvellous binding force over men's minds, as it has in Ireland and Switzerland, and more or less in all modern States.

If the union of villages was thus made more possible, as the idea of the land took the place of the idea of kinship, what may we suppose were the

[1] See Maine, *Early Institutions*, p. 72 foll.

motives which actually prompted union, or what circumstances suggested it ? We may discern two, with which we must be here content — (1) the necessities of self-defence ; (2) the renown of some prominent centre of religious worship. The two might act together in many instances, but we must deal with each separately and very briefly.

It is an almost self-evident proposition that village communities would stand in need of defence from enemies, whether neighbours or pirates. Thucydides, in the passages already quoted, has pictured their weakness as he conceived it ; and with his account it is interesting to compare those of modern travellers, *e.g.* that of Mr. A. R. Wallace, who, in his *Malay Archipelago*, has described the dangers to which the unprotected villagers are liable in the islands of that group.[1] At a very early period, we may suppose, these little units felt the first influences of a purpose which began to agglutinate them together. Several would unite for the possession of a hill or vantage-ground of refuge, which they would fortify, and to which they could retreat from danger. Such fortified hills are found in every country, including our own. In Italy the stronghold was known as *urbs*, or *oppidum*, or *arx* ; and in Greece as πτόλις, or πόλις.[2]   Here, then, we come upon

---

[1] *Malay Archipelago*, p. 341, ed. 1886.

[2] Schomann, *Antiquities of Greece* (Eng. trans.), pp. 121, 123. At p. 66, speaking of the Homeric πόλις, Schomann points out that the πόλις of Homer was not always a fortified place. Probably the word was acquiring its later sense when the Homeric poems were composed.

the first meaning of the word which has become so famous in the world's history. The citadel, as a centre-point of union, gradually gathers round it a city. A few famous examples are the Acropolis of Athens, the Cadmea of Thebes, the strongholds of Alba and Tusculum, the Palatine, and later the Capitoline hill at Rome. But any traveller with an observant eye may verify the process for himself in England, France, Italy, or Greece.

Together with this motive, the preservation of themselves and their property, the primitive villagers doubtless felt the influence of another, which they perhaps hardly realised as distinct from the first. Every community had its worship, as we have seen; every tribe or State had its deities, brought with it in its wanderings from its original home. The gods of the race were its guardians, for the essence of the idea of a deity lies in the fact that man looks to an invisible Power for aid in adversity, as he also expects punishment for neglect and sin. The desire to protect the protector, to keep the guardian from passing over to the enemy as a consequence of neglect, to prevent his holy place from falling into strange hands, was beyond doubt in part what led our forefathers so often to fix the site of their worships on hills and isolated rocks. They would gain protection for their gods in this way, and would also gain a double advantage for themselves—the aid of the gods who were necessary to their welfare, and the aid of the "rock-built refuge" behind which they would be secure. And thus it would come about that the

fame of some holy place, where a deity was worshipped whose protecting power was notorious,
would assist in the union of village communities.
" The forming," says Duncker,[1] " of the agricultural
communities around the Cecropia (*i.e.* the later
Acropolis) under the protection of Athena, around
Eleusis under the protection of Demeter, and the
community of shepherds in the South under the
protection of Pallas, is the oldest known fact in
Attic history." And indeed, wherever we turn in
Greek or Italian history, we find that all unions of
communities, small and great, are invariably held
together by the bond of a common worship, a special
devotion to some protecting deity, or combination of
deities. For, as De Coulanges has well said, it is
only a *belief* which could overcome the immense
difficulty which men felt in giving up old habits
and small liberties for the restrictions and discipline
of a more highly-organised life ; a belief, we may
add, not destitute of reason, but based on the actual
necessities of life, which themselves suggested union,
while religion made it practicable.

Before we turn to examine one or two examples
of this process of union, one question seems to call
for such an answer as we may be able to find for it.
Have we any evidence which will enable us to fix
with any kind of certainty the period during which
the City-State came into existence ? As regards
Italy, it may be said at once that we have no such
evidence. The traditional date of the foundation

---

[1] *History of Greece*, Eng. trans. i. 113. Cf. De Coulanges,
La Cité antique, ed. ii. p. 145.

of Rome (753 B.C.) has no historical value ; we know on archæological evidence that there must have been settlements on the site of Rome long before that date, but when Rome began its life as a City-State we can hardly even guess. With regard to Greece we are in a somewhat better position. There archæological evidence, though it is still *sub judice*, has accumulated with astonishing rapidity of late years ; and the fruitful discoveries of Dr. Schliemann can be compared with the pictures of social and political life preserved in the Homeric poems. The result of this comparison, in spite of endless differences of learned opinion, both as to the archæological evidence itself and as to the relative age and value of various parts of the poems, can now be presented in a tolerably certain form. We now feel comparatively sure that there was a civilisation in Greece before that of the πόλις, and out of the ruins of which the πόλις probably grew ; and that this civilisation, which may be called Achæan, and which is represented in Homer by the great kings of Mycenæ and Sparta, came to an end somewhere about the year 1000 B.C., and perhaps under stress of a Dorian invasion from the north. It is after that date that we may discern the beginnings of that later civilisation with which we are solely concerned. " There is a broad line dividing mythical from political Hellas, which seems to coincide with the great break made in the continuity of Hellas by the Dorian invasion. . . . On the more recent side of that line we see vigorous communities, choosing their own governments, carrying on trade

with all parts of the Mediterranean and Euxine.
. . . On the older side we see the castles of magnificent princes standing among the huts of their
dependants."[1]

With this older civilisation we have here nothing
to do. It is not the civilisation of the City-State,
which only began after the race of Agamemnon had
disappeared from Greece, approximately in the tenth
and ninth centuries B.C. Great indeed is the darkness that lies around the origin of this later wonderful civilisation, which made Greece all that it is for
us. But one City-State, and that the most famous
of all, preserved a tradition of its origin so lively
and so reasonable, that we can rely upon it as representing in outline at least what actually took
place in that instance.[2]

About the Synoikismos or political union of
Attica a great deal has of late years been written,
but our ideas of it are still based chiefly on the
account of Thucydides, which we may conveniently
quote in full. It represents the traditional ideas
of the Athenian, divested of much mythical setting,
and attested by what we should call scientific
reasoning. He says (ii. 15):—

" In the days of Cecrops and the first kings, down to the
reign of Theseus, Athens was divided into communes, having
their own town-halls and magistrates. Except in case of
alarm the whole people did not assemble in council under
the king, but administered their own affairs, and advised

---

[1] Gardner, *New Chapters in Greek History*, p. 97.
[2] For prehistoric Athens, references to modern researches will
be found quoted in Holm's *Geschichte Griechenlands*, i. 477.

together in their several townships. Some of them at times even went to war with him, as the Eleusinians under Eumolpus with Erechtheus. But when Theseus came to the throne, he, being a powerful as well as a wise ruler, among other improvements in the administration of the country, dissolved the councils and separate governments, and united all the inhabitants of Attica in the present city, establishing one council and town hall. They continued to live on their own lands, but he compelled them to resort to Athens as their metropolis, and henceforward they were all inscribed on the roll of her citizens. A great city thus arose which was handed down by Theseus to his descendants, and from his day to this the Athenians have regularly celebrated the national festival of the Synoikia, or union of the communes, in honour of the Goddess Athene." [1]

The net historical result of this passage, and of the corresponding one of Plutarch, is that at an early date the village communities of Attica, already perhaps grouped together here and there for mutual aid or worship,[2] and looking to the kings of the Acropolis for aid in serious danger, were induced to give up their local self-government, and the worships with which it was connected, and to own one government only, of which the seat was Athens. They did not migrate thither in a body—that would have been to leave their lands untilled. Many indeed of the noble families may have removed to the new centre, glad of the prospect of concentrating aristo-

[1] Jowett, *Thucydides*, vol. i. 104. Cf. Plutarch, *Theseus*, 24, 32.

[2] Thucydides uses the word πόλις ; perhaps indicating a stage of union midway between the κώμη and the true City-State. We know of at least one previous agglutination, that of the *tetrapolis* of Marathon, and we have traces of others. See Kuhn, *Entstehung der Stadte der Alten*, p. 48 foll. See also Beloch, *Storia Greca*, pp. 11, 114.

cratic strength ;[1] but Attica, which is about the
size of Kent, was too large for a general change of
such a kind ; and the consequence was that an
entirely new kind of community was formed, the
heart and life of which was in the πόλις *par excellence* — the city on and around the Cecropian
rock,—while all the smaller units counted this
centre as their own, and gradually came to consider
it as the visible expression of their united life and
strength.   Who was the real author of this great
work we do not know; and it is no more than
conjecture if we interpret the legend of Theseus as
indicating an invasion from the Peloponnese which
brought it about by force.[2]   It seems more likely
to have been due to the hand of a strong master
than to a common agreement of communities.   But
however it came about, it laid the foundation-stone
of Athenian greatness, and changed Attica into the
City-State of Athens, the first and the most perfect
in Hellas—a destiny to which her fortunate geographical conditions seem naturally to point.[3]

This, then, is the most famous example of the
birth of a Greek City-State, and of all prehistoric
foundations it is the best attested.   It would be a
mistake, however, to suppose that many other Greek
cities owed their origin to circumstances of exactly
the same kind.   There was beyond doubt local
variation everywhere—variation arising from the

[1] Plutarch, *l.c.* ; Kuhn, *Entstehung der Städte der Alten*, p. 167
foll.

[2] Abbott, *History of Greece*, i. 281 and note ; Gilbert, i. 107.

[3] Holm, *op. cit.* i. 455.

disposition of the people, the nature of their land, the force brought to bear on them, or the objects to be gained by union. In one or two cases such as that of Elis, where the " synoikismos " did not take place till after the Persian wars, we have traces of a form of union closely resembling that of Attica.[1] But in many others, where the territory was smaller, the inhabitants of the pre-existing villages or groups of villages seem to have been actually transferred to the new city. For example, the two Arcadian towns of Tegea and Mantinea, which lay at the southern and northern ends of a single long, flat plain among the hills, were made up of communities which probably ceased to exist when once the city had been formed ; for the territory on which the two towns subsisted was all of it within easy reach of the walls, and could be cultivated by the inhabitants without residing in the country.[2] It is possible that the City-State of Argos came into existence as such in the same way, though her territory was much larger. But the most famous instance of this kind of union—the one of which we know by far the most—is that of Megalopolis, the great city built in B.C. 370 under the auspices of Epaminondas, to overawe Sparta. It is true that it was rather an artificial than a natural union, born as it were out of due time ; but it shows plainly the way in which the Greeks would naturally go to work when a city had to be created out of disconnected units which were in no true sense of the word a State. Forty-one town-

---

[1] Strabo, pp. 336, 340.   [2] *Ib.* p. 337.

ships, or, as we may imagine them, village communities of various sizes and growth,[1] had their
population transferred to that imposing stronghold
which has lately been in part excavated by members
of the British school at Athens. The foundation
answered its purpose, and Megalopolis was destined
to play a great part in the last struggles of the
Greeks for liberty; but the forcible method used
was perhaps hardly well suited to the conditions
of the considerable territory which was laid under
contribution, for we know that the land became
eventually depopulated, and thereby deprived of its
natural strength.[2] In a Greek City-State, city and
land must be one whole, admitting of no disproportion or division of natural interest.

If we turn to Italy we find our knowledge of the
genesis of the City-State even more scanty; and of
the beginnings of any other Italian city than Rome
we may be said to know nothing at all. It has
been already said that the earliest inhabitants lived
in small communities (*vici* and *pagi*) within reach
of a fortified place of vantage and refuge, which
probably also served as a centre both for worship
and traffic. Each ring-wall, or citadel (*arx*, *urbs*,
oppidum), was common, so far as we can discover, to
several village communities, and was the object of
special religious observance and care, both in its
foundation and its maintenance,—a fact which be-

[1] Kuhn, *op. cit.* 229. The words used to describe them are πόλεις
and πολίχνια; but they were small and weak. Paus. vi. 12, 3;
Xen. *Hist.* vii. 5, 5; cf. Grote, vii. 196.

[2] Strabo, p. 358.

came the nucleus of the legend of the foundation of
Rome by Romulus and Remus. Thus we seem to
see from the beginning, as we might have expected,
a difference between the character of the Latin
village community and that of Greece. The latter
seems to have been comparatively isolated, and to
have found the process of union slow and difficult ;
and the same dislike of amalgamation was inherited
by the City-State of the Greeks from the communities which had generated it, and acted as a
centrifugal force, as we shall see, throughout Greek
history. But in Latium, if not elsewhere in Italy,
we can trace from the beginning a tendency in
the villages to gather in groups,[1] a tendency inherent in the race, and destined to give them a
very different future from that of the Greek peoples.
They were at all times a practical people, who
saw their own advantage and acted upon it ; and in
their early relations with each other, whether public
or private, they showed a power of *accommodation*
which eventually became the natural basis of Roman
law—their greatest contribution to civilisation.

There can be little doubt that at a very early
period the Latin people were grouped in " cantons,"
as they have been called, *i.e.* in clusters of village
communities, each owning a citadel of refuge and
worship ; and further, that the *whole* race had a
common worship and a common political centre on
the conspicuous Alban hill (Monte Cavo), whence
Jupiter Latiaris, the divine father, looked down upon
his people. One of the communities which shared

[1] Marquardt, *Staatsverwaltung*, i. 2.

his worship had occupied as their citadel a square hill, some 160 feet above the sea, whose steep and rocky sides fell sharply to the southern banks of the Tiber, and to the marshy ground which the river sometimes overflowed. Three communities seem to have had their residence as well as their refuge on this hill, while their farms (*pagi*) lay around it; these three oldest settlements of the oldest Rome were the Cermalus, the Velia, and the Palatium. The whole hill came to be called the Palatine; its natural strength was increased by massive masonry, fragments of which we may see still on its northern and western sides; and its position as commanding the Tiber, and as the outpost of Latium on the borders of Etruria, marked it out for a great future.

This triple community would probably have been called by the Greeks a πολίχνιον or πόλις in the earlier sense, as we saw it used of the Arcadian communities which went to form the city of Megalopolis. It could hardly have been deemed a real πόλις; nor can we name a time at which the City-State of Rome began its true existence. But we can trace two stages of its growth, in each of which the genius of the Latins for cohesion was the guiding spirit of its advance. There were other hills around the Palatine which invited settlement. Four communities on the Esquiline formed a union with the three on the Palatine, and this union was kept up in the memory of the Romans for centuries by the festival of the Septimontium on 11th December, which had not become quite forgotten even in the

days of the Empire.[1]   On the Quirinal hill, to the
north-east, there settled yet another community, or
group of communities, with its own worships and
its own citadel, and in due time a fusion took place
between this and its neighbours on the seven mounts.
The whole area occupied by all these settlements was
eventually encircled by one great wall and foss,
ascribed to Servius Tullius, of which fragments are
still to be seen ; a single arx or citadel was fortified on the small and steep Capitoline hill, which
had perhaps been hitherto unoccupied ; the worships were fused together, though always retaining
traces of a distinct origin, and in the end there
arose on the Capitoline a new and splendid temple
to mark the completed union of the component
parts of a great city.   But long before that temple
of Jupiter, Juno, and Minerva had been erected by
Etruscan conquerors, Rome had grown into a City-
State, with its king's house, its sacred hearth or
temple of Vesta, and its open market-place, placed
together in a central position between the Palatine,
Esquiline, and Quirinal.[2]

Such then, in briefest outline, were the beginnings
of the πόλις,—of the City-State of Greece and Italy.
From the cities thus formed there were born innumerable others, which had not to go through the
same slow processes of growth, but sprang at once,

[1] Plutarch, *Quæst. Rom.* 69 ; Suetonius, *Vita Domitiani*, 4.
[2] The position of the Regia and Vesta - temple between the
Palatine and Esquiline hills seem to suggest that they also
formed the centre - point of the united communities of the Sep-
tem montes, before the final union with the settlement on the
Quirinal.

like Athene from the head of Zeus, complete organisms and fully armed. By far the greater number of Greek cities were colonies from States already formed and often even over-populated ; but as these ultimately owed their existence to the conditions of growth which we have already been examining, the story of their origin does not fall within the scope of this chapter. Far less does that of the military colonies of Rome, which were never independent political units, but at all times a part, strange as it may seem, of the ever-growing City-State which founded them. We may safely leave these, and turn for a while to consider the nature of the State we have seen generated, and of the earliest form of its government.

CHAPTER III

THE City-State once realised, at the moment when
the smaller units gave up their separate existence
to become one powerful whole, a new era was
entered on in which the possibilities of advance
were boundless. A new *species* of community had
been developed, with the germs lying hidden within
it of such bloom and fruit as man had never yet
dreamed of. The first members of the new community can hardly have realised this ; but we, looking back into the ages, can see it, and the Greek
philosophers, when they came to turn their thoughts
upon the nature of the State they lived in, recognised it as a leading fact in the history of mankind.
It may be as well, before we go further, to consider
it for a moment in the light of their reflections, and
to ask the fundamental question with which Aristotle
enters on his discussion of the State,—In what way
did this new kind of community essentially differ
from those which preceded it ?

We can ourselves realise, without much effort, in the light of the highest ends of human life, how great is the difference between a highly organised State and all less perfect forms of association. We can compare the possibilities of progress in a well-knit State, and in an imperfectly civilised society, and see how art and literature, morality and material comfort, find a much more favourable soil in the one than in the other. We know, for example, how the conscience and the genius of Englishmen began at last to find utterance when the nation was strongly knit together under Henry VIII., and again under Elizabeth, after being choked by disunion for many generations. We can see how even the modern Socialist, who is apt to hanker after an economy like that of the Middle Ages, or even after the simplicity of savage life, is forced to assume an even more fully developed State-power than we have as yet attained to, for the realisation of the social perfection of his fancy. In spite of all its shortcomings, our modern State is all in all to us; it must seem capable of bringing about such human perfection as we can aspire to, for we can imagine nothing beyond it, except in the vaguest dreams of a far distant future.

Yet it may be doubted whether we can see into these things with a vision so clear and comprehensive as that of the Greek philosophers. Our State, as I said in the first chapter, is not so easily reasoned on; its life is not so visibly focussed for us as theirs. Plato and Aristotle, like Herodotus before them, seeing the peoples around them living in

village communities like the Ætolians or Macedonians, or in very imperfect States like those of the
Oriental nations, and themselves enjoying the ripe
culture, the liberty, the leisure, and the comfort
which the City-State had brought them, easily came
to believe that there was something almost divine
in the πόλις, enabling it to outstrip all other forms
of association in the power of developing man's best
instincts.   With that mysterious power of the Greek
to beautify and idealise everything he touched, Plato
immortalised the πόλις by the very perfection of his
ideal picture of it; and if all Greek history were
lost, and the Republic alone remained, we should
still be able to understand the depth of Greek conviction which connected political forms with the
moral and intellectual perfectibility of human
nature.   But in Aristotle this idealisation was
tempered both with the critical spirit and with a
strict adherence to the essential facts of Greek life,
and in seeking for the real distinction between the
City-State and all earlier and less perfect associations, we cannot do better than follow in his
footsteps.

There are only two or three points in Aristotle's
theory of the State to which we need at present
advert, but these are essentially axioms, which condition all his political thinking.

Let us place first his famous *dictum*, that while
the end of all earlier forms of society is simply *life*,
the end of the State is *good life*.[1]   What a world of

---

[1] *Politics*, i. 2, 8 ; 1252 B ; γινομένη μὲν τοῦ ζῆν ἔνεκεν, οὖσα δὲ τοῦ
εὖ ζῆν ; that is, the πόλις is the earliest association of which the

thought is suggested by this little sentence, and how true it is to the facts! Thucydides describes the Greeks before the era of the πόλις as scraping together just sufficient subsistence to live upon, and he was probably thinking of the conditions of life known to him in parts of Greece where the State had not yet been generated. Almost exactly the same language is used by Sir H. Maine of the village community in India, and the picture drawn by Mr. Wallace of life in the Russian *mir* suggests precisely the same limit to the field of human enterprise.[1] But in rising out of the life of the village into that of the State, man rises, or at least may rise, from the idea of material supply to that of moral and intellectual advance. Aristotle is careful to make us understand what he means by "good life"; it is the life which best realises the best instincts of man. The law and the education of the State will make the citizens good and just men, enjoying "a perfect and self-sufficing life," developing the unimpeded activity of their moral and intellectual excellence.[2] Art, literature, law, philosophy, could not ripen in the family or the village; the narrow limits, the insecurity, the constant toil of that earlier life, impeded all activity in such directions, though the instincts might strive to assert themselves. And so too with justice—the perfectly

"end" is good life. Cf. i. 9, 16 ; 1258 A. Cf. also Professor Bradley's Essay in *Hellenica*, p. 192 foll. The "end" of a thing, in Aristotle's view, is the perfect form in which nature strives to realise it.

[1] Maine, *Village Communities*, p. 175 ; Wallace, *Russia*, ch. viii.

[2] *Hellenica*, p. 193 foll.

harmonious relation of man to man in society—
" the State develops virtues unknown, or imperfectly
known, to the family and the village ; justice, in the
true sense, first appears in the State." [1]

The same idea of the State is further enforced
by the doctrine that the State is a *natural* growth,
i.e. that it is not the artificial result of a convention
or compact between individuals.   It is the natural
and inevitable result of man's desire to use his
faculties to the best purpose, to force his way onwards to his appointed end.   The family and the
village could not realise that end for him ; they
limited and hampered his activity at every point,
excepting so far as they enabled him to procure a
bare subsistence.   Not content with this he pushes
upward with an unconscious growth like that of a
plant, and at last produces a form of social existence
in which all his needs can be satisfied.   He is by
nature meant to be a member of a State, and without the State he cannot fully realise his true nature.
Here, as Mr. Newman admirably expresses it, " he
breathes at last his native air, reaches his full
stature, and attains the end of his being.   Society
is no longer a warping and disturbing, but an ele-
vating and ennobling influence." [2]   He only needs
to perfect the State itself,—a process which neither
Plato nor Aristotle believed to be complete in their
day, if indeed it ever could be completed,—in order
to raise human nature to the highest possible degree
of perfection.   It has been truly said that the Greeks

[1] Newman, *Politics of Aristotle*, i. 38 ; cf. p. 69.
[2] *Op. cit.* i. 557 ; Aristotle, *Politics*, i. 2, 9 ; 1253 A.

were essentially *seekers* ;[1] and if in some paths of search they sought and never found, in the problems of social life at least they laid hold on a great prize, and did not underrate its value.

Nothing can be clearer to the reader of the *Politics* than Aristotle's conviction that no higher form of social union was possible than that of the City-State. Of Empire—of the subordination of several States to one ruling State—he has nothing to tell us ; he must have looked on such a form of union as artificial and unnatural, and therefore as beyond the scope of his inquiry. Nor does he treat of Federation, or the union of several States under a common government for the common good ; to his mind the City-State should need no help from other States, and in combining with them would only be surrendering a part of its own essential vitality. The ideal State must be wholly independent of others, wholly self-sufficing ; it must be able to maintain its own character as a State, by itself and for itself, without aid or stimulus from without.[2] Its beauty and its order are the result of its own natural growth, and must be secured and enhanced by purely natural means.

And here Aristotle does but reflect the inborn tendency of the Greeks to dislike all larger political unions ; a tendency which, as we saw, was less strong, or at least less permanent, in the sister peninsula. To the Greek thinker, as to the ordinary Greek citizen, all federations were a step down-

---

[1] See the preface to Holm's *Griechische Geschichte*, p. xi.

[2] Aristotle. *Politics*. 1326 B.

ward, and all empires were destructive of man's best chances. The City-State could not join with others in any such union, whether by consent or by compulsion, without giving up some of those precious characteristics which Aristotle postulated as necessary to a perfect State, and therefore as equally essential to the production of perfect man. And in this instinct of his, which Aristotle thus reflected, it can hardly be denied that the Greek was right. So far as he could attain perfection at all, he could attain it only in his peculiar form of State. As that form of State decays, the value of Greek life diminishes with it. There came a time in later Greek history when the cities were forced to unite together in self-defence, and again a time when, falling under the dominion of Macedon and Rome, they were absorbed into a wider and grander system of political union than any they had themselves developed; but the Greek life of those later days was not the life to which we look back with most reverence; it was not the spring-time of the rarest gifts of humanity. It was the Hellas of the true πόλις which produced Sappho and Sophocles, Herodotus and Pheidias, and Plato. And in another way the same thing is true also of Rome; as a City-State she developed the germs of all that was most fruitful in her civilisation, and produced the noblest types of Roman character. In ceasing to be a City-State she lost her own individual genius, her stately *morale*, her inflexible courage. Assuredly it was in this form of union that the gifts and the virtues of both races found their best expression.

We have now to trace the steps by which the City-State reached such perfection as it was capable of attaining. In all cases it passed through many vicissitudes of fortune, and was forced to learn by the experience of failure and disaster. Its progress was attended by the drawbacks that seem to dog all human effort; for example, it could not exist without slavery, and it never wholly freed itself from the distinction of privileged and unprivileged. The citizen who really reached his full stature, and attained, in Aristotelian phrase, the true end of his being, was one of comparatively few: the great majority of those who lived around him either toiled for his enjoyment, or looked enviously on his advantages. We cannot call any City-State perfect; but as we turn from the philosophers to the reality, we can see humanity slowly struggling towards perfection in this form of social union, in spite of many obstacles never wholly overcome.

The first unquestionable fact which meets us in the life of this new kind of community is that it was originally governed by kings. The thing was expressed by various words—Basileus, Archon, Prytanis, Rex, Dictator—but, so far as we know, it was always there in the childhood of the ancient State.[1] Tradition, both in Greece and Italy, always told of a time when the essential acts of govern-

---

[1] "The king represents the national as distinguished from the tribal form of political development."—Freeman, *Comparative Politics*, p. 165. The lecture from which this passage is quoted is full of useful material for the study of kingship in general.

ment were performed either by or under the
authority of a single man; and in this case we
can be sure that tradition was right. Both Thucydides and Aristotle accepted it;[1] at conservative
Sparta the king himself survived throughout her
history; and at Athens and Rome kingship left
traces behind it when it had vanished, which the
"method of survivals" has co-ordinated with a
definite result.

We can best study kingship by comparing three
different forms of it, which seem roughly to represent three successive stages in its history. We
can see it in the Homeric poems, where on the
whole it appears as an undefined and therefore
early form; next in the earliest constitution of
Rome, which represents a later stage, and shows
it defined with tolerable exactness by custom and
tradition; and lastly, as a survival at Sparta, retaining its old characteristics of form, but much
modified in actual practice.

I. We no sooner touch the Homeric poems than
we are met by the question, Was the City-State
already in existence when they took their present
shape? In any case, are we justified in using
Homer as evidence for the earliest form of State
government? On the whole we are so justified,
in spite of the fact that the first of these questions
must be answered in the negative. It has already
been pointed out (see p. 47) that recent archæological discovery seems to indicate a clear line of
distinction between the civilisation of the age repre-

[1] Thucyd. i. 13, 1 ; Aristotle, *Politics*, i. 2, 6, and elsewhere.

sented in Homer and the civilisation of the πόλις. But it may now be assumed as certain, that the Homeric poems as we have them were put together on the later side of this line, and that they do not all represent the same age, or exactly the same state of society. The *Iliad*, or the oldest portions of it, seems to contain reminiscences of an older type of polity, in which great chiefs ruled over wide and loosely united territories, as the early kings of France or Scotland ruled over lesser chieftains whom they could only attempt to control.[1] The *Odyssey*, and especially those parts of it which are believed to be of the latest origin, gives us the idea of a society altered in some important features, and tending towards the development of that kind of polity which is the object of our study.

It is true, indeed, that there is little or no sign even in the *Odyssey* of the life of the fully formed State. The town is there, and it is frequently called πόλις; the king and the chief men seem to reside in it, and their dwellings show a comfort and affluence which mark an advanced civilisation; yet the life is essentially rural, the wealth is reckoned by flocks and herds, and we find few traces of that public interest and concentrated population which mark the true City-State. Perhaps we may pro-

---

[1] In the description of the shield of Achilles we do, however, see pictured something very like the life of the City-State (*Il.* xviii. 490 foll.); and this is by common consent allowed to be one of the oldest parts of the *Iliad*. On the subject of the Homeric polity, Fanta's little work, *Der Staat in der Ilias und Odyssee* (Innsbruck, 1882), will be found useful.

visionally conclude that the State appears in the
Odyssey as ripe indeed for formation, but not yet
really formed; all the materials are there, but the
building is not as yet complete. And if this view
be the right one, we may surely use Homer as
picturing for us, in outline at least, the features of
the kingship of the new-born State; for not only
have we abundant evidence that those same features
were retained long after the State had been formed,
but nothing is more intrinsically probable than that
an institution, which certainly existed long before
the State arose, should have been accepted as an
heirloom by the earliest "statesmen."

What strikes us at once about the Basileus in
Homer is, that he is one among many; there are
kings of all degrees, from Agamemnon, who in the
poet's fancy rules over wide territories, and appears
sometimes almost as master of an empire, down to
the most insignificant chieftain who bears the title
of Basileus.[1]   At once, therefore, we get a warning
against the mistake of supposing that there is anything of the nature of a fixed constitution to be
discovered in Homer. The king has no clearly
defined limits to his power of government; kingship is not an office, a magistracy, as we think of
it, with a certain sphere of duty and limit of action.
It is rather a social position, like that of the "eorl"

[1] Cf. the Homeric forms βασιλεύτερος and βασιλεύτατος (*Il.* ix.
69, x. 239). A single instance may here suffice of the multiplica-
tion of Basileîs; in Scheria there were thirteen (*Od.* viii. 390),
with Alcinous apparently chief among them. Cf. Gilbert, *Griech.
Alterthümer*, ii. p. 272, note 2, where the many Basileîs of the
Odyssey are contrasted with the great kings of the *Iliad*.

of our early history, with various grades depending
on varying wealth, and expecting rather than demanding reverence, obedience, and tribute from all
men of lower station.[1]   It is an ancient and a
hallowed institution, for all Basileîs are believed to
be of divine ancestry, and all carry the sceptre, or
rod of office ; no one questions their authority; they
are the best men, and it is by the inspiration of the
gods that they give judgment.   Their sons succeed
to their wealth and influence, and are watched with
loving care in their youth as the future leaders of
the people.   It is clear, then, that if we use the
word king of the Homeric Basileus, we must bear
in mind that he is rather a hereditary chieftain
than a constitutional king, and that his power
at home and in peace rests simply on aristocratic
sentiment.   It is, indeed, quite true to say that
this kingship was merely the formal expression of
an aristocracy, and rested on no independent basis
of its own.[2]

We must be careful to remember this in examining the nature of the powers exercised by the
Homeric Basileus.   These powers are generally
represented as being threefold—religious, military,
and judicial,—and this is in the main true ; but they
are very far from being distinctly outlined, and do
not answer to our notions of a clear-cut constitu-

---

[1] The word τιμή has been thought (by Fanta, p. 49) to express,
as a definite political term, the position and power of the Basileus ;
but this is not borne out by the passages quoted, e.g. Il. i. 278,
vi. 193. The word seems really rather to indicate the non-political
nature of the power.

[2] Henkel, *Studien*, p. 57, quoted by Newman, *Politics*, i. 283.

tional law. The king is indeed the representative
of the community in all its most important relations
with gods and with men. He knows how to propitiate the gods worshipped by the community, who
have given him the τιμή by which he rules. He
knows how to make war and to make peace, how
to receive the guest and the fugitive according to
the customs of the people and the will of Zeus.
But his duties are neither constant nor defined ; and
this must be borne in mind if, for convenience' sake,
we examine them briefly in the triple form in which
they are usually presented.[1]

The King as Sacrificer.—When we find Agamemnon sacrificing for the whole host,[2] we are
naturally inclined to ask, Where is the priest ? And
here we have to learn, once and for all, that there
was no such distinction in antiquity between magistrate and priest as our modern ideas would lead us
to imagine. As every father of a family was the
sacrificer for his own household, so was every king
a sacrificer on behalf of his people. Sacrifice was
the most universal and efficacious act of early
religion ; it was matter of daily performance, and
nothing could be undertaken without it.[3] Whoever was in authority must be able to perform it

[1] Perhaps the best general account of Homeric kingship is still
to be found in Schomann's *Political Antiquities of Greece*, p. 22
foll. (Eng. trans.)   See also Jebb's *Homer*, p. 46 ; Gladstone's
Homer and the Homeric Age, vol. i. p. 440.   But it is not a
laborious task to gather the material together from the poems
themselves.

[2] *Il.* ii. 402 foll.   Cf. *Od.* xiii. 281 foll.

[3] See articles "Sacrificium," "Sacerdos," and "Rex," in Smith's

rightly, *i.e.* according to traditional ritual, for to
him all looked for the due maintenance of salutary
relations with the gods. Every chieftain, great or
small, must have exercised this duty at home in his
own community, though in time of war it might
fall to the greatest only. To him and to his family
alone were known the secrets of the office ; it might
happen that even if he ceased to be king in the
Homeric sense,—if his kingship were merged in a
larger one, or if his family became only one among
other noble ones in a newly-formed City-State, it
still retained the sacrificial knowledge and the sole
right to minister to the deity of the community.
Hence arose the hereditary local priesthood of early
Greece ; it begins with the chieftain, and descends
as an heirloom in his family long after his secular
authority has passed away. Aristotle tells us that
the Homeric Basileus controlled all sacrifices except
those which specially belonged to priests ;[1] by which
I understand him to mean, not so much that there
was · a distinction between the kingly and the
priestly offices, but that already some noble (or
kingly) families had lost the one while they retained the other. It will be important to bear this

---

Dict. of Classical Antiquities (new edition). It was on this side of
the king's power that Fustel de Coulanges laid so much stress in
his brilliant book *La Cité antique*. He found the origin of early
monarchies almost entirely in the religious importance of the chiefs
of family, gens, and city. But this is not borne out by what we
know of the early history of the king, or by the etymology of the
names by which he was called. Sacrificial knowledge was a necessary condition, but not the only one, of his power.

[1] *Politics*. 1285 B.

in mind when we come in the next chapter to the period of aristocratic government.

The King as Commander of the Host.—All that needs to be remarked on this point is, that not even in war does the Homeric king appear to be absolute. Aristotle indeed says that he had the power of life and death in the field, and quotes Homer to prove it; but the words (πὰρ γὰρ ἐμοὶ θάνατος) of his quotation are not to be found in the poems as we have them.[1]   Such power would seem to postulate a much more clearly defined polity than that which Homer depicts.   We find the king in the *Iliad* deliberating with other chiefs,—with his council of elderly men[2] and wise, the Witenagemot of that day; and we find even the people present at these deliberations as listeners who may express their approval or disapproval.   Thus, though there is no constitution here, even in time of war, there are, in solution as it were, the elements of a constitution; the nobility is there to advise, and the people have a right to express their feelings.   And that these elements of a constitution, as we see them in time of war, also represent in the main the relations of king, council, and commons in time of peace can admit of no doubt.   We should, however, remember

---

[1] *Politics*, 1285 A.   Cf., however, *Il.* xv. 348.

[2] The γέροντες in Homer are not necessarily elderly men.   But he word itself, like *Senatus*, is proof of the idea on which the nstitution is based, *i.e.* chieftaincy of some degree, for which the on has had to wait till his father has died or stepped aside, and he himself is growing old.   At Sparta the fact as well as the word survived; no one under sixty years of age could be a member of the Gerousia.   Plutarch, *Lycurgus*, 26.

that in war the outlines of authority are likely to
be more sharply defined than in peace, and that a
long period of war would have a tendency to increase the king's authority, so long as he survived.
His normal power at home was probably of a very
gentle kind, as might be expected in a society that
was so entirely aristocratic.

The King as Judge.—In a full-grown State, such
as Athens, Rome, or any modern State, the executive,
as we call it, has a large amount of varied business
to perform. But in an early state of society, executive government consists almost entirely of the
decision of disputes; and even this sphere of judicial action was a limited one, for thieves and
adulterers taken in the act could be put to death
without ceremony, and the revenge of murder was
the duty of the family or clan of the victim,
unless a proper indemnity (ποινή) was offered by
the murderer.[1] Still disputes would arise, perhaps more often between families than individuals,
which could only be settled by bringing the force of
the community to bear on them : and wherein was
this force to be found concentrated but in the
Basileus ? It is just here that we see the value of
the idea of kingship—of a sanctity arising from
noble descent, in the discipline of peoples who are
preparing for life in a State. The kings of all
degrees, in virtue of their divine ancestry and nurture,
are provided with judgments or dooms by Zeus,
which are unquestioningly accepted by the people.
These judgments (θέμιστες) do not rest upon any-

[1] *Il.* ix. 632 : *Od.* viii. 347.

thing which we can call law, for Homer knew no law, and has no word for it. " They are separate, isolated judgments not connected by any thread of principle." [1] Only a firm belief in the divine source from which they proceed could give them a binding force in men's eyes.

It is true that the greatest Basileîs do not appear in Homer as themselves dispensing justice. It is the sages of the council who sit in judgment, as in the famous picture on the shield of Achilles. But the sanction of their decision was no doubt the same ; they too were chiefs of less degree, and enjoyed the confidence of the people by virtue of a divine descent. There is no trace in Homer of any decay of this confidence, nor of the growth of that mistrust which issues eventually in a demand for written law. And if we are right in assuming that the later Homeric society is close upon the beginning of the State, we shall also be right in concluding that the State sets out on its career not with questioning but with trust ; and that it has been made possible simply because men have shown themselves capable of discipline, ready to accept a divine ordering of society, and to obey those whom they believe to be better than themselves.

---

[1] Maine, *Ancient Law*, ch. i. p. 4. Maine perhaps puts this a little too strongly ; for there is a Homeric word (δίκη) which seems to indicate an idea of *usage*,—the course which the gods pointed out and which the people would accept ; while the θέμιστες are dooms which at once create this usage and conform to it. See Jebb, *Homer*, p. 48, and passages there quoted, to which may be added *Il.* xvi. 387 foll. ; *Od.* xiv. 83 ; Hesiod, *Theogonia*, 85, and *Works and Days*, 9 and 215 foll.

The strength of the earliest monarchies then, so far as we can gather from Homer, lay in no clearly defined powers or prerogatives, for definition implies limitation, and the Homeric monarchy knows no such thing, either as securing the king's power or confining it within certain bounds. It lay rather in the belief that the good relation of men and gods could be successfully cared for by those only with whose families the knowledge of divine things was deposited; in the belief that men of noble birth, and therefore as a rule of bodily beauty and prowess, could be the only leaders in war; and in the belief that obedience was owing to these in all questions between man and man in time of peace, because it was only through their judgments that the will of Zeus could be known. These three aspects of a single deeply-rooted conception lie at the base of all ancient aristocratic government; and this earliest monarchy, as we said just now, was but the outward expression of a truly aristocratic society. If we now turn for a moment to the earliest Roman constitution of which we have any knowledge, we shall find a marked change in the direction of definition and solidity.

II. Of the kings of Rome we have no direct contemporary evidence; we know them only from tradition, and from the traces they left behind them in the Republican constitution which followed. But the " method of survivals " has here been applied by a master-hand; and we can be fairly sure, not only of the fact that monarchy actually existed at Rome, but even of some at least of its leading characteristics.[1]

[1] See Mommsen, *Staatsrecht*, ii. pt. i. p. 3 foll., and *Roman*

Here we have kingship no longer denoting, as in Homer, a social position of chieftaincy which bears with it certain vaguely-conceived prerogatives, but a clearly defined *magistracy* within the fully realised State. The rights and duties of the Rex are indeed defined by no documents, and the spirit of the age still seems to be obedience and trust ; but we also find the marks of a formal customary procedure, which is already hardening into constitutional practice, and will in time further harden into constitutional law. The monarchy has ceased to be hereditary, if it ever was so ; and the method of appointment, though we are uncertain as to its exact nature, is beyond doubt regulated with precision, and expressed in technical terms. Let us fix our attention for a moment on one of these terms,—the most famous of them all, and the one which best exemplifies that stage in the government of the City-State which the Roman monarchy seems to represent.

The functions of the Rex show the same three sides as those of the Homeric Basileus. He was priest for the whole people, he commanded the army in war, and he dispensed justice at home. But the Romans have learnt to sum up the whole of this power in one technical term of wonderful force and meaning. This word, *imperium*, introduces us at once to a new range of ideas, which we may call political, and which belong to the newly realised life of the City-State. *Imperium* is a technical term, the first we

History, vol. i. p. 66.   Cf. Prof. Pelham's article "Roman History" in the last edition of the *Encyclopædia Britannica*.

meet with ; for there is no Homeric word which can be regarded as such politically. It marks the power of the king as distinguished from the power of the head of a family or a village community ; it expresses the supreme power of the chief magistrate *in an organised State.* The *imperium* of the Rex was technically unlimited, both in peace and war ; the idea of State authority is fully expressed in the word, and had therefore been fully realised. All power exercised by any individual beside the Rex is *delegated* to its holder by the Rex, and emanates directly from his *imperium.* To him alone belonged the regal insignia, and above all the rods and axes carried before him, symbol of a power which could punish the disobedient with instant death. And this power, we must notice, was not his by hereditary right, but was given him by a formal vote of the citizens ; whatever might be the mode of his appointment or election, it is certain that he only became supreme after this vote had been passed. Here, then, we plainly have a fixed constitution, expressed in formal procedure and in technical terms ; and the leading feature of it is the concentration of political power in the king, and the remarkable clearness with which that power is conceived.

But all this was by no means incompatible with a customary limitation to the absolutism of the Roman king. In the Roman mind there was an instinct, which was never lost, to define, and at the same time to check authority ; to make the clearness of legal definition itself assist the influence of moral limitation. This moral limitation can be traced very plainly as acting even on the Rex. He is expected to ask advice, and probably also to take it. His advising body was the Senate, the equivalent of the Homeric γερουσία, of which we shall have more to say presently; and the principle which in form, if not always in fact, governed the Roman magistrate for ever afterwards, that he should not act without the advice of this council, became so much a necessary law of the Roman mind that we may be certain that it had its origin in the monarchy. Again, we have reason to believe that in the trial of accused persons of importance the king was expected, though by no means legally bound, to submit the question of life and death to the people for their decision; if this be so, another great principle which became the charter of republican liberty as the *jus provocationis*, a right of appeal against the decision of the magistrate, also had its origin in the moral obligations of the Rex.[1]

In the Roman monarchy, then, we see the earliest form of State government completely and judiciously developed. Order and discipline, so necessary to man in his political childhood, are there represented by the technically unlimited power of the Rex; while in the salutary moral obligations which the good sense of the people has imposed on this magistrate, we find customary rules of conduct

---

[1] Both these principles may have grown out of germs of great antiquity, and were not the peculiar invention of the Romans. But it is not given to every people to fertilise such germs, and convert them into plain and formal principles of constitutional action.

which are capable of growing into invaluable
constitutional principles. Two things seem necessary to a young State which is to have a great
future,—the full realisation of authority and of the
obedience due to it, and a sense of the moral limits
which reason sets both on obedience and authority.
Both these were present in early Rome, as in early
England.

III. The third form of monarchy which we are to
consider in this chapter is that of Sparta. Of the
early history of the Spartan kingship we know
hardly anything; but as a late and most curious
survival into historical times it well repays study.
As in the Homeric Basileus we have the undefined
stage of early magisterial authority, and in the
Roman Rex its complete and defined realisation, so
in the history of Spartan kingship in the sixth and
fifth centuries we have a picture of the way in which
life might slowly leave an old and valuable institution, while its venerable framework remained, as
much respected and cherished as ever.

The Spartan resembled the Roman in many
ways, and one of them was the tenacity with which
he clung to old ideas and institutions. When the
Romans got rid of their kings they retained not
only many of the outward signs of kingship, but
also the *imperium* itself—the very essence of the
king's magisterial power. The Spartans, on the
other hand, kept the kingship throughout their
history, but allowed it by slow degrees to moulder
away into a picturesque ruin. The explanation of
this is to be found not only in the dual form of

Spartan kingship, which probably weakened it from the first, but in the radical difference between the Greek and Italian conception of monarchy. At Sparta, as in the Homeric age, the kings were of divine descent, and the position and power passed from father to son ; to break the sacred line of the children of Herakles would be simply to make light of the divine ordering of things. Just as the Greek conceived of his gods as bodily presences rather than as spiritual essences, so it was the personality of his kings, their ancestry and breeding, rather than their constitutional powers, which filled his mind with reverence.[1] There is little trace of this feeling among the more prosaic Romans. They did not think of their gods as beings in human form ; nor was it the glory of the person or the family which overawed them. As it was the power of the gods and their use of it which conditioned their religious thoughts and acts, so it was the king's power and his use of it on which they fixed their eyes as citizens. Thus, as will be seen in the next chapter, they could abolish the king, yet retain his *imperium* ; while at Sparta the powers were suffered to decay, the king himself remaining.

At Sparta there were two kingly families, and two kings with equal authority ; and however this is to be explained, it will not surprise any one who

[1] This is curiously illustrated by Herodotus's account of the funeral ceremonies of the Spartan kings (vi. 58). No absolute monarch could be the subject of more universal lamentation, however formal it might be ; yet this was no homage rendered to power.

recalls the multiplicity of the Homeric kingship.[1] The division of sovereignty probably led to that period of distress and anarchy which is the one almost certain fact of the earliest Spartan history ; and the result was a reconstruction, attributed to Lycurgus, at a date which may be assumed to be not later than 800 B.C. This must have been the era when the Spartan institutions were fixed on a system compatible with the life of an organised State, and is at the same time the point from which the decay of the kingly power may be traced.

When Herodotus, who had himself been at Sparta, described the duties and privileges of the Spartan kings as they existed in the latter half of the fifth century, the monarchy still retained the triple powers which we have seen outlined in the Homeric poems, and gathered into a single conception in the Roman kings. It will be as well to quote the very words of Herodotus, for they give us a life-like picture of an ancient moss-grown monarchy.[2]

" The prerogatives which the Spartans have allowed their kings are the following. In the first place, two priesthoods, those of Zeus of Lakedaimôn and celestial Zeus ; also the right of making war on whatsoever country they please, without hindrance from any of the other Spartans on pain of exile ; in the field the privilege of marching first in the advance and last in the retreat, and of having a hundred picked men for their

---

[1] For different explanations see Abbott, *Hist. of Greece*, i. 206 ; and for further detail G. Gilbert, *Griech. Alterthumer*, i. p. 4 foll.

[2] Hdt. vi. 56. Rawlinson's translation.

bodyguard while with the army ; likewise the liberty of sacrificing as many cattle in their expeditions as seems to them
good, and the right of having the skins and chines of the
slaughtered animals for their own use.

" Such are their privileges in war ; in peace their rights
are as follows. When a citizen makes a public sacrifice, the
kings are given the first seat at the banquet ; they are served
before any of the other guests, and have a double portion of
everything. They lead the libations, and the hides of the
sacrificed beasts are their perquisite. Every month on the
first day, and again on the seventh of the first decade, each
king receives a beast without blemish at the public cost,
which he offers up to Apollo ; likewise a medimnus of meal,
and of wine a Laconian quart. In the athletic contests they
have always the seat of honour ; they appoint the citizens
who have to entertain foreigners. . . . They have the whole
decision of certain causes, which are these, and these only ;—
When a maiden is left the heiress of her father's estate,
and has not been betrothed by him to any one, they decide
who is to marry her ; in all matters concerning the public
highways, they are judges ; and if a person wants to adopt
a child, he must do it before the kings. They likewise
have the right of sitting in council with the twenty-eight
senators ; and if they are not present, then the senators
nearest of kin to them have their privileges, and give two
votes as representing the kings, beside their own as councillors."

In this picture we see, as it were, an ancient
and hallowed building, with all the graceful details
of its architecture still preserved ; a building which
was once the central point of the common life of the
State, but is now comparatively little used except
for religious purposes.

The king is here still high-priest for the community ; but his priesthood is limited to two special
worships. The religious system has been organised

so as to suit the needs of a City-State, and the various worships have their appointed priests. And those which the kings hold, they hold, not like the Homeric Basileus, as part of an undefined τιμή, but as γέρα, *i.e.* privileges specially reserved to them. So it is also with the administration of justice. In jurisdiction Herodotus mentions but two kinds of suits which came to them for decision, and both are of a special and limited character—the one relating to certain contingencies in the devolution of property, and the other to the maintenance of the public roads. In cases of bloodshed the kings shared jurisdiction with the Gerousia, and all ordinary disputes seem to have been decided by the Ephors, *i.e.* by magistrates of later origin than the City-State itself.[1] Only in war, *i.e.* outside of the ordinary range of State-life, does the Spartan king still seem to be supreme, and even here he is beginning to be mistrusted. As early as the end of the sixth century B.C. Cleomenes I., the most original and remarkable of all the Spartan kings, was brought to trial for alleged misconduct; and several other instances, both of trial and punishment, are recorded in the two following centuries.[2] Being thus made responsible for their conduct in war, they gradually lost the essential part of those military prerogatives which Herodotus describes. In the fourth century B.C. they were little more than nominal kings, while the Ephors, an elected board

[1] Aristotle, *Politics*, iii. 1, 10 ; 1275 B.
[2] Thucyd. v. 63 ; Hdt. vi. 72 and 82.

of five, whose powers were not defined by ancient and hallowed custom, and could therefore be easily extended as convenience or necessity suggested, raised their authority to such a pitch that Plato could describe it as "exceedingly like that of a tyrant."[1]

We need not here enter into the question how all this change was brought about, nor does it belong to the scope of this chapter. Spartan history is extremely obscure, and we know neither details nor dates of the rise and progress of the Ephorate; nor can we certainly discover how far the other elements in the constitution, the Gerousia and the Assembly of the people (*apella*), also had a share in trenching on the original prerogatives of the kings. Enough has been said to show that a monarchy might survive in a State of conservative tendencies long after kingship had disappeared both from Greece and Italy, but that it survived in outward form rather than in reality, still bearing unmistakably the signs of its origin in the heroic age, yet ceasing gradually to do the work of an effective State-magistracy.

But Sparta in this, as in many other ways, stands alone in the history of the City - State. She never was a pioneer in political development. Shut away in her "hollow" valley among the mountains, she did not feel the influences which, from the eighth century onwards, began in the rest of Greece to change the simple form of

[1] Plato. *Laws.* iv. 712 D.

society which made kingship possible and salutary ;
or if she felt them, she took her own way in
responding to them. Those influences, and the
changes they brought about, are now to be considered in the next chapter.

CHAPTER IV

IN the earliest form of the City-State there were
three prominent factors. First, the king, with
his three functions, religious, military, and judicial;
his powers resting not on written law, but on custom, and constituting no real absolutism, but being
apt to gain in strength as custom hardened, provided
that the kings themselves and their families were
equal to the task of maintaining their prestige.
Secondly, the lesser chieftains, who in their own
domain were probably quite independent of the
king, like the feudal lords of the middle ages.
These acted as the advising council of the king,
whose influence became stronger or weaker according as he was of a character to need help or to
dispense with it. Thirdly, the people, *i.e.* all those
who did not belong to the families of any of these
powerful chiefs, and could boast of no divine descent,
nor of any large estates, but in time of peace went
about their daily work as husbandmen or artisans,
and served on foot in time of war. Of the people

we shall speak more fully later on. But we may pause for a moment here to point out that in these three factors of the earliest State we see, in embryo, all possible forms of constitution. In all governments the sovereignty must be either in the hands of one, or of few, or of the many ; it must be either monarchical, or aristocratic, or democratic. Each of these three forms of constitution may indeed take a different colouring, as, according to Aristotle's doctrine,[1] monarchy may become tyranny, aristocracy may, and indeed always did, pass into oligarchy, and democracy in the best sense may become democracy in the worst sense, or, as Polybius styles it, government by the mob. Or there may be transitional forms, such as are often called " mixed " constitutions, in which, for example, as at Athens after Solon, the political privileges of the few were being gradually extended to the many ; or as at Sparta, where we saw that during a long period the monarchy continued to survive alongside both of oligarchic and democratic elements. But in all cases, whether the constitution be natural, or lebased, or transitional, it can always be traced oack to one or other of these social facts which meet us at the very outset of our study of the City-State. Even tyranny, which will at first sight appear to have no direct connection with early forms of monarchy, was really only a reaction towards a traditional concentration of authority, brought about by the many, as suiting them better than the rule of the few. The social predominance

[1] *Pol.* iii. 6 *fin.* and 7 ; 1279 A. Cf. Polybius, vi. 4, 6.

of one family, or of a few, or of many,—such is the simplest way of expressing the long series of changes in constitutional form which we have to trace ; and looking forward from the age of monarchy we can guess without much difficulty how such changes would be likely to run.

We might naturally suppose that if the monarchies gave way at all, they would give way, not to the people, who had neither knowledge, experience, property, renown, or high descent, but to those noble families who surrounded the king, supplied him with advisers, and were on the same social level as his own family. And so it was. Universal tradition, both in Greece and Italy, told of the displacement of the kings by these noble families, and of a long period of aristocratic government which followed. When history really begins in Greece and Italy, hardly a single kingship of the old type is to be found.[1]

Of the immediate causes of this universal change we have scarcely any positive knowledge, and we may be fairly sure that ancient writers had no more than we have. Aristotle, in mentioning it, writes in quite general terms, and does not, as his habit is, quote examples to support what he tells us.[2] The causes that he suggests are disagreement among the members of the kingly house, and a tendency to arbitrary government by the kings

[1] In other Italian towns besides Rome we know nothing of the change ; but that it took place is almost certain. See Mommsen, *Hist. of Rome*, i. 255.

[2] *Politics*. 1313 A.

themselves, such as would be likely to break into the traditional and willing acceptance of monarchy as a natural and inevitable institution. This is no more than we might have guessed for ourselves. Weakness arising from whatever cause—disunion or other,—and on the other hand ambition and arbitrary use of power, are the causes which have throughout all history been apt to destroy not only monarchies, but all governments. And when the monarch is but the chief among a number of lesser potentates, it is easy enough to guess not only at the causes but at the results of revolutions which have at least much apparent resemblance to those of the early modern State.

Perhaps it may be said that we have at least one glimpse of a monarchy on the point of falling to pieces,—though even that glimpse is one into a region that is mythical and misty. Odysseus was king in Ithaca ; and during his twenty years' absence his kingship barely survives the attacks made upon it by the aristocracy of the island, the lesser βασιλεῖς. There seems to be indeed no idea of abolishing monarchy as an institution. Telemachus assumes that some one will be king, even if it be not one of the true kingly family.[1] "There are many other chiefs of the Achæans in sea-girt Ithaca—kings young and old ; some one of them shall surely have this kingship since goodly Odysseus is dead." But if the kingship be removed from the family which has so far held it, the first step is taken towards its destruction ; and Antinous says angrily

[1] *Od.* i. 394 ; Butcher and Lang's translation.

to young Telemachus, " Never may Cronion make
thee king in sea-girt Ithaca, which thing is of
inheritance thy right!"[1]   And Eurymachus, in
kinder tone, tells him that though it is unjust for
the lords to devour the substance of Odysseus, yet
" it lies on the knees of the gods what man is to
be king over the Achæans in sea-girt Ithaca." And
in the assembly which follows in book ii., where
Telemachus seems to appeal to the " folk " for help
against the lords who are living on his substance
and wooing his mother, he shows weakness himself,
and can get no support from the people.[2]   Ithaca
is in confusion ; there seems to be no hope for the
house of Odysseus ; the heir can hardly procure the
ship to carry him to Pylos to seek for news of his
father.

The *Odyssey* is in great part ancient myth and
folk-tale ; but these first two books contain no such
element.   They are clearly a picture,——a fancy
picture it may be,——of such confusion as might
have arisen in any monarchy about the time when
the *Odyssey* took its present shape.   War might
strengthen a king's hands if he returned successful,
but it might also shake his house to its foundations
if he never returned at all.   The plot of the *Odyssey*
brings the king home at last to wreak vengeance on
the traitor lords, and we can imagine his power
thereby greatly increased and handed down intact
to his son.[3]   But in many a case the king may never

---

[1] *Od.* i. 386.   [2] *Ib.* ii. 1-320.
[3] It is to be noticed that when Odysseus finally recovers the
kingship, it is confirmed to him by a "covenant with sacrifice"

have returned, or from some other cause his family
may have given way before the aspiring chiefs, and
the kingship, if not yet destroyed, must have passed
out of the house which had long held it, and so have
lost its oldest traditional claim to loyalty.

But the Homeric poems, as we saw in the last
chapter, seem to point to a time when the City-
State was not yet fully formed, but rather in process of formation. The picture of Telemachus and
the suitors hardly helps us to understand why a
monarchy which had become hardened by usage, as
at Rome, into something resembling a constitution,
should have easily given way to aristocracy, and
why this revolution should have been so universal.
Historians, in default of positive knowledge, are
at pains to bring forward explanations *a priori*.
Grote, for example, and Montesquieu before him,
observed that monarchies are apt to last longer in
large territorial States, while small States, like the
Greek and the later Italian republics, seem naturally
to develop an aristocratic or democratic constitution.[1] The observation is a just one, and the reasons
given in support of it are also worth attention. The
smaller the State, and the more distinctly its life
is centred in a city, the more obvious will the
king's shortcomings be to the eye of his rivals and
of the people. The monarchy of a mediæval State
was hardly an object of criticism, even to the great
lords who surrounded it, except when it impinged

(*Od.* xxiv. 483, 546), an artificial prop which can hardly have
existed in the earliest and most natural form of kingship.

[1] Grote, *Hist. of Greece*, vol. ii. ch. ix.

too closely on their traditional rights ; and even then concerted action against it was not easy to organise. The mass of the people had very little knowledge of it, and accepted it, as they for the most part accept it still, without a hostile thought. Only in great capital cities, such as London or Paris, where the misdeeds of a monarch are obvious, and where discontent can easily gather and grow to a head, have violent anti-monarchical outbreaks found place in modern times. The inference seems to be a safe one that when a State is practically a city, and not a large territory, the traditional institution of kingship, with which political history seems everywhere to begin, is almost sure to be comparatively shortlived. The weakness or cruelty of a king, or a kingly family, would in a City-State be known and felt by all, and would be inevitably brought to an end, whether by sudden revolution or by gradual process. Thus the small size of the Greek State, which has been so often called in as an explanation of the phenomena of its history, or more truly indeed its peculiar nature as a City-State, is almost the only certain fact to which we can have recourse in order to account for this universal change from monarchy to aristocracy.

But there is another consideration which calls for attention before we go farther. It has already been said that monarchy was in one sense only a form of aristocracy ; and the meaning of this *dictum* would seem to be that monarchy, though found everywhere in the world, does not everywhere of itself serve as an adequate political expression for

a certain social condition. It is, in fact, in one
sense a less natural form of constitution than either
aristocracy or democracy. Each of these is the
direct and natural political expression of *a state of
society*. If the rich or the well-born exercise a pre-
dominant influence in a State, the resulting political
form is aristocracy or oligarchy; if the poor or
the low-born carry the full weight which their
numbers would naturally bring them, the resulting
political form is democracy. But of what is
monarchy the political expression ? Neither in an
aristocratic nor in a democratic state of society is
monarchy entirely secure, because it cannot fully
represent the needs, the feelings, or the prejudices
of that society. When, as we shall see in the next
chapter, it was called in to lead the first popular
impulse in the cities of the Greek world, it was
speedily rejected as soon as that work of leadership
was accomplished—the Greek tyrannies were pro-
verbially of short duration. And in the age of
which we are now speaking, where it existed in
an aristocratic society, though much longer lived,
it could not be permanent, simply because it represented that society ever more and more in-
adequately.

All history teaches us that aristocracies have a
strong tendency to grow steadily narrower; that
their sentiment and privilege alike increase in
strength with time. Now a monarchy may serve
fairly well as the political expression of an aristocratic society, but the narrower and more prejudiced
that society grows, the less chance will the monarchy

have of surviving. The king may even be forced
out of sympathy with the class to which he naturally
belongs, and into more intimate relation with the
poorer and unprivileged classes. If then we can
show that the Greek aristocracies had a tendency
to grow narrower, and that the facts and ideas on
which their predominance rested were such as might
easily increase this tendency, we shall at once have
an explanation of the decay of monarchy, even if
we cannot trace the causes of decadence within the
monarchy itself. And at the same time we shall
be providing ourselves with some account, imperfect
though it be, of the characteristics of the aristocracies we are concerned with. Then we may pass
on to consider the few known facts as to the *method*
by which the destruction of monarchy was brought
about.

Aristocracy literally means the rule of the best.
But in what sense of the word " best " did the
Greeks use their word ἀριστοκρατία, and by what
standard did they estimate the class which dis-
placed the early kings ? Aristotle, whose knowledge of the early aristocracies was certainly not
large, writes as if he thought that the rule of the
" best " were an ideal which had never been attained
to in Greece, and warns his pupils not to fall into
the popular error of confusing it with the oligarchical forms of government prevalent in his own
day.[1] He thus attaches a distinctly ethical meaning

[1] *Politics*, 1293 B. He is ready, however, to use the word
ἀριστοκρατία in a modified sense for a very few mixed constitutions, such as that of Carthage. See Newman, i. 497. To the

to the word " best," and seems to contrast the virtue of the true aristocratic ruler with the wealth of the oligarch. But was he right in his belief that the government of the *best* had never been realised ?

Undoubtedly the Greek aristocracies, like all modern ones, did not owe their political power simply to superior moral qualities. They obtained it as the result of certain advantages which they possessed, of which the chief were wealth and high descent. But we can hardly be wrong in believing that the excellence (ἀρετή) which they claimed for themselves—a claim which survived into much later times in the expressions καλοὶ κἀγαθοὶ, ἐπιεικεῖς, γνώριμοι, etc., applied to oligarchs who did not merit them—had at one time had a real existence. We must indeed, in order to understand what it was that they claimed, get rid for the moment of much of our modern notions of virtue or goodness ; but there will still remain an element of ethical superiority which we may predicate of this nobility without misgiving. With them, so far as we can see, began the idea, so fruitful afterwards for Greek civilisation, that the mind and the body alike of each individual should be cultivated to the utmost for the benefit of the State. Here, if anywhere, we must look for the origin in Greece of the culti-vation of the beautiful, in the human body, in the products of art, and, to some extent at least, in conduct too ; and at Rome for the beginning of the

word ὀλιγαρχία Aristotle attaches the meaning, usual in Greece, of government by a few families, distinguished not by excellence but by wealth.

idea of duty, as extending beyond the family to the
State. Naturally, application of this idea was limited
to the members of their own class, from a deeply-
rooted conviction that all others were not worth
the cultivation, and could not repay it by any valuable results ; these were in no true sense a part of
the State, but only, as it were, the natural append-
ages of it, whose destiny was to do the necessary
and inferior work without which it could not exist.
But they themselves, the nobles, were the real men
of the State ; on them devolved all its higher duties ;
and if in the early life of the City-State these nobles
really worked out an idea of public duty which first
made the position of the citizen an honourable and
arduous one, they made a discovery for which the
later Greeks and Romans might well have been
more thankful than they were.

And we may reasonably believe that this discovery was really theirs, though we have little
positive evidence of it. When history opens, the
aristocracies were indeed a thing of the past, but
the idea of the good citizen was there, and can
only be due to their influence. The passionate
lamentations of Theognis over the overthrow of the
" good men " in his own city carry us back in
imagination to a time when Megara was not yet
governed by a narrow oligarchy, but by a nobility
which was really excellent, as well as rich and
high-born, and was bent on developing all its
best powers, bodily and mental, for the good of
the whole community. Even as late as the fifth
century the same idea is seen in the Odes of Pindar,

commemorating the deeds as well as the high descent of men who had brought renown to their cities. And a century later still, the reflection of it may be caught in the writings of Plato and Aristotle, the central feature of whose political teaching is that a man's duty to his State can only be performed at the best when he has fully and rationally developed all his mental and bodily capacities. Such an ideal could never have been formulated by the philosophers, if it had not been already existent in the spirit of the best Greek life. And we may be fairly sure that it originated, not with oligarchy, or tyranny, or democracy, but in an age preceding them all ; in an age when it was possible, to use the language of Prof. Duncker,[1] for the ideal of life and conduct to be realised in the man " capable in body and mind, strong and agile in limb, brave in fight, free from personal greed, zealous for the general good." It was the Greek nobles, then, who first recognised the true nature of the State, and of its infinite capacity for ennobling man ; they realised " the good life " (τὸ εὖ ζῆν) of the citizen in contrast to the mere life (τὸ ζῆν) of the village community. With them begins the development of art and poetry, of education and discipline, of law and public order, in immediate and healthy relation to the State and its needs. And in a different way the Roman aristocracy too, though narrower and less gifted than the Greek, had its own unconscious ideal, and its own peculiar " virtus "; to them and them alone were

---

[1] *Hist. of Greece*, ii. 307 (Eng. trans.) ; cf. p. 214 foll.

due the habits of discipline and self-sacrifice for the good of the State, and the ideas of self-respect and of duty correlated with wealth and station, which forced on all Romans such a vivid conception of the nature of citizenship, and enabled them to survive so many fierce struggles for existence.

An aristocratic class of this kind, in whose bringing up the self-regarding instincts were only so far encouraged as they might contribute to the common good of the youthful State, might co-exist with a monarchy, and probably did so for many generations. There was no natural antagonism between their interests and those of a kingly family which was only the first among many. But their ἀρετή, that combination of self-respect with devotion to the State which we have been describing, was the indirect result of two advantages which in themselves constituted no virtue—the pride of a noble descent, and the possession of wealth, especially in land. Birth and wealth alike may call for self-respect, for courage, and for public spirit, in those who possess them, and the call may be responded to ; the noble may be and should be worthy of his ancestry, and the rich man worthy of his wealth ; but in each of these advantages there is always a certain poison hidden, which is apt to deaden the force of its claim for virtue. An honest family pride may degenerate into mere exclusiveness, and wealth may too easily become an object for its own sake. Some such subtle process must have been at work in the aristocracies of the young City-State, gradually narrowing their ideas and in-

H

terests, and bringing them into antagonism, perhaps almost at the same time, with the kingly family as well as with the unprivileged masses. Let us see how it might have acted.

1. We saw that the Homeric chieftains believed themselves to be διογενεῖς—of divine descent ; and this idea was kept up for centuries by the great families in most Greek States. Even in democratic Athens Alcibiades could boast to his teacher Socrates that he was descended from Zeus, and in other States examples are abundant.[1] At Rome too the same boast could be made ; the Julii, e.g., were descended from Venus and Anchises. Thus the claim of high birth was a much more powerful one than it has ever been in England, or even in France. But there was another and yet stronger reason why in the City-State these families should tend to become peculiarly exclusive. Let us recall the fact that the State had grown out of smaller communities, which survived within it as gentes or γένη, each a close corporation, with its own religious rites, its own government within the State, its own traditions and prejudices. Whether these corporations consisted entirely, as at Rome, of patrician families, or included others belonging to the lower population, as was probably the case at Athens, they were always strongholds of an exclusive nobility. To marry outside the circle of this nobility was a desecration of the sacred rites and traditions of the noble family or gens, and continued to be thought so long after those outside

[1] See Schomann, *Political Antiquities of Greece* (Eng. trans.), p. 124.

it had begun to force their way within the pale.[1]
Thus it is easy to see how the honourable pride of
a noble descent, which for a while might help to
engender the first feelings of duty to self and state,
might also in course of time, under the continued
influence of these groups of kin, serve to cherish
and increase a spirit of exclusiveness. If a family
grew weak or threatened to die out, there was no
possibility of recruiting it from the class below,—
a process which has always been the safeguard of
our English nobility;[2] it might be kept alive by
intermarriage within the class to which it belonged,
but by no fresh blood imported from the lower
orders. At the very time when the noblest qualities
of mind and body were being cultivated for the
good of the State and the service of its king, these
same qualities were beginning to be regarded more
distinctly as the exclusive property of the members
of the groups of ancient kin ; while as the outside
population increased in numbers, or the king increased his power, these groups were more and
more brought into mutual alliance in opposition
both to monarch and to people. This is the first
illustration we meet with of the surviving power of
the kinship groups in the city of which they were
the original constituent elements ; and it is most

---

[1] Schomann, p. 125, notes that in Greece such intermarriage
was not strictly illegal ; but in early times it must have been
practically so. At Rome it had eventually to be sanctioned by
law, which is proof that custom had previously rigidly forbidden
it. See Livy, iv. 1-6.

[2] See e.g. Boutmy English Constitution (Eng. trans.), p. 108
foll.

important to bear it in mind as we pursue the
history of the City-State.

2. Besides noble descent, the chief characteristic
of these aristocracies was *wealth*, and chiefly wealth
in land. The Homeric chieftains are all land-
holders; so were the patricians of Rome, and so
also the aristocracy of Athens when first we catch
a glimpse of it. Land was almost the sole source
of wealth in the economy of the early State, and
wealth was reckoned by the flocks and herds which
the land supported. The Greek aristocracy, and
perhaps originally the Roman too, were distinguished in war from the lower population by the
fact that they were able to supply themselves with
horses, like the chivalry of the middle ages, while
the "people," if they served at all, served only on
foot.[1] This was the result of the possession of large
estates, which would enable them to indulge in the
rich man's occupation of horse-breeding. Another
result no doubt was that they were able to let or
to give land to their inferiors, and to supply them
with stock for it—a practice common to aristocracies
at all times.[2] Their wealth might thus be used
entirely for the benefit of the community, and in a
generous spirit worthy of its noble holders; but it
has never so been used for long by any aristocracy.
When, later on, we get any positive knowledge of
the economy of any City-State, we find troubles

[1] Arist. *Pol.* 1297 B. But this was not the case in all
aristocracies; only where the land was suitable for horses.
Holm, i. 309.

[2] See Maine, *Early History of Institutions*, ch. vi. esp. p. 168.
Mommsen, *Hist of Rome*, i. 199 (Eng. trans.)

arising from the narrow and selfish spirit in which
the noble families used this source of wealth. There
was a secret poison in the possession of it, which
would sooner or later begin to act. So long as
wealth was not an end in itself, and did not cause
friction with their dependants, this poison did not
work ; but there must have come a time when it
began to narrow their views of life and its ends,
and brought them into collision both with the king
and with the people. The earliest glimpses we get
of ancient law show us that the disputes to be
decided were disputes about property ; and the
earliest political revolutions of which we have any
knowledge arose out of unequal distribution of
wealth. It is not too much, then, to conjecture that
at a very early period these noble families found it
convenient to take into their own hands the control
of the unwritten law, and that one reason at least
why the monarchies had to disappear was because
they stood in the way of this. The king, as we
saw, was the fountain of justice ; and if his decisions
interfered with the interests of the nobility in their
dealings with their inferiors, his power must be
limited or got rid of entirely. The assembly of
nobles which had acted as his advising body must
also be able to control him, or the executive power
he possessed must pass directly into the hands of
the members of it.

Thus narrowed and strengthened both in the
pride of birth and in the power of wealth, the aristocracies both in Greece and at Rome set their hands
to modify the form of government so as to bring it

more into harmony with their own particular interests ; and we must now turn to examine briefly
the way in which this change was accomplished.
We know something of it at Athens, and have
recently learnt more ; we have also some knowledge
of it at Rome, and in one or two other States.

The revolutions at Athens and Rome may be
described, so far as we can understand them, as
generically the same but specifically different. They
seem to offer a contrast in more than one important
point. At Rome there is every sign that the
monarchy came to an end suddenly, and that this
was the result of attempts on the part of a powerful monarch to override the aristocracy. But at
Athens we may guess that the king's power fell to
pieces gradually, and that what brought it to an
end was not increasing strength, but increasing
weakness. As we saw (p. 49), the noble families
had, in part at least, migrated from the country to
Athens, and thus found their opportunity of slowly
closing in upon the king, whose power might have
grown much more conspicuous had not his councillors
been constantly around him. He seems never to have
struggled against them with any serious effort or
success. There is no Attic tradition of misdoing or
tyranny on the part of the king. The word Basileus
was never held in execration by the Athenians.
We do not hear that any attempt was made by the
king to " take the people into partnership," and
play them off against the nobility. There is no
trace in later Athenian feeling of any memory of hot
blood or evil doing in this revolution ; the develop-

ment of the constitution must have proceeded gradually and rationally, as it also continued to do in later stages of its growth, until complete democracy was reached. There are few surprises in Athenian political history : the constitution grows with the growing intelligence of the people, whose love of order and sterling good sense is obvious throughout.

With the aid of the recently discovered Aristotelian tract on the Athenian constitution,[1] we may now believe the change from monarchy to aristocracy to have been in outline as follows. Codrus, the last king in the full sense of the word, was succeeded by a line of *Basileis* who held the kingship for life, *but not by simple hereditary right.* This line, the Medontidæ, or family of Medon, son of Codrus, remained the kingly family ; but any member of it might be selected to fill the kingly office, and this selection was in the hands of the aristocracy. How this selection was managed, whether by lot or by voting in the council of nobles meeting on the hill of Ares, we do not at present know. But it is plain that we have here, in the new expedient of selection, the first appearance of something like a constitutional magistracy, as distinguished from the traditional and hereditary power of the king. And this is seen still more plainly in the fact—if such it be —which we have but just discovered, that the king has now to share his powers with other authorities, to whom we can give no other name but that of magistrate. A Polemarch was appointed to help the king in war ; and later on an Archon, who

[1] 'Αθηναίων πολιτεία, 1-3.

probably relieved him of some of the judicial work which must have been his chief civil duty.

Then came a time when the Basileus had so far sunk in reputation in comparison with these two magistracies that it was possible and advisable to deprive him entirely of his military functions, and also to leave him only a part of his judicial power. There remained to him only the sacrificial duties which were traditionally associated with the title of Basileus, and the cognisance of certain crimes of a religious character. To take these from him would be a violation of divine law; but no such scruple need be felt in passing his other prerogatives into alien hands. As the most important of these were no doubt the judicial, it is the Archon who now rises to the first place in consideration, with the Polemarch below him as General, while the Basileus occupies a place midway between the two. The Archon, however, is not to step into the place which the kingly family held; he henceforward holds his position not for life, *but for a period of ten years.* At first it seems that both he and the Basileus, if not the Polemarch too, were selected from the family of the Medontidæ; for it was not easy to get rid of the idea that the "ruler" must be a person qualified by the divine right of descent, as well as by ability or prowess. But at a date which is usually fixed as 752 B.C., the Archonship at least came to be thrown open to all the noble families. And in the seventh century (682 B.C.) we find the constitution passing without further difficulty into a real republican form of government;

for at this time the tenure of all three offices is said to have become annual in duration, and six more Archons were added to help in performing the growing business of the State. These came to be known as Thesmothetæ. All nine magistrates must now have been chosen from the whole body of the aristocracy, and at the end of their period of office have passed into the aristocratic council for life.

Here, then, is aristocratic government complete and organised. There are two leading features in it as we see it at Athens. First, we have a close corporation of privileged noble families who call themselves Eupatridæ—a word which shows that it was high descent which they conceived as constituting their chief claim to predominance. They were privileged, because they alone could hold office in the State, and they alone could select the officers; they only, in fact, were in the true sense of the word πολῖται, citizens. The political organ which represented this corporation was almost without doubt the council of the Areopagus. Secondly, we find a distribution of the functions of executive government, including, of course, religious duties, among a certain small number of officials, elected by the whole body of the privileged. These two features were probably common to the Greek aristocracies of this period, and they are indeed of the essence of all aristocratic or oligarchic government. We shall find them also at Rome, though naturally varying in some points from the Athenian type.

At Rome the power of the king had been stronger than at Athens, stronger perhaps than in any Greek

State. The Roman aristocracy consisted of farmers
on a large scale, who probably spent much of their
time in the country; thus, unlike the Athenian
nobility, they may have failed to act as a timely
obstacle to the free exercise of the monarch's personal power. However this may have been, that
power was in itself vividly realised at Rome, and
capable of being used with a high hand. Two
unmistakable facts show this distinctly. First,
as we have already seen, the Roman genius for
politics had by this time produced a technical word,
imperium, for plenary magisterial and military power,
and this proves that they had a more definite conception of what such power meant than the Athenians, who had no such word. Secondly, there can
be no doubt that the last of the Roman kings tried
to carry the exercise of this *imperium* beyond the
limits which a reverential custom had set upon it
—to turn it, in fact, into a tyranny. Tarquinius
Superbus is no mythical figure in Roman history.
Though we need not believe the stories told of him,
some of which can be traced to non-Roman sources,
we may take it for granted that there was really
such a king, that he was an Etruscan by birth, and
that he used the *imperium* in a way which was
foreign to Roman custom.[1] Had there been no such
king, it would doubtless have been found necessary
sooner or later to modify the practical working of
the *imperium* in the hands of a single man; but
the conduct of Tarquinius hastened the critical
moment.

[1] Mommsen, *Hist. of Rome*, vol. i. p. 255.

Here, then, the executive power *had to be in some degree restricted*; and the way in which the Roman aristocracy contrived this is most curious and interesting. They could not part with the *imperium* they had created. Like the *patria potestas* of their home life, it had come to be a part of their mental furniture as social beings; and more than this, to abolish anything was all but impossible to the Roman mind. Institutions might grow, change, decay, fall into desuetude, or become mere forms; but as descended from the fathers of the State they could not be wholly done away with. They had once been useful, and might in some way be useful again. To those familiar with Roman history many examples will occur of this peculiar tenacity of conservatism; but the change from monarchy to aristocracy in 509 B.C. is the first and perhaps the most striking.

The *imperium* of the Rex was not abolished. His title only, and some of his insignia, disappeared from the political system. From religious observance, however, it was not possible wholly to sever the title of the priest-king, or the relations of the State to the gods might be compromised. A Rex, who resided in the king's house (*regia*), continued to perform the kingly sacrifices, and held the first place on certain formal occasions among all the Roman priests, but he had no *imperium*, and was disqualified from holding any civil office.[1] The *imperium*, however, remained, but it was now

[1] For the survival of the title also in the form *interrex*, see the last edition of Smith's *Dict. of Antiquities*, s.v.

entrusted to two magistrates instead of one, and not for their lifetime, but for one year only, at the end of which they were morally, though not legally, bound to resign it. So long as they held it they could use it undiminished in war, and with hardly a single direct limitation in the city itself. They were nominally quite independent of each other; and if the action of the one crossed that of the other, the result was simply that *imperium* was hampered by *imperium*, not by any new factor in the constitution. These two yearly kings could imprison, scourge, and put to death, could issue edicts and command armies, and could appoint their successors, just as the king for life had done. In the eye of the law the *imperium* was undiminished; it only changed hands once every year.

Yet while keeping this precious political conception to all appearance intact, the aristocracy contrived to prevent its being so used as again to override the custom of the State, or indeed to interfere with their own interests. We saw that the king had been expected to consult his Senate—a custom said to have been neglected by the second Tarquinius. No law was passed, now or at any time, which compelled the magistrate to ask or take advice, but the altered conditions under which the *imperium* was now held made it practically necessary for him to do so. He would be himself an adviser after his year of office was over, and moreover he would be, as a private individual, liable to criticism in the Senate, and to accusation before the people. He would wish to strengthen himself against such chances by following the general voice of the aristocracy assembled in the Senate. And it was not long before habit had made this practice into a definite constitutional principle, affecting all the magistrates of the Republic, with results of the greatest importance ; for it eventually raised the Senate from the position of an advising council to that of a supreme administrative body, whose advice became the utterance of an authority which even the holder of the *imperium* was morally bound to obey.

Again, it was now laid down by law, according to the universal tradition of the Romans, that the *imperium* should not be used to put to death any Roman citizen without allowing him that right of appealing from the magistrate to the people, which the king had usually perhaps been willing to allow, but might certainly refuse if he chose. For this purpose, as well as for others to be mentioned hereafter, the convention of the whole number of citizens in their military array (*comitia centuriata*) was now made to serve as a political assembly, answering yes or no to the question (*rogatio*) of the presiding magistrate. The consul was now bound by law to allow this appeal, and this was perhaps the only direct legal limitation placed on his *imperium*. It was a necessary one, if the aristocracy were really to control their executive, or even to secure themselves against it ; and as they had a majority of votes in this new form of assembly (to which we shall return later on), their security was practically complete.

The *imperium*, then, though in theory it remained

as free and absolute as ever, was practically restricted in civil matters—(1) in respect of the time for which it was held, and the relation to each other of the two magistrates who held it; (2) in respect of the relations of these magistrates to the other parts of the nascent constitution, the Senate and the centuriate assembly. But in the sense of a military command it was still free from all limitations save that of the duration of a campaign. The good sense of the Romans retained for their consuls in the field a temporary absolutism as complete as that of the king. They were free from the necessity of consulting the Senate, and they held the power of life and death unhampered by the right of the accused to appeal to the people. Hence arose a distinction between the *imperium* in the city (*domi*) and the same *imperium* in the field (*militiæ*), which was maintained throughout the life of the Republic, and which must be clearly grasped before the Roman system of government can be understood adequately. It was only when that government passed once more into the hands of a single man that this distinction vanished, and Cæsar and his successors held a single undivided and unrestricted *imperium*.[1]

Our knowledge of this revolution at Rome rests on no contemporary records, only on the traditions of the Romans and on scraps of learning collected by their antiquaries, sifted and supplemented by the modern "method of survivals." Yet it is the most

---

[1] Mommsen, *Staatsrecht*, i. 59 foll. ; article "Imperium" in *Dict. of Antiquities* (new edition).

consistent account we have of any such revolution, and the mutilated beginning of the lately discovered " Constitution of Athens " has not placed the corresponding change at Athens equally beyond doubt in its leading features. At Rome we can see quite plainly how an aristocracy with a strong political and legal instinct went about the difficult task of getting the executive into its own hands, neither diminishing its efficiency on the one hand, nor yet leaving it so uncontrolled as to be capable of further misuse.

But from Athenian, as from Roman, history we may learn at this point a most valuable lesson. Our complicated modern constitutions make it hard for us to realise the fact that the earliest form of government was simply an executive power, and nothing more. It consisted of a single man's power to command, unrestricted save by moral checks. Such a power, such a discipline, were necessary to the infant State, as they had been also to the family. There might be a council of high-born advisers, and there might be assemblies of the people held from time to time, but neither of these had any direct share in the government of the State, which was the task of the king alone.

Now it must be placed to the credit of the aristocracies that just as they first developed the idea of duty to the State, so they transformed this executive government from a primitive contrivance into a part of a real constitutional system. Had they destroyed the executive power, they would probably have destroyed the State too; had they attempted to pass it over to their council, and so to share it amongst their whole number, they would have weakened it irretrievably. As it was, they kept the power intact, but they made it a duty as well as an honour—a duty to be shared by the holder with one or two others, and for a set time only; a duty for the good performance of which the holders would be made responsible as soon as they returned to the life of private citizens.

This, then, is the point at which the constitutional history of the ancient State really begins. It is a great epoch, for now begins also the idea of political order; not of order only in the sense of traditional and trustful obedience to a hereditary monarchy, but order in the sense of conscious organisation by an intelligent body of privileged individuals. From our better knowledge of later history we are apt to see both Greek and Roman aristocracies in a bad light; we do not easily recognise the value of their contribution to political history, because we find them acting as a purely conservative social force, and acting usually from self-regarding motives in the later series of political changes. But it was really to them that even the democracies themselves owed those traditions of solid government which enabled them to govern at all; and it will hardly be going too far to say that all the three constitutional germs which we find in the infant State—the king, the council, and the people, or the executive, the deliberative and the legislative elements in the later constitutions—owed both their survival and their development to the political intelligence of the aristocracies.

CHAPTER V

TRANSITION FROM ARISTOCRACY TO DEMOCRACY
(GREECE)

THE picture given in the last chapter of the rule of
the aristocracies was necessarily a somewhat ideal
one. We were dealing with a period of which
we have no direct historical evidence; we had to
interpret the work of the aristocracies by attri-
buting to them a certain stage of development in
the life of the City-State, which cannot, so far as
we can see, be accounted for in any other way.[1]
That work must have been partly destructive,
partly constructive. The loose fabric of ancient
monarchy was pulled down; but a new fabric
slowly arose, more compact, and better suited to

---

[1] From what is now called the Mycenæan age, *i.e.* the age of
the art treasures found at Mycenæ and elsewhere, to the seventh
century, there is a gap in Greek history, generally supposed to be
occupied by a Dorian invasion of the Peloponnese, by a series of
colonising movements, by the settlement of the constitution at
Sparta, and the abolition of kingship elsewhere. All these events
belong to the age of aristocracy, or (what is the same thing) to the
age of declining kingship.

I

the society which was to shelter under it.   In the
council of nobles men must have begun to learn
what government means—how to deliberate with
due regard for order, for the opinions of others, and
for the good of the State.   Here were learnt, if we
are right, those necessary lessons in the grammar of
politics, which are so much a part of our own mental
furniture that we can hardly conceive of a time
when they had still to be slowly and painfully
acquired.

But the very learning of this lesson was a process
which must in time have narrowed the interests
and prejudices of the learners.   Where we first meet
with aristocracies in records which may be called
historical, we can see that while much progress has
been made in the art of government, the governors
have become a class whose sympathies are limited,
and whose motives are self-regarding.   Government
has in fact become a science known only to the few,
and as the few were also the rich, their political
education has taught them not only how to govern,
but how to make government protect and advance
their own interests.   Some indication was given in
the last chapter of the way in which this might
come about, when we endeavoured to explain how
the nobility found it expedient to put an end to
kingship.   We must now look at the same tendency from a different point of view, and show how,
perhaps at the same time, the few began to slide
into a sharper opposition to the many than had as
yet been felt since the beginning of the City-State.

Greek history proper may be said to begin in the

seventh century B.C., and to increase in value greatly
in the sixth. Here we begin to find our footing
firmer, meeting as we do with the earliest lyric
poetry, with archaic works of art, with an inscription here and there, and with historical traditions
preserved in later writers such as Herodotus, Thucydides, Aristotle, and Plutarch.[1]   Roman history
proper begins later, in the fifth century, and is less
certain, depending entirely on tradition, or on records
of a doubtful character used by Livy and Dionysius
as late as the age of Augustus. But both in Greece
and Italy, as soon as the mist begins to lift, what
we dimly see is much the same. We see aristocracies narrowed in interests, and brought into
sharp opposition with the class below them ; in
some cases they triumph, as at Sparta, and prolong
the age of aristocracy into a hard and barren period
of oligarchic rule; in others they are gradually
forced to give way, and to learn another and yet
more difficult lesson than that of the art of government by a class. When this new lesson is learnt,
new prospects of prosperity, both material and
moral, are opened to the State which has had
sufficient patience and good sense to learn it.

But how has this sharp opposition arisen between the few and the many ? In the age of kingship, as we saw, the functions of government were
religious, judicial, and military. These functions

---

[1] To these should be added the poems of Hesiod, and especially
the *Works and Days*, which gives us a picture of the conditions of
life in Bœotia at a very early period ; but we do not know the
exact date of these poems.

have now passed out of the hands of the king, and belong to the magistrates and council of the aristocracy. Let us see how they might be used so as to favour the interests of the few as against those of the many.

The secrets of religion consisted of a knowledge of the *ritual* proper to each occasion ; the knowledge, that is, of the art of keeping the human inhabitants of the city on good terms with its divine members. Every public act was accompanied by a sacrifice, and all sacrifices must be performed in exactly the right way. The sacrificial hymns must be rightly sung ; the omens must be taken, the purificatory processions conducted, exactly in the received manner, or the gods would not answer and bless.[1] The whole life and happiness of the State depended on the proper performance of these necessary duties.

Now in a State made up, as we have seen, by the union of lesser communities, each of which had its own peculiar worship conducted by its own noble family or families, it is plain that all these worships, now embodied in the State, must have remained in the hands of the aristocracy. The whole organisation of the State's religious life was theirs also. The regulation of festivals, of marriages, of funerals, of holy places and land belonging to the

[1] No better example of this principle can be found than in the great inscription from Iguvium in Italy, which gives at great length the ritual of a purificatory procession round the city. A single slip necessitated the returning of the procession to the point last started from.—Bucheler, *Umbrica*, p. 21, etc.

gods,—all that the Romans understood by the words
jus sacrum,—was theirs and theirs only.   For a
person to meddle with such things, who was not
qualified by birth or education or tradition, nor
expressly invited by the State as a reformer, was
not only to interfere with the rights of a class,
but positively to disturb the good relations of the
city with its gods, and thus to imperil its very
life.[1]   Of these relations, and of this life, the noble
families were in a way *trustees*; what wonder,
then, if their trusteeship increased their pride
and narrowed their sympathies, raising in them a
growing contempt for men who knew nothing of
the will or the needs of the divine inhabitants of
the city ?

So it was also in the region of profane law, as
it slowly disentangled itself from the law of religious usage.   Here, too, the rule held good that all
solemn acts must be performed according to prescribed order, if they were to have any binding
force.   Rules governing the tenure of land, rules
governing the transference of all property by suc-
cession or sale, rules governing the treatment of
evil-doers and the adjustment of all disputes, so
far as they came under the cognisance of the State
at all, were known and administered by the aristocracy only.   They were as much matter of technical
and traditional knowledge as the religious law, and
could not be administered save by those to whom
a divine order had entrusted that knowledge.   The
executive of the State, in fact, was in the hands of

[1] See *e.g.* Livy, iv. chaps. 2 and 6.

the only true *statesmen* (πολίται).[1] What wonder
then, once more, if these men and their families
believed themselves to be the only lawful possessors
of secrets of government, as well as of religion,
which they might turn to their own particular
advantage ?

Even in military matters—the third department of government—the same tendency is seen ;
for the aristocracy took the greater risk in actual
warfare, and were at greater expense than the
commons in providing themselves with horses and
superior arms.[2] They, like the chivalry of the
middle ages, were the flower of the State's army ;
they had a greater stake in the State and they bore
the greater burden. What wonder, then, if they,
like their mediæval counterparts, came to look down
on the people as louts who could not or would not
fight, unworthy alike of honour on the battlefield,
and of power in the constitution ?[3]

Thus we may be sure that in course of time
there came to be a greater distinctness of outline in

[1] In Homer the πολίτης is literally the dweller in the πόλις as
opposed to the dweller in the ἄγρος : *Il.* ii. 806 ; *Od.* vii. 131,
xvii. 206. The latter two passages may indicate a time when the
word was beginning to be used in its later sense ; for it is the
nobility that dwells in the πόλις, as in the Mycenæan age it was,
perhaps, only the βασιλεύτατος.

[2] Aristotle, *Pol.* 1297 B ; Gilbert, ii. 274.

[3] This contempt is visible even in Homer, where, however, it
may be rather a reflex from the age of the compilers (ninth to
seventh century) than a feature of the " Mycenæan " age : *Od.* i.
411, iv. 64, vi. 187 ; and even in *Il.* xiv. 126, xvi. 570. Fanta,
Der Staat, etc. p. 14. The next point at which we meet it is in
he poems of Theognis.

the position of the class to whom all these secrets
and advantages belonged. While the' State was not
yet fully realised, while its elements were still in
solution, this distinctness was less strong. But
when the various elements of population came to
face each other in the well-knit State, the idea of
privilege began to make itself felt. The holders of
the secrets which we have been describing, so soon
as they began to use them for their own advantage
as a class, would cease to be thought of as heaven-
appointed trustees, and would come to be considered
as *privileged*.

And as such we find them when history opens.
Their right to exclusive advantages is already questioned, and they are themselves responsible for this.
They have initiated a period in which the established order is called in question. They claim to be
the only true *men of the State*, and thus suggest the
question of what citizenship is, and who is a citizen.
They absorb the land, by lending money or stock
on the security of estate or person, and thus they
raise questions about the justice of the unwritten
law, and the power of the executive which enforces
it. In manners and bearing they show an increasing contempt for all who are not born and educated
like themselves, and for all employments which are
not after their own kind; and here again they
unconsciously invite questioning as to the order of
things in the world—the difference between freeman and slave, rich and poor, noble and ignoble.
It is this questioning that is the chief characteristic
of the age we now have to deal with—an age in

which the old order of things ceases to be thought
of as divinely dispensed, the old worships are to be
no longer the only ones which claim the attention
of the State, and membership in the old groups of
noble *clans* no longer the sole test of real citizenship.   Aristocracy, in fact, has ceased in any
real sense to be the rule of the best, and has become the rule of the few and rich.   It has lost its
essential character, and men begin to ask questions
about it,—to call in question its claim for reverence;
it is known now as *oligarchy*, the rule of the wealthy
few, and continues so to be known, wherever it is
found, throughout Greek history.[1]

As yet we have said little or nothing about the
population from which the aristocracy thus came to
be more and more vividly distinguished, and on whose
interests it now began seriously to encroach.   But
it is the rise of this population into prominence
which has made both Greek and Roman history
really valuable for us ; and before we exemplify that
rise in any single State, we must form some idea
of who they were.   The aristocracies did their
part, as we have seen ; but the essential fibre of a
people is not to be found in an upper class only,
and any *class*, however gifted, must sooner or later
dwindle and decay.   The questioning, the fermentation, which appears in Greece in or about the
seventh century, indicates the growth in intelligence and aspiration of this lower population ; it
shows that the lessons of public duty and of the
art of government, which the nobles have been

[1] Aristotle. *Politics.* 1290 B ; cf. 1293 B.

learning, have had an influence beyond their own ranks.

Those free persons who are not dwellers in the city, *i.e.* the fortress, like the king or the leading nobles, appear in Homer as either ἀγροιῶται, *i.e.* tillers of the soil, shepherds, and herdsmen, or, on the other hand, as τέκτονες ἄνδρες, or δημιόεργοι, namely, craftsmen, tradesmen, and what we should call professional men.[1] All these clearly formed part of the community (δῆμος),[2] as distinguished from the slaves; they served in war κατὰ φῦλα κατὰ φρήτρας (*Il.* ii. 362), *i.e.* according to the groups of kinship in which they lived at home.[3] On the whole, the "people" of the Homeric age must be thought of as numerous, industrious, and content with their position as labourers on the land or artisans in the city.[4]

We do not know for certain what part of Greece the Homeric descriptions represent; but in historical times the lower populations of many States do not accord with them, owing to changes caused by migrations and conquests, of which the greatest was

[1] Fanta, *Der Staat in der Ilias u. Odyssee*, p. 42 foll.

[2] This is the word in Homer for the city and its land taken together, *e.g. Il.* ii. 547. Fanta, p. 12.

[3] This population may have been gradually increased in certain ways, *e.g.* by liberation of slaves, and by reception of foreigners skilled in some craft; as *e.g.* in *Od.* xvii. 383, "craftsmen of the people, a prophet or a healer of ills, a shipwright, or a godlike minstrel"; but whether such persons were admitted into the φῦλα and φρήτραι must be very doubtful.

[4] These last would live, as seems to have been the case at Mycenæ and the Acropolis of Athens, not in the citadel, but in the suburb below.

the invasion of the Peloponnese by the Dorians. The
" people " in most Peloponnesian States were not
really a part of the State at all, but had been
reduced to subjection by conquest, and so remained.
But in Attica, which had never been completely
overrun by invaders, we get glimpses of a population which strongly reminds us of Homer. In
contrast to the Eupatridæ or nobles was a class
sometimes called Georgi[1] (husbandmen), sometimes
Demiurgi (artisans) ; and we may think of these as
partly small landowners, together with shepherds
and herdsmen on the high lands, partly as artisans
and labourers for hire, living at the foot of the
Acropolis, and fishermen on the sea coast. Perhaps we may generalise so far as to conclude that
in most Greek States, ere yet the slaves had become
very numerous, such a class existed, whose occupations enabled the great to live in affluence ; in some
cases, as at Sparta, these were almost in the position
of serfs, and in no sense citizens, while in others, as
at Athens, they were all included in the groups of
Attic kin,[2] and formed a part of the State proper,
though they had no share in the government except
in so far as they might be occasionally summoned
to an assembly.[3] And as the aristocracies grew

[1] Or Geomori, Pollux, 8, 111. There is much confusion about these
names : cf. Gilbert, i. 111 note. In the *Ath. Pol.* ch. 13, the Georgi
appear as Agroiki, and the classes are three.

[2] See Gilbert, i. 111 ; Holm, i. 457.

[3] In the colonies, or at least the western ones, the conditions
were again different ; the first settlers constituting an aristocracy
so soon as new settlers arrived, and the latter becoming a body of
" outsiders " desirous of sharing in land and government. See

narrower, the occasions of meeting became naturally fewer.

It was among this lower population that the
questioning we have spoken of was first heard.
Some of them may have advanced in position and
wealth in an age which developed a great commercial system,[1] and in some States numbers left
their homes and settled in the colonies which the
same commercial enterprise was now forming. But
in Attica, which shared but little in this colonising
movement, the mass of the people became steadily
depressed, as we shall see, by the aristocracy, or, as
we may now call it, the oligarchy ; and social discontent and economical difficulties began to have
their natural result upon politics. The age of
fermentation sets in. In the rest of this chapter
we can only trace the leading characteristics of this
fermentation in Greece, and especially at Athens,
where alone we get any comprehensive view of it ;
later on we shall deal with the parallel movement
at Rome.

Let us note in the first place that in Greece the
disturbance almost everywhere took the form of a
tendency to set up an executive power stronger
than that of the existing oligarchy. The few had
formerly suited their own interests by appropriating the executive power of the kings, which was
not usually a difficult process, as they belonged to
the same class as the king. It was now becoming

Freeman, *Hist. of Sicily*, ii. 11 foll., and cf. the early history of
Cyrene in Herodotus, iv. 159 foll.

[1] Thucyd. i. 13.

the instinct of the many to consult their advantage also by appropriating the executive of the few; but this was a much harder task, and the many were almost always compelled to begin, not by abolishing or directly attacking it, but simply by setting it aside and creating a new and still stronger government in its place. This was a rude expedient, though perhaps the only possible one. It was in some instances so violent a remedy as to become in itself a formidable disease. It weakened the ideas of law and order,—the very ideas which the long ages of aristocratic government had created or confirmed; it set class against class; it roused dangerous ambitions in the minds of men who loved power and wealth; it broke roughly into the natural and tranquil course of political advance. Yet it was so universal in Greece in this age that we must believe it to have been a necessity; one which arose from the over-long acquiescence by the people in the aristocratic monopoly of wealth, education, and power.

To this strong executive, which practically meant absolutism, the Greeks gave two different names answering to the two ways in which it might be constituted. If it were set up by the general assent of the community, or by the action of an oligarchy more reasonable than usual, with the temporary object of adjusting the constitution to the needs of the age, its holder was called Aisymnêtês, or arbiter. If on the other hand an individual citizen, either with good or evil intent, pushed himself into the position of an autocrat, or rose to it by the action of the unprivileged class only, he was called tyrant.[1] In either case the immediate result was the same; the oligarchic executive disappeared, and in most cases could never be re-established on the old basis of social prestige. But the indirect results were often different; for the tyrant was apt to leave behind him a legacy of revolutionary tendency, the natural fruit of his own violence and self-seeking; while the arbiter had at least the chance of leaving a well-ordered State as the result of his labours, which in spite of subsequent difficulties and dangers might never wholly forget the lesson it had received. The government of the arbiter was a government of reason, based on law and begetting law;[2] the government of the tyrant was often one of passion, begetting a spirit of lawlessness utterly alien to the true Greek nature.

The position and work of the arbiter may best be studied in the history of Athens. The tyrant is also to be found there, and, strange to say, immediately following on the arbiter; but the rule of the latter had here preserved the instinct of order, and the tyranny is for the most part of so mild a nature as hardly to be characteristic. I shall therefore postpone the consideration of the real tyrant to the end of this chapter, and keep for the present to Athens, where, in spite of the un-

---

[1] Freeman, *Sicily*, ii. 49 foll. Aristotle defines the position of the Aisymnêtês as αἱρετὴ τυραννίς (*Pol.* 1285 B), the τυραννίς as μοναρχία πρὸς τὸ σύμφερον τὸ τοῦ μοναρχοῦντος (*Pol.* 1279 B).

[2] Cf. Butcher, *Some Aspects of the Greek Genius*, p. 57 foll.

certainty of historic details, we shall be able to
detect the fermentation which called for the en-
trusting of abnormal power to an individual
arbiter, and to see something of the use he made
of it, as well as of the excellent results he left
behind him.

The period of fermentation begins at Athens
towards the close of the seventh century. Three
successive events illustrate its progress.

The first of these (though their order is indeed
somewhat uncertain) is the appearance for the first
time of a code of written law, attributed to the
aristocrat Draco, in the year 621 B.C.[1] The recent
discovery of the Aristotelian treatise on the Athenian
constitution has so far only added confusion to our
ignorance of this man and his work; for the new
account is so strange, and so much in contradiction
with what little we knew before, that grave sus-
picions have been aroused as to the real origin and
application of the chapter which contains it. But
for us at present it will suffice to note the simple
fact that law is now for the first time in Athenian
history set down in writing, and the task entrusted
to a leading individual with full powers. About
the same time, or later, we find the same phenomenon in other parts of Hellas. The lawgivers of
the age, such as Zaleucus of Locri in Italy, and
Charondas of Catana in Sicily, do not indeed offer
an exact analogy to Draco; they correspond rather
with Draco's great successor. But the lesson for us
is the same in all these cases, and also in the legisla-

[1] Aristotle, *Pol.* ii. 12. 1274 B; *Ath. Pol.* ch. iv.

tion of the Decemvirate at Rome, which we shall
notice in a later chapter. Whether the customary
law was substantially changed or simply committed to writing, it is plain that it is to be no
longer the private possession of a class. The secrets
of aristocratic rule are being revealed to the whole
community ; questioning has begun—questioning as
to the rules which the oligarchic executive ad-
ministers. And the first signs of distrust in the
executive and its administration are perhaps to be
seen in the fact that the task of writing down the
law is entrusted to a single individual, and not to
that executive as a whole.

The next event is a deliberate attempt at tyranny
on the part of an Athenian who had married the
daughter of Theagenes, tyrant of Megara. This is
none the less significant because it was a failure.
Like Theagenes in the neighbouring State, Cylon
probably represented a popular feeling ; but the
State was not yet ripe for tyranny. The oligarchic
executive was too strong for him, and according to
the story, he made the mistake of using Megarian
troops to seize on the Acropolis. This brought the
oligarchy and the people for the moment into sympathy, and the Cylonians were besieged in the
stronghold. Cylon himself escaped, but Megacles
the archon, of the great family of the Alcmæonidæ,
put the rest to death after promising to spare their
lives ; some were even slain at the altar where they
had taken refuge. The story is most striking, as
pointing to an unwholesome and surprising dis-
regard of honour and sanctuary in the oligarchic

executive, which looks as though they felt they
were living on a volcano ready at any time to
break out in eruption, and must at all risks endeavour to check the popular tendency.[1]

The third event which shows disturbance in
Attica is the most singular of all. Plutarch, in
describing it, uses language which implies that the
Athenian State was suffering from a malignant
disease in religion and morals, and that the happy
relations between the human and divine inhabitants
of Attica were seriously deranged. As in the case
of bodily disease, this cannot be ascribed to a single
event only, such as the Cylonian sacrilege; it indicates an unhealthy condition. Fear, pestilence,
disaster, are only symptoms of a general demoralis-
ation, caused in part perhaps by the rise of new ideas
and the introduction of new and strange worships
among the lower classes. The remedy was curious;
they sent for a wise man, as a minister of religion,
to set them right. The mission of Epimenides the
Cretan to Athens is a singular example of that
readiness to submit their troubles to a master-mind
which is characteristic of the earlier Greeks; it is in
fact no more than the tendency towards absolutism
taking an unusual form. It may be that we should
see in it the first public recognition of certain new
worships which had crept into Attica, and which
were afterwards embodied in the calendar of public
feasts by Pisistratus, on behalf of the lower population whose interests he represented.[2] Epimenides,

[1] Thucyd. i. 126; Plut. *Solon*, 12. Cf. *Ath. Pol.* i.
[2] Dyer, *Gods in Greece*, p. 125 foll. For Epimenides, read

according to tradition, ordered the public religion anew, purified the country, and tranquillised its inhabitants for a time.

These three events, showing stir in the Athenian population, prepare us for the approach of democracy, and through democracy for the ripening of the choicest fruit that the wonderful Greek people ever produced. But democracy could not even approach without still greater pain and trouble than we have yet met with in Attica. It is always social discontent and economical distress which causes friction between a people and its rulers to become a positive danger and to lead to revolution and anarchy;[1] while an unprivileged class is still materially comfortable, it does not feel keenly its want of privilege. The unprivileged at Athens, according to our accounts, had been long growing more and more uncomfortable, and the oligarchs were probably well aware that revolution was at hand. Neither the laws of Draco nor the purification by Epimenides had sufficed. At the root of all the troubles lay an economical distress, which is thus briefly described by the author of the treatise on the Athenian constitution :—

"Not only was the constitution at this time oligarchical in every respect, but the poorer classes, men, women, and children, were in absolute slavery to the rich. They were known as Pelatæ and also as Hektemori, because they culti-

___

Plut. *Solon*, 12, and cf. the mission of Demonax to Cyrene in Herodotus, iv. 162. In later times Timoleon affords a parallel on the political side : see Plutarch's *Life of Timoleon*.

[1] Aristotle was aware of this : *Politics*, 1297 B.

vated the lands of the rich for a sixth part of the produce. The whole country was in the hands of a few persons, and if the tenants failed to pay their rent, they were liable to be haled into slavery, and their children with them.   Their persons were mortgaged to their creditors . . . ; but the hardest and bitterest part of the condition of the masses was the fact that they had no share in the offices then existing under the constitution. . . . To speak generally, they had no part or share in anything." [1]

This is nothing but the familiar story of the accumulation of wealth in the hands of a few, with the usual ethical results : the deterioration of aristocratic character into plutocratic, and the shifting of the sense of duty from the State as its object to individual interests.   It is entirely confirmed by the poems of Solon, the only contemporary evidence we possess, which formed no doubt the basis of later accounts, such as that just quoted.   The author of the treatise himself quotes most appositely four lines which exactly express the new spirit of questioning as well as its chief cause—

" But ye who have store of good, who are sated and overflow,
Restrain your swelling soul, and still it and keep it low ;
Let the heart that is great within you be trained a lowlier
    way ;
Ye shall not have all at your will, and we will not for
    ever obey." [2]

---

[1] *Ath. Pol.* ch. 5.   Cf. the words of Plutarch, *Solon,* ch. 13 at end.

[2] ὑμεῖς δ' ἡσυχάσαντες ἐνὶ φρεσὶ κάρτερον ἦτορ,
    οἱ πολλῶν ἀγαθῶν ἐς κόρον [ἠλ]άσατε,
ἐν μετρίοισι τ[ρέφεσθ]ε μέγαν νόον· οὔτε γὰρ ἡμεῖς
    πεισόμεθ', οὔθ' ὑμῖν ἄρτια τα[ῦτ'] ἔσεται.

I have borrowed Mr. Kenyon's spirited translation.   These lines were new to us when the treatise was discovered.

In the last few generations it is plain that the
privileged of Attica have become richer, and the
unprivileged poorer. This was a disease to which
the City-State was always peculiarly liable, as
Aristotle well knew,[1] and we shall have to recur to
it later on ; it was indeed one of the leading causes
of the ultimate decay of this form of State. And
in Attica wars, bad harvests, increasing commerce,
pestilence, and the harsh law of debt, all had their
share in magnifying the disproportion between
wealth and poverty, and between the political
power of the rich and the political helplessness of
the poor.[2] Yet it was the peculiar good fortune of
Athens that, severely attacked as she was by troubles
of this kind, she found a physician so single-minded
and so self-restrained that she had good reason to
be for ever grateful to him. Solon, the friend of
Epimenides, was Archon in 594 (the traditional
date) ; and in due accordance with the tendency
we have been pointing out, he was also then or
shortly afterwards entrusted with an abnormal
power which placed him in the position of arbiter,
and was even pressed in some quarters to become
tyrant—a temptation he steadily refused.

Solon and his work form a most important landmark in the history of the City-State. He made
it possible for one such State at least to reach the
highest point of development of which this form of
social union was capable. He was at once the
prophet and the lawgiver of Athens, whose memory

---

[1] *e.g. Politics*, 1301 B.
[2] Read Plut. *Solon*, 8, 12, 13.

was cherished by his people with profound reverence. Whether his laws gave satisfaction at the
moment, whether they were retained in the next
generation, whether they were wholly the issue of
his own reasoning or based in part on the work
of a predecessor,[1]— these are questions of minor
moment compared with the undoubted fact that the
spirit of Solon's life and character never wholly
vanished from Athens. And if we are to explain
this immortality of a great man's life, we can do so
by applying to it a commonplace epithet, with a
tinge of special meaning in this instance : it was
eminently *reasonable*. In a famous passage Aristotle defines law as *reason without passion* ;[2] of this
principle Solon was the personification. And his
importance to us in following out the history of the
City-State lies in the fact that with him, in the
development of the most perfect state of antiquity,
begins the age of reason as applied to politics.
Long ages of acquiescence had been followed by an
age of discontent and questioning ; under the guid-
ance of the wise spirit of Solon's life, passion is
eventually stilled, and reason takes its place. This
benevolent influence is visible, not only in the
gratitude of the Athenians, but in the true ring
of Solon's own poems, in every story that is
told of him by Herodotus, and in the life which,
seven centuries later, the last of the true Greek

---

[1] The Solonian division of the people is ascribed by the author
of the "Athenian Constitution" to Draco in the first place ; see
chapters iv. and vii.

[2] *Politics.* iii. 16. 5. 1287 A.

men of letters compiled with evident delight and
reverence.

Without going unnecessarily into the details
of an oft-told story, let us briefly see in what
the reasonableness of Solon's work consisted. All
political progress of which the conscious or unconscious aim is to develop the resources, material
and intellectual, of a whole people, ought to be
accompanied by social and economic reform. We
in England, after 1832, were slow to realise this
principle. Our political leaders did not at first
perceive that a new population had arisen among
us, suggesting many new problems which could not
be solved by political legislation alone.[1] It is partly
owing to this that our proletariat is still in fermentation, *i.e.* socially and economically uncomfortable,
though, owing to political changes, it has a powerful
hold on the executive which governs it. Now
the reasonableness of Solon is seen in the fact that
he combined social, economic, and political reform.
The problems before the Greek statesman were
always simpler and on a smaller scale than those
of the modern State; and Solon was able to take
in at a glance the whole of his field of work, and
to deal with it step by step. He did not give the
" people " political weight without also giving them
the material means of maintaining it; nor, con-
versely, did he aid them economically without

---

[1] It is worth noting that the man of that generation who saw
this fact, and gave utterance to it, was a Tory man of letters. See
the list of Southey's proposals for social and economic reform, in
Dowden's Life of him (English Men of Letters Series), p. 154.

giving them a political status by means of which they might care for themselves in future. His work is therefore complete; and if we would speak of him in terms appropriate to Hellenic life, we might call him the perfect Greek artist in the region of politics, who breathed a new spirit into what was conventional, and whose sense of proportion, order, and beauty were all kept in due subjection to the needs of everyday life.[1]

The intent and the general character of Solon's first measures have an objective reality for us which is rare in ancient history, owing to the preservation of large fragments of his poems. It is plain from his own words that he meant not only to relieve immediate distress, but to prevent the poor of Attica from ever falling into servitude a second time. In other words, he wished to see a vigorous and industrious class in Attica, which should stand midway between the rich on the one hand, and the increasing slave population on the other. All outstanding debts incurred on the security of land or person were absolutely cancelled; the families who had been in a condition of serfdom were thereby freed; those who had preferred exile to bondage could return

---

[1] The admirable words used by Professor Butcher of the Greek artist might almost equally well be applied to Solon : " We are always conscious of a reserve of power, a temperate strength which knows its own resources and employs them without effort and without ostentation. . . . He is bent on seeing truly, on seeing harmoniously, and on expressing what he sees. The materials on which his imagination works are fused and combined according to the laws of what is possible, reasonable, natural."—*Some Aspects*, etc., p. 332.

home; and the marks of hopeless mortgaging disappeared from the land. Men who had lost their land entirely could not indeed recover it; but Solon seems to have tried to give these a new start in life by turning their attention to art and trade. To cheapen the ordinary products of the country he forbade their exportation, except in the case of olive oil, of which there was the greatest abundance. To bring Athens into closer connection with the great trading and colonising cities of Chalcis and Corinth he introduced the Euboic coinage, which was in use there, in place of the older system of Athens' natural enemies, Ægina and Megara. Many other measures are mentioned, of which the general purpose seems to have been the same—to revive native industry, to keep the population employed, and so to enable all to acquire a certain amount of wealth.[1]   Equality in the distribution of wealth has never yet been realised, but absence of startling inequality was the safeguard of the City-State. Aristotle long afterwards pointed out this law in an admirable chapter, which is as true now as on the day on which he wrote it.[2]   It is destruction, he teaches, for a city to be made up of masters and slaves, and not of men who are really, as well as technically, free. The State is a social union of friends, and would be, if it could,

---

[1] For the Seisactheia, read especially Plut. *Solon*, 14-17, *Ath. Pol.* 6, and Solon's *Poems*, fragments 4 and 36. Useful summaries of other evidence will be found in Busolt, *Gr. Gesch.* i. 524, and Gilbert, 1. 130.

[2] *Pol.* 1295 A and B, on the advantages of τὸ μέσον.   Cf. Newman. vol. i. 502. note 1.

composed of men who are equal in wealth and influence. With a strong intermediate class of moderate wealth it may most nearly realise its aim, and avoid the supreme danger of all small States—the bitterness of party strife. Aristotle reasoned thus from the facts of Hellenic life as they had been for a century and more before his time. He knew that the mischief for which he was prescribing a remedy had already half ruined Greece, and that the instinct of the best Greek statesmen, such as the ideal Lycurgus, Solon, Charondas, had led them to foresee and attempt to avert it. His chapter is a protest, on behalf of the State, against the greed of the individual, and strikes the keynote of all truly Greek political reasoning.

But if Solon had contented himself with simply shaking off the burdens from the shoulders of the poor, his work would have been left but half done. They must also be secured against the binding of these burdens afresh on their backs by an oligarchy of wealth which also held the reins of government. As we saw at the end of the last chapter, the strength of the executive power is the chief characteristic both of the early monarchies and aristocracies ; and in this chapter we have already seen how a degenerate aristocracy could use that strength for their own advantage, rather than for the benefit of the State as a whole. Somehow the ruled must be protected permanently against their rulers. If they were not yet ripe to rule themselves,—and Solon's reasonable mind fully recognised the fact that they were wholly ignorant of the art which it had been the task of the aristocracies to discover,—they were at least qualified, by sad experience, to judge of the use of such power, and to name the persons whom they would wish to see exercising it.[1]

Whatever doubt may exist as to some parts of Solon's constitutional changes, we may treat it as a fact that he gave the ordinary Athenian citizen exactly that share of power for which he was naturally fitted ; and here again he stands out as representing a great epoch in the development of the City-State. His object was gained chiefly by two simple and efficacious changes. First, the body of Athenian citizens, comprised in the ancient tribes, phratries, and γένη, was classified afresh on the basis of the yearly return from the land owned by each individual, without any regard to his descent, whether noble or ignoble. The first class must have a minimum return of 500 medimni, or roughly a capital of one talent (£244) ; in the fourth and lowest (Thetes) were all who had a less return from land than 150 medimni, or derived their income, not from land, but from trade. Secondly, on this economic basis, in place of the old social one of Eupatridæ, Georgi, and Demiurgi, was fitted what was practically a new constitution. The Archonship was reserved for the first class, or Pentakosiomedimni ; the other offices were open to the three highest classes, to those, that is, who had the neces-

---

[1] Cf. Aristotle, *Politics*, iii. 11, 1281 B ; a valuable chapter, which may at this point be studied with great advantage. Aristotle is here discussing the question in the abstract, " What share may the many justly have in a constitution ? "

sary education, and a considerable stake in the welfare of the State. But Solon's great stroke was the elevation of the lowest class, not indeed to the executive itself, but to a position in the constitution whence it could, as it were, survey and control that executive. They were to share in the elections of the magistrates, and all over thirty years of age were to have the right of sitting in an assembly which should judge of the conduct of the magistrates after their year of office was over. If these constitutional changes were maintained, no magistrate, whatever his birth or wealth, could ever with impunity use his power to trample on the rights of the poorest Athenian. It is possible that he also guaranteed to the whole people in their ancient assembly (ἐκκλησία) the right, which must have in theory been theirs always, of deciding on questions of war and peace.[1]

These changes did not constitute Democracy,—a form of government then unknown, and for which there was as yet no word in the Greek language. But they initiated the democratic spirit, and were indeed changes vital enough to alarm men who did not know the reasonableness of the Athenian people and its lawgiver. As if aware that he was bringing into political prominence a new stratum of

---

[1] Busolt, *Gr. Gesch.* i. 536, note 1. For Solon's constitution, read Plut *Solon*, 18 foll. ; Solon, fragment 5 ; Aristotle, *Pol.* ii 12 ; *Ath. Pol.* 7. Cf. Busolt and Gilbert, *ll cc.* The reader, perhaps, needs to be reminded that in any independent study of Solon's work, he must weigh the value of the ancient authorities both in regard to their intrinsic excellence and to the sources to which they may be traced.

population whose temper was uncertain, and who could not be held responsible for their public conduct, Solon himself endeavoured to guard against any misuse of their power. To the old Council of the Areopagus, consisting of ex-Archons, he entrusted the task,—probably no new one,—of superintending the working of the constitution, and of guarding the interests of public and private morality. To him also is ascribed the establishment of another Council of 400, of which we shall hear more, constituting a committee of the whole people, but chosen yearly from the first three classes. And lastly, it is probable, though we cannot indeed be sure of our details here, that Solon endeavoured by other laws to educate the people in morality and self-respect, to curb luxury as he discouraged idleness, and as he had freed them from the hard bondage of custom and convention, so also to direct them on the road towards intellectual as well as political liberty.[1]

Solon's work did but aid the natural development of germs already in existence. It was simply the turning of the light of a rare and sympathetic wisdom on the opening bud at a critical moment. In spite of cloud and storm, the bud expanded slowly and naturally into bloom, and ripened at last into the choicest fruit. Athens, thus fairly started on her way,—emancipated from the discipline of aristocratic schoolmasters, and growing into an age of manly liberty and self-restraint,—came

[1] Abbott, *Hist. of Greece*, vol. i. 419 foll. ; Holm, i 472 ; Plutarch. *Solon*. 21-23.

eventually nearer to the ideal of "the good life" (see p. 59) than any other State in Hellas. But we must now leave Athens for a while, and turn to see how, in other parts of Greece, this natural development of the City-State was for a while retarded, and in many cases permanently checked.

The tendency towards absolutism, or, if we like so to call it, the reaction to monarchy, which was so characteristic of this age, might, and did, show itself even more often in the shape of what the Greeks called tyranny, than in the milder form of the philosophic arbiter. What, then, precisely did a Greek understand by a tyrant,—a word probably borrowed by him from some Oriental tongue? Herodotus, writing some century and a half later than Solon, but with all the traditions of that period fresh in his mind, describes the tyrant in memorable words put dramatically into the mouth of a Persian.[1] "How can a monarchy be a convenient thing, wielding power as it does without responsibility? *The best man in the world, in such a position, will find himself outside the pale of the ideas in which he has been trained.* A reckless pride is bred in him of his present good fortune, while envy is natural to him as to every man. In these two

---

[1] Herod. iii. 80. Here Herodotus, as more or less throughout his work, does not exactly distinguish monarchy and tyranny, as Aristotle did later. It should in fact be noted that a legitimate Basileus might become a tyrant (*e.g.* Pheidon of Argos), though a tyrant of the genuine kind could never become a Basileus. See Freeman, *Hist. of Sicily*, ii. 53, and 431 foll. Cf. Herod. v. 92, sec. 20, where Cypselus in the oracle is styled Basileus, as being a tyrant descended from a royal family. Cf. v. 44.

flaws he possesses every vice ; filled full with pride,
he commits many reckless acts, and the envy in
him has the same result. . . . He is jealous of the
best men, his contemporaries, while they survive,
and rejoices in the worst of the citizens.[1]   He
hears slander with the utmost delight. He is of
all men the most inconsistent ; for if you praise
him but moderately, he is angry with you for not
making more of him, while if you adore him to the
utmost he hates you as a fawner.   And now I
shall sum up with the worst of all his wickednesses :
he disturbs the traditions of his State, he violates
women, and slays men without trial." To this
graphic picture we may add the concise definition
of Aristotle : "Tyranny is monarchy used for the
advantage of the monarch." [2]

These two passages may suffice to show us what
the thinking Greek understood by the word, and
how he regarded the thing. The typical Tyrant
did not represent the State and its needs ; he represented his own interests only.[3]   Tyranny in this
aspect was therefore a thing utterly alien to that
true and fruitful Greek life which was inseparable
from the State both in thought and fact.   Even the
best of tyrants, as Herodotus puts it in his own
inimitable way, must leave the circle of ideas in
which he has hitherto lived.   He lives no longer

[1] Herodotus is here intentionally using the language of the Greek
oligarch. See p. 119. It is not clear that he is here stating his
own view of tyranny ; but his description represents one view
which was current in Greece in his day.

[2] *Pol.* iii. 7, 5. More fully in vi. (iv.) 10 (1295 A).

[3] Thuc. i. 17.

in the air which every true Greek must breathe, the air of the free πόλις, invigorating both to body and mind. When Self takes the place of State, as the pivot on which social life works, that life ceases to be natural, loses its sap and its principle of growth, develops abnormal tendencies and strange monstrosities of character. And we cannot be far wrong in concluding that as, in Aristotelian language (see p. 60), the *end* (τέλος) of tyranny is not "the good life," but the good of an individual, it must be considered as marking a backward current in the stream of social development. It is a disease, not a natural growth; a return to monarchy, but to monarchy in a debased form.

Yet it is possible to criticise the trite definition of Aristotle, and to correct, even from his own history, the view of Herodotus which has just been quoted. It does not follow that the interests of an individual autocrat need be irreconcilable with those of his State, nor that every such autocrat should be drawn into weak and wicked conduct such as Herodotus describes. However true it may be in the main that tyranny was a backward movement, it is quite possible that the hatred of the high-born men tc whose rule the tyrants put an end,[1] and the inborn dislike of the average Greek for all individualism, may have handed down the memory of many tyrants in an unjustly evil light. Let us note two or three points in which the interest of the tyrant might,

---

[1] These are the men, it should be noted, in whose hands was the literature of that age.

and in many cases actually did, coincide with the interest of the State.

If an oligarchy were particularly narrow and oppressive, and affairs were rapidly drawing towards an epoch of party violence, a tyrant might for a time disarm both combatants, and by weakening the stronger might relatively strengthen the weaker. Most of the great tyrants of Greece rose to power by the help of the people, and all set themselves in self-defence to weaken the oligarchies.[1] In a certain sense, as in our own history with the absolutism of the Tudors, the disease of tyranny had eventually in many States a healing effect; it brought out latent possibilities in the State by bringing forward a new population with new ideas and new worships, and in some cases, as in the Peloponnese, one of a different race from the oligarchies which had so long ruled it.[2]

Again, the tyrant, if he were a man of education (and he frequently belonged to the cultured oligarchy itself), would naturally use his power to adorn his city with works of art. He wished his fame to spread through Hellas, and he knew the kind of glory that would appeal to the Hellenic mind. He would try to make his city, as it were, a university of literature and art; and in fact we find that Simonides, Pindar, Æschylus, and other

[1] Ar. *Pol.* viii. (v.), p. 1305 A ; cf. Herod. iii. 80, 8, as quoted above, and the memorable advice given by Periander to Thrasybulus, or, as Herod. has it (v. 92, 26), by Thras. to Per. Busolt, *Gr. Gesch.* i. note.

[2] Of this our best example is Cleisthenes of Sicyon ; cf. Herod. v. 67, vi. 126.

poets could make long journeys to visit a large-hearted
and open-handed tyrant, and were not ashamed to
enjoy his patronage or to sing his praises. It is
beyond doubt that both poetry and the plastic arts
owed much to the wealth and to the honourable
pride of these despots. Here and there, at least,
a tyrant's self-regarding aims, so far from hindering
the education of the Greek mind, positively did
much to advance it.[1]

And once more, the tyrant, in the very fact that
he was out of harmony with the true Greek social
life, was of some use in widening its boundaries,—
always apt to be somewhat confining. He stepped
for the moment beyond the limits of the πόλις, and
as he rose to fame might venture on alliance or
friendship with the despots of distant cities, or even
with the great monarchies that lay beyond Hellas.
Such startling steps could hardly be taken by the
City-State in its ordinary and natural life, which, as
we saw, must be as independent as possible of aid
from other States.[2] But the great tyrant rose altogether beyond these limits, and modelled himself
rather on Eastern than on Greek ideas ; he dreamt
perhaps of empire, he built a navy, he stimulated

[1] Hiero of Syracuse, in the fifth century, is the most splendid
example of this tendency of the tyrants. See especially Freeman,
Hist. of Sicily, vol. ii. 256-289. Polycrates, Periander, and the
Pisistratidæ can all be studied in Herodotus from the same
point of view.

[2] The contrast between the far-reaching plans of the tyrant
and the strict conventionalism of the typical πόλις is expressed
with all Herodotus's consummate skill in the interview between
Aristagoras of Miletus and Cleomenes of Sparta (v. 49).

commerce, he allied himself with the lower or trading classes. And in such ways, even while seeking his own glory, and violating the most vital principles of the older Greek life, he opened the eyes of the Greeks to things that lay beyond their narrow bounds, and had never been dreamed of in their philosophy since the age of Mycenæ, before the true State had come into being. Even in plotting with the Persians against Greece, his very selfishness revealed to the Greeks the dangers which surrounded them, and the want of union of which their system of City-States was the chief cause.

It is not possible, within the scope of this chapter, to illustrate these and other characteristics of tyranny from recorded facts. But the reader has only to take up his Herodotus, and to read the stories of men like Cleisthenes of Sicyon, Periander of Corinth, Gelo of Syracuse, Polycrates of Samos, Aristagoras of Miletus, and Pisistratus at Athens, in order to realise for himself how in various ways, both for good and for evil, the tyrant overstepped the limits of "the ideas in which he (and all Greeks) had been trained." Only let him remember that every word and every phrase of Herodotus are worth close attention, and that he is not to be read like a modern book in which words and phrases are often of little more account than the paper on which they are printed. To use the felicitous language of a true Greek scholar, Herodotus' finished art "preserved unimpaired the primitive energy of words;"[1] and in the fresh light of those words we

[1] Professor Butcher, *Some Aspects*, etc., p. 16.

can still see in clearest outline, if not always the actual facts themselves, at least the impression they had left on the mind of the open-eyed Greek of an age when knowledge was not derived from books, but from memory and the spoken word.

But let me conclude this chapter by a rapid glance at a single mighty tyrant, as he lives for ever in the pages of Herodotus. The City-State of Samos, with its territory of the island of the same name, had been ruled by an oligarchy till about the year 537 B.C.[1] "Then Polycrates, son of Æaces, rose up and laid his hand on Samos. At first he shared his power with his two brothers; but soon he slew one and drove out the other. Then he sent gifts to Amasis, king of Egypt, and receiving others in return, became his friend and ally; and to such a pitch of prosperity did he attain that his fame was spread abroad throughout Ionia and the whole of Hellas. Wherever he set out with fleet or army, good luck followed him; he owned a hundred ships of war, and had a thousand archers for a bodyguard. He went about capturing and plundering without respect of persons, for he used to say that he could oblige a friend more by returning what he had taken from him, than by leaving his property wholly untouched. His power extended over many of the islands and over many towns on the coast; and when the Lesbians came to help Miletus in warding off his attack, he beat and captured them with his fleet, and those Les-

[1] Herod. iii. 39, 120; Polyænus, i. 23, 2. The passage in the text is paraphrased from Herodotus.

bians had to dig in fetters the whole circle of the
foss around his city-wall at Samos."

Nothing can show more clearly than these graphic
sentences that Polycrates had passed the boundary
of "the ideas in which he had been trained." He
is not only the master of a πόλις, but the founder
of a naval empire in the Ægean.[1] He knows no
law, civil or moral; he respects neither property
nor person, but appropriates the one and binds the
other in chains. And yet, while the end of all his
actions was his own glory, he made his city famous
in Greece; for even if the three wonders of
Samos,—the great tunnel,[2] the mole in the harbour,
and the magnificent temple,—were not all of them
projected or even completed by him, he left behind
him a name as a great employer of labour, and as a
munificent patron of artists. Theodorus, the en-
graver of the tyrant's famous ring, and Rhœcus,
the architect of the temple, were natives of Samos
in his age. We know, too, that poets were welcome
at his court, and that Ibycus and Anakreon lived
and sang there; and the greatest physician of that
age, Democedes of Croton, was glad to obtain his
patronage.[3]

In two other points Polycrates is typical as a
tyrant. First, he held out a friendly hand to the
empires beyond Hellas. When Amasis repudiated
his alliance, he offered help to Cambyses in his attack

[1] Herod. iii. 122. He stands half-way between the legendary
empire of Minos and the later Athenian empire.

[2] Herod. iii. 41, 60. The tunnel, or aqueduct, has recently
been discovered. Busolt, Gr. Gesch. i. 603.

[3] Herod. iii. 121, 131 : cf. 125.

on Egypt, doing a black deed in despatching to the
Persian's aid a fleet of forty triremes, manned by all
the high-born Samians whom he most feared and
hated, in order to bring them to an evil end. And
secondly, his power is short - lived ; for while
negotiating with a Persian satrap for the acquisition of wealth which would have made him
master of Hellas, he fell into a trap, little recking
that he was in the way of the Persian power, and
died a cruel and disgraceful death.[1] Nemesis, so
the Greeks thought, must assuredly lay her aveng-
ing hand on all who overstepped those limits of
power and fortune within which the State, and not
the Individual, was the true end of life.

One more word before we leave the tyrants.
The love of gain, of power and position above the
laws and conventionalities of the State, was a
common phenomenon in Greek history, and is seen
not only in tyrants like Polycrates, but in kings
and even ordinary citizens of the best ordered
πόλεις, such as Cleomenes and Pausanias of Sparta,
and Themistocles and Alcibiades of Athens. And
the explanation is surely to be found in the very
nature of the City-State itself. In its normal type
it was too small, too narrow, too much bound down
by fixed traditions, and by a single rule of life, to
give the individual free play, or even always fair
play. To its model he must conform, or overstep
the limits of " the ideas in which he has grown up."
Human nature is everywhere such that there will
always be found rebels against the drill of a social-

[1] Herod. iii. 43, 44, 120-126.

istic system; and the stricter that drill, and the smaller the State, the more lawless will be the rebellion of the individual. Athens alone among Greek States, and that not without risk both for herself and Greece, solved for a time the problem of developing the best fruits of individual genius and ambition through, and together with, the full glory of the City-State.

CHAPTER VI

I SAID at the end of the last chapter that Athens alone, of all the City-States of antiquity, solved for a time the problem of freely developing the talent of the individual, while maintaining fully that identification of the individual with the State which was the very essence of Greek social life. This proposition I wish to prove and explain in the present chapter. By keeping steadily to it, we shall obtain, I believe, the best idea of such "good life" as it was possible for the City-State to realise; and we shall learn to identify that "good life" with the form and spirit of Democracy, the last phase taken by this kind of social union in the course of its natural development, before decay set in. I say the *form and spirit* of Democracy; for though Democracy is often treated as a form of government only,[1] we surely may not be content so to treat it, if we are really bent on understanding what the πόλις in its perfection could do for the education of mankind.

[1] *E.g.* by Sir H. Maine in *Popular Government*, ch. i.

Let us start by taking as a text some memorable words of the statesman who above all other Athenians, in the golden days of Athens, perceived what the State might do for the individual, and the individual for the State, towards the realisation of " the good life." When Athens at last became involved in war with Sparta, at the funeral of the first victims of battle Pericles was chosen to deliver an oration over them, of which Thucydides the historian, himself doubtless among the audience, has preserved for us the spirit and the thoughts in his own weighty and subtle phraseology. One passage in this immortal speech seems to embody in living words the statesman's idea of what life in democratic Athens ought to be, expressed as though it actually were so ; as in moments of deep emotion we are apt to speak of one whom we profoundly admire and love with an enthusiasm suggested and justified by his character, even if it fall short in truth of the perfection with which our strong feeling invests it. But Pericles must have known well the shortcomings of the Athenians, as well as their wonderful capacities ; and if at this moment of supreme feeling he expressed not only the bare truth about them, but also his own hopes for them, and his ideal of a perfect civic life, we need not shrink on that account to take these words of his as the best possible text from which to set about learning what Athens actually was in his day. I shall quote the passage in full.[1]

---

[1] Thucydides, ii. 37. I quote from Jowett's translation ; but

"Our form of government does not enter into rivalry
with the institutions of others. We do not copy our neighbours, but are an example to them. It is true that we are
called a democracy, for the administration is in the hands of
the many and not the few. But while the law secures equal
justice to all alike in their private disputes, the claim of
excellence is also recognised ; and where a citizen is in any
way distinguished, he is preferred to the public service, not
as a matter of privilege, but as a reward of merit. Neither
is poverty a bar, but a man may benefit his country whatever be the obscurity of his condition. There is no exclusiveness in our public life, and in our private intercourse
we are not suspicious of each other, nor angry with our
neighbour if he does what he likes ; we do not put on sour
looks at him which, though harmless, are not pleasant.
While we are thus unconstrained in our private intercourse,
a spirit of reverence pervades our public acts ; we are
prevented from doing wrong by respect for authority and
for the laws, having an especial regard for those which are
ordained for the protection of the injured, as well as for
those unwritten laws which bring upon the transgressor of
them the reprobation of the general sentiment."

Now what Pericles here wished to impress on
the Athenians, as the ideal at which their social
life should be aimed, may be expressed mainly in
two propositions. First, the whole Athenian people
were identified with, actually were, the State, in a
higher and fuller sense than had so far been realised
by any Greek city ; all shared equally in its government, in its education, and in its pleasures.
Secondly, this equality of right and advantage, so
far from reducing all to a dead level of intellect,
actually gave freer play to individual talent than

it is only from the Greek, and from the laying to heart of every
phrase of it, that Pericles' meaning can fully be apprehended.

it could be sure of obtaining in other States ; for at
Athens alone poverty was no hindrance to the
development of genius. If these two propositions
were in any real sense true of the Athenians of
that day, then surely we may find here the " good
life " which Aristotle claims as the true *end* of the
City-State—the full and free culture of the individual
aiming at the advantage of the community.

We have now to see how far these two propositions hold good of Athens in the time of Pericles.
Very different views, it must be said at once, were
taken by later writers and orators of the Athenians
and their democracy. Plato, for instance, makes
Socrates say in the *Gorgias*,[1] " I hear that Pericles
made the Athenians a lazy, cowardly, talkative, and
money-loving people, by accustoming them to
receive wages." Isocrates describes democracy at
Athens as passing into disorder, freedom into lawlessness, equality into reckless impudence.[2] Aristotle, too, never shows enthusiasm for Athenian
institutions, nor does he connect Pericles with any
attempt to realise his own ideal of τὸ εὖ ζῆν.[3] But
Plato, Isocrates, and Aristotle knew Athens only
when her best days were past, and when the gifted
and animated population of the golden age had been
thinned down sadly by war and pestilence. It is
not scientific to judge of the working of Athenian
institutions in the fifth century B.C. by the opinions

---

[1] P. 515.   [2] *Areop.* 20.
[3] To these unfavourable verdicts must be added that of the
treatise on the Athenian constitution formerly attributed to
Xenophon.

of men who knew them only as worked by a
degenerate population in the fourth.   Let us keep
for the present to Pericles himself as a guide.
Following his lead, we may try and form some idea
of Athenian democracy first as a political whole, and
secondly, in respect of the education and capacity
of the individuals composing that whole.

I. Let us recall, to begin with, the position in
which Solon's legislation had left the Athenian
people.   Having freed them from the bondage of
debt, and cleared the way for their progress towards
social independence, he gave to the whole people,
including the poorest class, a powerful hold on the
executive which governed them.   All had a share in
electing the magistrates, and all had a share in the
right of judging of the conduct of these magistrates
at the end of their year of office.   He added to the
constitution a new Council of 400, also elected by
the whole body of citizens, but retained the old
Council of the Areopagus to watch over the general
interests of the State, both material and moral.
And by a re-division of the existing citizens on the
basis of property instead of descent, and by restricting
the right of holding magistracies to the richer
citizens, he destroyed the purely aristocratic character of the executive, while securing that this
executive should not pass into the hands of persons
ill-educated or poverty-stricken.

The general result of Solon's work was therefore
to identify every individual Athenian very closely
with the State, but to keep the reins of government
in the hands of men who were qualified to wield

them.   Under the oligarchical regime the ordinary
Athenian had little benefit from the government,
little interest in the State ; he was a part of the
State only in a very doubtful sense, and politically
was not on a much higher level than the Attic
slave.   After Solon he could feel that the government was of advantage to him, that he himself had
a distinct share in it, and a very lively interest in
its good management.   He is raised a whole stage
higher in the social system, and removed far above
the level of the slave.   But this identification of
the interests of individual and State might be made
still more complete and fruitful.

If we could in imagination transport ourselves
to the Athens of a century and a half later, and
mingle in the city and the port of Piræus with the
busy crowd of citizens, we should find a very different state of things from that left by Solon.   Not only
has the city greatly increased in size, population,
and magnificence, as well as in fame and influence ;
not only has a new port arisen, in which a splendid
navy is sheltered, and whose streets are thronged
by strangers from all parts of Hellas and the surrounding countries ; but by questioning and observing we should discover as a fact beyond all doubt,
that every Athenian citizen is now a citizen in the
fullest sense of which the word is capable.   The
words πόλις and πολίτης have here a closer relation than they have ever yet reached in Greek
history, and express the fact that the full identification of the State and the individual is here at
last achieved.

Every citizen has now not only a right to hold office,[1] and to serve on the Council, but also a very good chance of exercising that right in his turn. Every citizen can take part in the meetings of the general Assembly (ἐκκλησία), which takes place regularly forty times every year, and on many other occasions when special business was to be transacted;[2] and in these assemblies final decisions are taken on every matter which concerned the interest of the State as a whole. Every citizen over thirty years of age can further sit as a judge in one of the large panels of 500 into which those thus qualified by age are now distributed; and before one of these panels almost every case of importance must come, for the judicial functions of even the highest magistrates are now limited to the mere direction of business in the courts, or to the settlement of suits of a petty nature. Lastly, the council of the Areopagus, which Solon retained as a body of experienced men occupying their seats in it for life, in order to place the working of the whole State under a wise and efficient control, has wholly lost this undefined power of supervision; the Athenians are now quite emancipated from any such paternal authority, and commit their interests to no trustees save their yearly elected magistrates,—and to these only in a very limited sense. The people, like the

---

[1] Whether the Archonship was open to the lowest class in 450, either legally or practically, is doubtful. At the end of the following century it was practically open to all. See *Ath. Pol.* ch. vii. *fin.*

[2] Gilbert, i. p. 255 and notes.

young sovereign who puts aside his father's too insistent counsellors, has taken the conduct of its affairs entirely into its own hands, confident in its own abilities and in its own reasonableness. The State, not only as the shelter and home but as the property and occupation of the people, truly *is* now the whole body of Athenians, and not a part only, as under the oligarchical rule. The individual is identified to the full with the State.

To explain how these great changes have come about would be beyond the scope of this chapter. Even after the discovery of the treatise on the Athenian constitution, the political history of Athens from Solon to Pericles is still a very difficult and complicated study, and there is hardly a point or a date in it which is not still matter of dispute. I am more concerned just now to illustrate a little more fully the actual working of this wonderful democracy ; but before attempting this I must recall the history of Athens in broadest outline, in order that we may see, if not precisely by what steps the democratic spirit went forward, at least how it was possible that it should make such rapid and effectual progress.

This progress, we may be sure, was not merely the result of a series of fortunate circumstances, for in the course of it Athens underwent such perils as would have crushed any ordinary state of her size. Four times at least, within a period of some thirty years, Attica was invaded by enemies, and twice her sacred Acropolis was desecrated by their forcible occupation;[1] yet the progress continued, steady and sure as ever. We must rather look for an explanation to that quality of her people which we saw exemplified so admirably in Solon, and which the student of her literature and art ever contemplates with delight; I mean the sanity, the reasonableness, of the Athenians and their leading men. I have pointed out how Solon's work was *reasonable*, because it embraced in one series of laws, social and economic, as well as political, reform; in all his legislation he was animated by the same reasonable object of developing the resources of the State in due proportion and harmony. The same quality is to be noted even in the tyranny which followed. Little as we know of the government of Pisistratus, it is quite enough to convince us that under this absolutism Athens was not, like so many other States, swept into a back-current, or left floating idle and exhausted. Pisistratus did not abolish Solon's laws, nor did he play false to the spirit which dictated them. On this point Thucydides is emphatic; let me quote his exact words.[2]

"The general character of his administration was not unpopular or oppressive to the many; in fact no tyrants ever displayed greater merit or capacity than these. Though the tax which they exacted amounted only to five per cent., they improved and adorned the city. . . . The city was permitted to retain her ancient laws, the Pisistratidæ only taking care that one of themselves should always be in office."

---

[1] By Cleomenes of Sparta in 509 B.C. after expelling Cleisthenes (Herod. v. 72); and by the Persians in 480 B.C.

[2] Thucyd. vi. 54, 5 and 6.

It is plain from this passage, and from what little else we know about him, that Pisistratus was one of those tyrants whose personal interest coincided with that of the State. He helped, rather than retarded, the development of the people in well-being, in commerce, in art, and in religion.[1] The words in which Thucydides describes his quality, ἀρετή and ξύνεσις,—a right spirit and an intellectual sanity,—would prove this sufficiently even if we had no other evidence at all.

Pisistratus died in 527 B.C. In the hands of his sons the tyranny gradually degenerated into one of the worst type; and on the expulsion of Hippias, in 510 B.C., the natural result followed—faction and anarchy. The oligarchs lifted up their heads again, and for a moment treachery and intrigue threatened to ruin the growing State. But again Athens found a reasonable man to help her. Cleisthenes, who perhaps began with the idea of making himself tyrant, ended by " taking the people into partnership," and working out more fully the reasonable policy of Solon and Pisistratus. Of the man himself we know little or nothing, but we know at least in outline what was his chief contribution to the development of democracy. When the leaders of the French Revolution wished to undermine the influence of the ancient feudal nobility, they did away with the old division of the country into provinces, in which the local magnates and their privileges were

---

[1] The evidence connecting Pisistratus with the popular Dionysus-worship at Athens will be found stated in Mr. Dyer's *Gods in Greece*, p. 125, note 3.

paramount, and adopted a new division into a much larger number of departments, on which the whole political system was to be based without fear of local aristocratic influence. Cleisthenes struck out a plan of much the same kind. Attica had been divided into four tribes, twelve phratries, and three hundred and sixty clans (γένη), *each clan having as its nucleus an aristocratic family.* Cleisthenes was too reasonable actually to abolish these; but he saw that if Athens was to enjoy repose, now that the people were familiar with the idea that they had a direct interest in the State, these old aristocratic groups must practically cease to have political importance. He re-divided the Athenians into ten new tribes, each comprising, as administrative units, ten demes or townships; the demes in each tribe *not being contiguous,* but situated in different parts of Attica, so as to be wholly free from the old local traditions and influences. In these new tribes and demes he included every free Athenian, together with many residents in Attica and enfranchised slaves, who had never been inscribed on the registers of the old divisions. On the basis of this new local system the constitution was henceforward to be worked; for example, the Council was increased to 500, so that fifty were elected to it yearly from each of the ten new tribes. If this new system were adhered to, oligarchy could never rear its head again, and tyranny would have but a poor chance. And surely we may see, in the loyal submission of the oligarchical party to this sweeping change, one more proof of the reasonableness of the Athenian people in all grades of social life. For the change was perhaps the most far-reaching in all Athenian history. The tissue out of which the State had been created,—the clan village with its religious aristocracy,—was no longer to be essential to the State's vitality; it might survive, but its place was henceforth to be supplied by a new organisation, in which there would be no aristocratic centres to influence the people's will.

Thus finally delivered from oligarchic tutelage and faction, "united and penetrated with a single spirit," [1] Athens was ready to face her greatest trial. The reasonableness of her leaders, and the strength which unity had given her, enabled her to act as the real champion of Hellas against the Persian invader; and the heroism of her successful defence, in which every citizen directly or indirectly took a part, at once made the completion of democracy certain, and spread throughout Greece the fame of democratic institutions. In the generation succeeding the Persian wars, the changes were brought about which produced the constitution of which I just now indicated the leading features. Aristides, another leader of the true Solonian type; Ephialtes, a man "with a reputation for incorruptibility and possessing a high public character"; [2] and lastly Pericles, whose character and abilities are immortalised by the greatest of Greek historians, completed the work, and brought Athens to such a pitch of greatness that she roused the hatred and jealousy of the City-

---

[1] Abbott, *Hist. of Greece*, I 484.

[2] *Ath. Pol.* 25.

M

States of Greece, and was forced to embark in a
struggle which ended in her own downfall. Of the
meaning of this jealousy and its fatal results, so far
as it concerns the history of the City-State, I shall
have a word to say later on; at present, leaving
aside the question as to the precise steps by which
complete democracy was realised under the leaders
just mentioned, let us turn for a moment to consider
what democracy really meant at Athens in the short
period of its best days.

Just as the City-State differed as a *species* from
the modern State, so did its democratic form differ
from what we now understand by Democracy. For
example, when we speak of our British constitution as having become a democracy, we mean that
we are governed by a ministry which has at its
back the majority of a democratically elected House
of Commons. We are not governed by the people;
this is impossible, even with the aid of representative institutions, in the large territories of the modern
State. Some approach can be made to it, in the
way of local government, which may enable the
people in each district to understand and in some
degree to manage their own local affairs; [1] but great
questions of national interest can only be presented
to the people at periodical elections, and it constantly happens that on such questions the government of the day is actually for a year or two at
variance with the feeling of the majority of the

---

[1] This may perhaps be best seen in the working of the Swiss
democracy. See Adams and Cunningham's *Swiss Constitution*,
chapters on the Commune and Canton.

people. When at last an election takes place, that
feeling is expressed, and the new government is, for
a time at least, in accordance with it. But this is
very far from what the Greeks meant by δημοκρατία
—government by the people. We have borrowed
their word, and given it a new meaning, as far less
simple as our form of State is less simple than
theirs.

When the Athenians called their constitution a
δημοκρατία, they meant literally what the word
itself expressed,—that the people undertook itself
the work of government. I must now try to explain briefly how this could be in any sense true ; and
I can best do so by considering three several points,
viz. (1) the legislative and judicial power ; (2) the
magistrates and lesser officials, together with the
council ; (3) the manner in which these were
elected.

1. I have already said that every Athenian citizen
could sit and vote in the Ecclesia, and that all over
thirty years of age could sit and vote in the law-
courts. This meant, no doubt, that practically the
dwellers in Athens and the Peiræus alone habitually
did so ; for not even in a City-State could democratic institutions be made absolutely perfect. They
met in the open air, listened to orators debating the
questions presented to them, and by their votes
finally decided them. Their assembly thus constituted the *sovereign body* of the State, from which
there was no further reference ; their Dikasteria
were also courts of final reference, from which there
was likewise no appeal whatever. And to secure

that all alike, poor as well as rich, should not only have the right, but also be able to exercise it, of taking part in these assemblies, and thus bringing their individuality to bear on the conduct of the State, Pericles introduced a small payment for attendance, sufficient to enable the poor to forgo their usual occupations on the days of meeting.

Want of space forbids me here to enter into detail on the subjects of discussion and decision which were brought before the sovereign assembly of Athenians. It will be sufficient to point out that they included every matter of vital interest to the State as a whole ; decisions of war and peace, negotiations with other States, the management of the military and naval forces, general questions of finance and of religion, complaints against the public conduct of individuals, and lastly—though in the best days of Athens, as we shall see, this was an unusual subject of debate—the passing of new laws and the amendment of existing ones. In all such matters the voice of the Athenian people was supreme and final.[1]

2. So far we have seen that the *sovereignty*, or as Sir H. Maine defines that word, the supreme social force, lay at Athens with the people themselves, and not with any set of delegates or officials elected by them. But what share had they in the actual administration,—in the conduct of all the complicated business which abounds in an active and

[1] On this subject read Schomann, *Ant.* p. 379 ; and for the form of popular decrees see examples in Hicks, *Greek Historical Inscriptions*, pp. 53, 62, 105.

prosperous State, and which cannot possibly be transacted in a vast popular assembly ? In other words, did the individual Athenian transact public business himself, as well as direct or judge those to whom it fell ? Was he in any degree familiar with the details of the business which he ultimately directed in his assembly, or was he, like the vast majority of the members of our own so-called democracy, wholly ignorant of them, utterly inexperienced in the burdens and responsibilities of office ?

The answer to these questions is, that if the constitution actually worked on the lines indicated by the researches of modern scholars, almost every Athenian must at one time or other in his life have taken part in the conduct of public business. This will not be fully apparent until we have explained how Athenian officials were elected ; but for the moment we will take a rapid glance at the two chief classes of officials,—those who constituted the Council of 500, and those who filled the long series of administrative posts, from the Archons and Generals at the top of the ladder to the lowest kind of overseers who looked after the police, the markets, or the victims for the public sacrifices.

The Council was simply a large committee of the whole people, elected afresh every year. Its business was of very various kinds, and need not be specified in detail here ; two points will be sufficient to provide us with an answer to our questions, so far as this institution is concerned. First, it prepared all business for the Ecclesia, and it had to

see that the decisions of the Ecclesia were properly
carried out; in a word, the whole of the ordinary
business of the State passed through its hands. The
preparation of all such business, as well as the
execution of Acts of Parliament, is in our own
constitution the work of permanent officials, skilled
men whose lives are given up to it as a profession—
statesmen, permanent secretaries, judges, magistrates,
and inspectors. At Athens all this work was done
by the ordinary Athenian elected to the Council,
who brought only his native intelligence and reasonableness to bear upon it. Secondly, it was hardly
possible for any councillor to shirk this business;
for the Council did not usually sit as a whole, but
in successive sections of fifty relieving each other
during ten divisions of the year. A member's
absence might easily be unnoticed in a large
assembly, but he would be missed if he failed often
to be present in a committee of fifty only.[1]

To the 500 members of Council who thus
became familiar, for a time at least, with the most
important practical side of public business, we must
now add the whole number of officials who assisted
the Council in administrative work in its minutest
details. It would be tedious to enumerate these;
but the point to notice is that the Athenians entrusted these details, not to single individuals, but
to *boards*. There were nine Archons, ten Strategi or
Generals, and other boards for finance, education,

---

[1] Much interesting information on these points, and others that
follow, will be found brought together in Mr. J. W. Headlam's
Election by Lot at Athens (Cambridge Historical Essays, No. iv.).

religion, dockyards, and every other department,
great and small, of public administration.   One
important board, the Logistæ or chief accountants,
were even thirty in number.   The whole number
of individuals serving the State in this way in any
one year cannot be computed for the age I am
speaking of; but for the age of Aristides the author
of the "Athenian Constitution" reckoned them at
1400.[1]   If we take the same number for the age
of Pericles, and add to it the 500 councillors, we
get a total of 1900, out of an adult male population of about 30,000.[2]

3. All these officials, with a very few excep-
tions, of which the Strategi are the most important,
were elected by *lot*, and to the best of our knowledge were rarely if ever re-elected.[3]   The exact
details of the method of election by lot are still
unknown to us; but there can be no reasonable
doubt that this method, which to us seems so
strange on account of our very different conception
of democracy, was meant to secure that every
Athenian should at some time in his life have the
right or bear the burden (in whichever way he

[1] *Ath. Pol.* 24.   Half of these were ἔνδημοι, and half ὑπερόριοι ;
but it is not clear who are meant by the latter,—the magistrates
"beyond the borders."   If we were to exclude these, the 1900
would be reduced to 1200.

[2] This number represents the general impression of the Athenians
themselves in the fifth century : Beloch, *Bevolkerung*, p. 59.   The
same author, at p. 99, concludes that it was 35,000 at the opening
of the Peloponnesian war.

[3] See Headlam, *op. cit.* p. 90, note 1.   But the author of the
Ath. Pol. states that in his own day membership of the Council
could be held twice, and military offices any number of times.

might consider it) of assisting in the performance
of some part of public business. Nineteen hundred
places of office, if the lot worked as we believe it
was meant to do, would circulate among the whole
body of citizens about once in sixteen years.[1]

Now if we take this in connection with the
universal right of citizens to take part in the
Ecclesia, and of those over thirty years of age to sit
as jurors in the courts, it becomes at once plain
that the Athenian people did actually conduct its
own government, and that the State was a true
δημοκρατία. Here is no privileged class, no class
of skilled politicians, no bureaucracy; no body of
men, like the Roman Senate, who alone understood
the secrets of State, and were looked up to and
trusted as the gathered wisdom of the whole community. At Athens there was no disposition, and
in fact no need, to trust the experience of any one;
each man entered intelligently into the details of
his own temporary duties, and discharged them, as
far as we can tell, with industry and integrity.
Like the players in a well-trained orchestra, all
contrived to learn their parts and to be satisfied
with the share allotted to them.

Nor was there any serious chance that this
system of government by the people should lead to
want of respect for law and tradition. The Athenian
of the best days of Athens never dreamed of thinking loosely about the law. Much of his time, as

[1] Read Aristotle's account of the general characteristics of
democracy, *Pol.* 1317 B; noting especially those passages which
are evidently a reflection from the practice at Athens.

we have seen, was spent in carrying it out himself,
or seeing that others did so. It was inevitable
that this should be so, where the interests of State
and individual were so wholesomely identified as
they were at Athens. Assuredly the democratic
leaders would never have done away with the
supervising authority of the Areopagus, had they
not been filled with the conviction that the laws
(that is, the constitution) were now in complete
harmony with the feelings of the people, and that
the people was itself capable of acting as their
guardians. In fact, the true justification for this
bold transference of trusteeship from an irresponsible
body to the people themselves is to be found in the
speech of Pericles quoted at the beginning of this
chapter.[1] "While we are thus unconstrained in
our private intercourse, a spirit of reverence pervades our public acts ; we are prevented from doing
wrong by respect for authority and for the laws"
(τὰ δημόσια διὰ δέος μάλιστα οὐ παρανομοῦμεν,
τῶν τε ἀεὶ ἐν ἀρχῇ ὄντων ἀκροάσει καὶ τῶν νόμων,
κ.τ.λ.).

And these memorable words were indeed no
empty boast. All through his civic life it was the
work of the Athenian to watch over the laws and
their administration. When as a youth just entering manhood he was enrolled with solemn religious
ceremony in the ranks of the Ephebi,[2] he swore not

---

[1] Thuc. ii , last words of ch. 37.

[2] *I.e.* the youths just ready to enter on their first military service. For the oath see Lycurgus *contra Leocr.* 77. Telfy, *Corpus
Juris Attici*, p. 6.

only to fight bravely for his city, but " to obey those
who bear rule, and the laws which are in force, and
all that the sovereign people shall decree." When
he came to take his turn as an official, he had to
undergo a preliminary examination as to his quali-
fication,[1] and when his term of office ended he had
to present his accounts to the Logistæ, and otherwise to show that his conduct had been in accordance with the law. It probably fell to his lot, at
least once in his life, also to help in conducting
such scrutinies. And as a councillor his work was
done *in public,* and not in any secret session ; for
the Council worked under the eye of the people,
and from its very nature could never become a
body apt to warp the constitution from its true
intention, as the Areopagus might have done, and
the Senate of Rome actually did. And lastly, the
Athenian, if he should ever desire to propose a
change in the existing law, had to do so at a risk
serious enough to deter him from all hasty trifling
with legislation. He made himself liable to an
indictment " for informality, illegality, or uncon-
stitutionality " (*Graphê Paranomôn*) ; and if, when
threatened with this, he still persisted, he incurred
after conviction a very severe penalty. The law,
which in the theory of the City-State was one and
unchangeable, was at Athens in her best days as
nearly so as was practically possible. It is of the
essence of true democracy to be intensely conserva-

---

[1] For the true nature of this examination (δοκιμασία) see Headlam, *op. cit.* 96 foll. ; Schomann, *Ant.* 403.   For the εὔθυναι, *ib.*
407 ; G. Gilbert, *Alterthumer,* i. 214.

tive ; conservative, not necessarily of petty customs which do not affect the vitality of the State, but of all great principles, written or unwritten, on which the constitution is based. Nowhere, since the days of Athens, has this conservative tendency asserted itself more strongly than in the great democratic State of the modern world.[1]

I hope I have now said enough to indicate the line of study to be taken by any one who really wishes to understand the nature of this most perfectly developed form of the ancient City-State. He should set himself to discover in detail, first, how it was possible for the Athenians to govern themselves, or in other words, what they meant by calling their constitution a δημοκρατία ; secondly, how such a government could be carried on, and must necessarily be carried on, in strict accordance with the law. Following closely this plan of inquiry, if I am not mistaken, he will come to appreciate the truth of the proposition, that in the golden age of Athens the interests of the State and the individual were more perfectly identified than in any other State of antiquity ; that we here reach the highest development of which the πόλις was capable. That there were drawbacks even here,

---

[1] See Bryce's *American Constitution*, vol. i. chaps. 31-34 ; or Maine, *Popular Government*, Essay 4. For the securities for the maintenance of the Athenian constitution, see especially Grote, vol. iv. 116 foll. ; but the student cannot do better, if he would see for himself how hard it was to effect a revolution when once the democracy was complete, than examine carefully the difficulties with which the oligarchical party had to contend in B.C 411, in Thucyd. viii. 47 foll.

and weak points in the system, is indeed true
enough, and of these I shall have a word to say at
the end of this chapter; but I must now turn for
a moment to the other claim which Pericles made
for Athens, that her political system, so far from
crushing the individual, gave him and his abilities
freer play than he could look for in any other
Greek State.

II. A people actually employed day by day in
the details of its own government must necessarily
be undergoing a process of education. If every
individual Athenian was expected, some time or
other in his life, to have to do such work as audit-
ing accounts, superintending public workmen, or
arranging contracts for the supply of sacrificial
victims (I select these simply as specimens of the
minor sort of duties which might fall to him), it is
obvious that a degree of intellectual alacrity would
also be expected from him which no one would look
for in the humbler classes of an oligarchically-
governed State. In such a State, as, for example,
at Rome in the best age of senatorial rule, the
intelligence of the governing class might be of a
high average, but there would be no call, no stimulus, for the mental education of the people. Sparta
is an even stronger example of the same tendency;
for there not only was the mass of the population
kept in a state of rude and rustic ignorance, but
the ruling class itself was educated on a system in
which intellectual ardour was rigidly discouraged.
But at Athens the individual had every inducement
to train his own intelligence for the benefit of the

State; and when he came to serve his State, the very fact that he was associated with others on official boards, on juries, and in the Ecclesia, must have still further sharpened his wits, while at the same time it taught him how to subordinate his own judgment to that of his fellows, and to reserve his own opinion till it was clearly called for. Even if we stopped here in considering the reasonable freedom of the individual at Athens, we should find Pericles' proud boast in great measure justified, for however low a man's birth or circumstances, he would still be able to bring his individual intelligence to bear upon public affairs, " ἔχων τι ἀγαθὸν δρᾶσαι τὴν πόλιν."

But there was another aspect of Athenian life which goes to confirm our impression that Pericles' ideal was in some degree realised. At this I can only glance very hurriedly. We may perhaps best appreciate it by considering how the public wealth was spent at Athens. At Sparta, owing to the peculiar constitution and discipline of the State, there was no surplus public wealth at all,—none, that is, except the land and its products. At Rome the resources of the State had a constant tendency to pass into the hands of individuals of the ruling class, and were as constantly spent by them on their own private and material advancement. At Athens such a tendency was practically impossible. There were moderately rich men at Athens, such as Nikias, who had large property in Attica, or Thucydides the historian, who owned mines on the coast of Thrace; but they had to contribute heavily to public objects,[1] and there was no obvious opening for the accumulation of a vast capital in the hands of an individual. The spirit of moderation, the inheritance of Solon's reasonableness, so far as we can see, survived in Athens for at least two centuries.

The truth is that the surplus public wealth—I leave aside for the moment the sources from which it was drawn — was spent on the intellectual and æsthetic education of the whole Athenian people. It was not spent only on the powerful navy which secured to Athens her commanding influence in Greece, or even on the splendid religious festivals which called on every Athenian at stated times to come out and feast and enjoy himself, or on the *gymnasia* which were to develop the bodily beauty and strength of boy and man alike. It was spent on the erection of those magnificent buildings on the Acropolis, of which the ruins still stand; on those inimitable sculptures which still serve to educate the imperfect artistic feeling of our modern world; on the exhibition, open to every citizen, however poor, of the tragic and comic dramas, in some of which the most perfect of languages lives still in its most perfect form. To put it briefly, it was spent in raising the whole level of the εἰωθότα νοήματα of Athens,—of the ways of thinking and feeling in which every citizen grew up. It may

---

[1] Schomann, *Ant.* 454 foll. ; Boeckh, *Public Economy of Athens* (new German edition), vol. i. 533 foll., 628 foll. I am compelled to omit here further reference to liturgies, trierarchies, and the general incidence of taxation on the rich. But the matter is of the greatest importance in forming an estimate of the influence of democracy on the distribution of property at Athens.

be that the ordinary Athenian did not see the
policy in this light; that he thought of it as
tending rather to increase his comfort than his
culture. But between comfort and culture Pericles
himself can have drawn no real distinction; in his
view, if Thucydides reports him rightly, the well-
being of the citizen would naturally enable him to
develop his individual faculties for the good and the
glory of the State.

And we have sufficient evidence that he succeeded in great measure. In no other age or State
has so small a population produced so many men of
genius, whose rare taste and ability were not wasted
or misdirected, but stimulated and called into healthy
action by the very circumstances of the everyday
life they lived. I do need but mention such
names as Æschylus, Sophocles, Euripides, Aristo-
phanes, Thucydides, Lysias, Pheidias, Socrates, and
Pericles himself, and others whose gifts enabled
them " to do some good to their city," to show
that individual genius found free play at Athens,
and was spent on gaining for her not only a
transient glory, but an immortal one. All these
poets, artists, and statesmen, and many others of
more ordinary fame, found Athens in need of them.
What their individual talents could supply was
exactly that which was called for by the daily life
as well as by the loftier aspirations of the people.
To use a modern phrase, they were in harmony
with their environment; there was no friction in
this golden age between the man of genius and the
world he lived in. Truly it cannot be said that

the Athenians were jealous of those whose talents raised them above the crowd. In some famous instances, indeed, they laid a heavy hand upon their great men ; they fined Pericles, they punished Pheidias, they drove out Anaxagoras, they put Socrates to death. But they were never angry with their men of genius because they were men of genius ; they merely declined to place absolute confidence in them as men who could do no wrong. And, after all, it was a plague-stricken and hard-pressed Athens that dealt unjustly with Pericles, and an Athens conquered and ruined that gave Socrates the hemlock. For years they had let Pericles, not indeed rule them, but lead them, and it was no more than the consciousness of a weak point in the Greek character that persuaded them that he or Pheidias could be guilty of peculation. For years they let Socrates go about the city teaching strange doctrines,—doctrines that were inconsistent even with the high level of the εἰωθότα νοήματα of the average Athenian mind. In spite of these mistakes, one of which at least has left a stain for ever on their glorious record, the proposition holds good that here " the good life " was realised more fully than in any other City-State, and the interests of the State and the individual more completely identified in the endeavour to attain it.

I said some way back that I should have a word to say about the weak points in this wonderful political creation of the Athenians. Drawbacks

there always have been, and always will be, to
every social organisation which human nature can
devise and develop; and at Athens these were so
serious and so far-reaching in their consequences
that the remainder of this chapter must be occupied
in a brief consideration of them.

In two ways, while thus realising " the good
life " to such extent as was practically possible in a
City-State, Athens impinged upon what we may
be disposed to call the rights of other individuals
and States.   She was, in the first place, a *slave-owning
State*, a character which she had in common with
all the City-States of the ancient world.   Secondly,
in this golden age of hers she was an imperial State
whose so-called " allies," including nearly all the
most important cities in and around the Ægean
Sea, were obliged to follow her lead, to contribute
to her treasury, and generally to obey her orders, or
risk the chance of severe punishment.   Had she
been neither a slave State nor an imperial State, it
is hardly possible to suppose that she could have
attained the high political and intellectual level
which I have been describing; and this reflection,
a somewhat melancholy one, needs a word of explanation.

I have been all along treating Athens as a
democracy, and such, in the view of every Greek,
she actually was.   But we must not entirely forget
that, judged by the standard of the nineteenth
century, she was not really a democracy, but a
slave-holding aristocracy.   It is true that she did
not thus violate any of the sentiments or traditions

N

of the Hellenic world ; other States had the same
advantage, and most of them used it in a much
narrower spirit than Athens. The number of
slaves in Attica is now estimated at 100,000 at
the beginning of the Peloponnesian war, as against
a free population of about 135,000.[1] And this
means that all their menial work, and no doubt a
great part of the work which is now done by what
we call the industrial classes, was done for the
Athenians by persons who were in no sense members of the State, who had neither will nor status
of their own, and whose one duty in life was to
obey the orders of their masters. The citizen at
Athens had leisure to attend to his public duties,
to educate himself for them, to enjoy himself at
festivals and at the theatre, chiefly because he had
at home and in his workshop a sufficient number of
slaves to carry on his affairs in his absence. It
need hardly be said that from all such education,
public business, and enjoyment, the slave was most
carefully excluded.

This is not the place to enter into a discussion
of slavery, either at Athens or in the ancient world
generally.[2] I shall be content with hazarding the
remark that, all things considered, it is hard to
grudge Athens her 100,000 slaves, if they really
were, as I think we must believe, essential to the
realisation of that " good life " of the free minority

[1] Beloch, *Bevolkerung*, p. 99. Former calculations placed the
slave population at a much higher figure.
[2] Read especially Aristotle, *Pol.* i. 3-7, 1253 B, and Mr Newman's valuable remarks (vol. I. 139 foll.).

which has left such an invaluable legacy to modern civilisation. And indeed the generous and reasonable spirit of Athenian democracy was itself not without influence on the condition and prospects of the slave population. In no ancient State were the slaves so materially comfortable; in none, perhaps, were they so exclusively drawn, not from Greek, but from foreign and semi-civilised peoples. Though their disabilities would form a long list, their discomforts were certainly few, and their prospects of liberation by no means small. If liberated, they would be in the same position as the resident stranger, and might eventually arrive at citizenship; and when, in great stress of war, they had served the State honourably as a citizen might do, they were more than once received into the citizen body by public vote of the Ecclesia.[1]

In Aristotle's view, the *raison d'être* of slavery was to make a noble life possible for the master;[2] and where the master actually lived such a life, and at the same time did his duty by his slaves, the institution might be justified. Tried by this test, Athens is not to be wholly condemned as a slave-holding State; she may, at least, claim far more indulgence than Sparta or Rome.

Not so justifiable, at least from a Greek point of view, was the other great advantage, without which Athens could hardly have merited the panegyric of Pericles. I just now put aside for the moment the considera-

On slavery at Athens see Wallon, *Histoire de l'Esclavage*, vol. i. ch. 9.

[2] Newman. *Politics*. i. 144.

tion of the sources from which that surplus wealth was drawn, which was spent on the intellectual and æsthetic education of the Athenian people : let us return to it now. That wealth, supplying the means of paying the citizens for attendance in the law-courts, and later in the Ecclesia, of providing them with constant recreation in the theatre and at the festivals, and of adorning the city with splendid temples and other public buildings, was drawn, in part, indeed, from the ordinary resources of the State, but chiefly from contributions coming from the cities subject to Athens ; contributions not voluntary in amount, but carefully assessed by Athens herself, and as rigidly exacted by her.[1]

It was Pericles himself who introduced this policy—a policy which met with strong opposition even in the Athenian assembly, and was one of the chief factors in rousing against Athens the bitter animosity of the majority of Greek States. It is of the greatest importance for us, for it marks an epoch in the history of the City-State. It was an essential characteristic of that form of State, as I have already pointed out,[2] that it should be independent, and as far as possible self-sufficing. All that I have been saying in this chapter about the realisation of " the good life " at Athens is so far proof of this, that if Athens had been the subject of another State she could not have lived her keen political life, or have called into play the gifts of

[1] See the quota-lists in Hicks's *Greek Historical Inscriptions*, Nos. 24, 30, 35, 47, 48.

[2] See p. 62.

so many men of genius. The whole tone of her life would have been duller, without the same intensity and the same resonance. But now we have to face the fact (to which I shall have to return in another chapter) that the small City-State,—even such an one as Athens, with her peculiar advantages of situation and climate, and with all the great natural gifts of the race,—could not reach the highest level of human life attainable in that day, without sacrificing the freedom and interests of other States whose capacity for good may have been as great as her own. Athens deprived the subjects of her empire of independence,—of the true political life of the Greek State,—and used their resources for her own glory and adornment. And in doing so, she showed at the very same time that she herself was no longer in the true sense self-sufficing ; she could not supply even her daily wants from within her own territory,[1] much less could she live the noble life of which Pericles spoke without encroaching on the rights of others.

Pericles sought to justify his own policy, and the new and startling position into which Athens had drifted, by an argument such as Cicero used in defence of the Roman Empire, though nobler indeed and more generous. Athens was to be teacher of Greece ; to inspire the Greek States with her own lofty spirit, and to be a central light diffusing warmth and vitality throughout the Hellenic world. To him, first perhaps of all Greeks, the system of the πόλις must have seemed small and petty, unequal

[1] See, e.g., Schömann, Ant. p. 526.

to the attainment of that real unity, strength, and security, which alone could guarantee the Greeks against attack from without and slow decay within. And as we contemplate his grand conception now, in the light of later Greek history, we may reasonably think him right. But great ideas are of little practical use, unless they are in harmony with the conditions of life and the feelings of the age; and Pericles, and with him Athens, had clearly overstepped the limits of the εἰωθότα νοήματα of the Greeks. As the tyrant, however excellent his intention, could not but find himself sooner or later outside of the circle of ideas in which he had been trained, so it was with Athens. The consciousness of this is only too apparent in Pericles' own words; for he does not hesitate to tell the Athenians that their empire is a tyranny, and their state a tyrant. "You have come by this tyranny," he tells them, "and you cannot go back from it; you have outrun the tardy motion of the Greek world of political ideas; you must keep your power, but use it for the noblest ends." [1]

No wonder, then, that Athens was at last attacked, and that the ruling ideas of independence and self-sufficingness rebelled against her claims of light and leading. The City-State, in reaching its highest point of development, had broken through the limits of its own proper nature, and was tending to become a different kind of political unit; the πόλις threatened to grow into an empire, one State menaced the healthy freedom of the rest. The Peloponnesian war

[1] Thuc. ii. 63.

put an end to the claims of Athens and to the ideas
of Pericles ; the tyrant city fell.   That fatal war
was in one sense a struggle between new and old
ideas, between the received notion of Greek political
life and a new doctrine wholly at variance with it.
The new heresy was put down by force, but the old
doctrine had received a shock from which it never
recovered ; the genuine old conception of the πόλις,
strong as was its hold upon the Greek people, lives
more vividly in the ideals of Plato and Aristotle than
in the history of any City-State after the great
struggle was over.   Of all the great wars of antiquity, the Peloponnesian war was the saddest and
most useless ; for while it humbled the tyrant city,
it was the means of irretrievably weakening the
true leader of Greek culture ; and while the enemies
of Athens believed themselves to be asserting the
true doctrine of the City-State, they were in reality
playing into the hands of another and a far worse
tyrant.

I shall recur to this subject in another chapter :
we must now once more turn our attention to the
progress of the City - State in Italy, where we
shall have to notice the same tendency to break the
bounds of the πόλις, and with a very different result.

CHAPTER VII

WE must now return for a while to that earlier age of popular stir and uprising, the ultimate results of which we have just been noting at Athens. Great as is the obscurity of this period in Greece, it is even greater in Italy. Of the early history of other cities besides Rome we have hardly a trace. The early Roman Republic has indeed what is called a history, but it is one which crumbles away at the first touch of scientific criticism. In the corresponding period of Greek history the poems of Solon and Theognis afford us here and there a solid footing of fact. But in the early Roman Republic literature was unknown; such meagre records as were made after the art of writing came in,—records of the priestly colleges, or official records preserved by noble families,— were probably all destroyed when the city was captured by the Gauls in 390 B.C. The earliest annalists wrote more than a century later than this catastrophe, and what they put together must have been traditional only, filled out and ornamented by their own invention, by stories adapted from the Greek, or by the untrustworthy pride of patrician houses. Others followed their example with even less conscious regard for truth, and in the Augustan age Livy and Dionysius worked up the whole mass into an artistic form, making use at the same time of much antiquarian lore which the scholars of that day had unearthed and were trying to interpret.

In its stories of war and conquests, in its speeches and dramatic incidents, this history is quite worthless. Yet there are certain landmarks which stand out with tolerable clearness in the general mist, and which become realities for us when our knowledge of later Roman institutions is brought to bear on them. The Romans, it should never be forgotten, had always a very clear conception of the salient features of their own legal institutions, and a very steady tradition as to their origin. Whatever doubt there may be as to dates and details, certain laws mentioned by the annalists may be taken as historical facts which fixed themselves on the memory of the Romans at a time when very few could read or write ; and of one great piece of legislation some fragments survive even now. These laws, and such explanations of them as are generally received, must form the material of the present chapter. They will provide an outline of this period of transition, of which we can thus recover the leading features, though the relation of the events to each other cannot always be made quite certain.[1]

[1] What follows is a sketch in mere outline of a period in which

But as a preliminary step we must look for a moment back to the period of the monarchy. We saw that the aristocratic government which succeeded the last king was probably the result of a reaction from an exaggerated use of kingly power. That the monarchy had undergone a change in the last century of its existence there is hardly a doubt. As often happened in the history of City-States, the monarchy in this case changed into something very like a tyranny, without the interposition of an aristocratic regime between the two; a change which was all the more natural at Rome where the conception of magisterial power (*imperium*) was so remarkably clear and strong. And the explanation of this change is not wholly wanting. There is much evidence that the last three kings were not of Roman descent. The very name Tarquinius is not Roman but Etruscan, and it was believed by Etruscan annalists that the original name of Servius Tullius was Mastarna. Both these names have been

almost every fact is matter more or less of controversy and doubt. To give full references would be under these circumstances impossible without overburdening the text, and I prefer to tell the reader at once that besides Livy and Dionysius, and the first volume of Mommsen's *History*, the most valuable works he can refer to are Mommsen's *Staatsrecht*, either in the German original or in the French translation, so far as it has yet appeared, and Willems' *Droit public Romain*, which is a concise and useful compendium of Roman political institutions, superior to Ramsay's *Roman Antiquities*, which is still the only book of the kind we have in English. Professor Pelham's article, "Roman History," in the *Encyclopædia Britannica*, about to be republished in a separate form, contains a masterly analysis of the events of this period. Ihne's *Roman History* is pleasant reading in its English form, but of very inferior value to Mommsen.

found inscribed on Etruscan wall-paintings in the forms *Tarchnas* and *Mestrna*. They are recognised by most scholars as genuine Etruscan, rather than as Etruscan forms of Latin names.

Now it is not possible to believe that the Romans should have willingly elected a king outside their own patrician gentes. Nor is it easier to believe that the powerful Etruscan aristocracy should never have been able to subdue Rome as they had subdued the original inhabitants of half the peninsula. Though Roman tradition naturally refused to allow that the great Etruscan power, which extended north and south of Latium, had at one time swallowed up the city on the Tiber, it yet unconsciously betrays the secret in many ways. We are justified in believing, in spite of the doubts of many critics, that an Etruscan dynasty ruled for a time in Rome, and ruled with something of the spirit of the tyrant.

Can we make out, in any degree of certainty, what policy these foreign kings pursued ? Roman tradition universally ascribed to them some at least of the features of the Greek tyrant; but this tradition, it may be said, is hardly to be trusted, and may be due to the influence of Greeks who read into Roman history the characteristics of their own form of City-State. On the other hand, there must have been a substratum of fact to which such stories could attach themselves. Extension of Roman territory, intercourse with other peoples, especially Greeks and Etruscans, oppression of the aristocracy, development of the army and of the less privileged

classes, reproduce exactly the policy of the tyrant;
but it would be going too far to assume that they
were ascribed without any reason to a certain Servius
and a certain Tarquinius. We may, however, leave
the stories to the critics, and turn our attention for
a moment to two facts which stand out clearly in
this period—facts which all Romans connected with
the name of Servius Tullius, and which may beyond
doubt be attributed to the last age of the monarchy.
These are (1) the organisation of the army in classes
and centuries, and (2) the division of the city and
its territory into four local tribes. The two are
closely connected with each other, and they begin
the story which we have to tell in this chapter.

What was the nature of the change which these
two facts indicate? We may think of the earlier
form of Roman State as a union of small communities
retaining in some degree the tie of kinship, or at
least the idea of it. But the influence of the land
(see p. 42) had long been felt, disintegrating the
original force of this tie. Alongside of the gentes,
which formed the basis of the original union, there
had grown up, as in Attica, another population which
stood to these in a position of inferiority and dependence. The gentes had the prestige of high
descent, of religious knowledge, of wealth and
prowess in war; they were the true citizens, *cives
optimo jure, ingenui, patricii*.[1] The others were

---

[1] Both words, *ingenuus* and *patricius*, suggest the idea of the
tie of kinship and descent surviving in the City-State as a mark
of superiority, as against those who were born outside the sacred
circle of *gentes*, or born in imperfect wedlock.

attached to them as those who hearkened and
obeyed (*clientes*), and the clear logic of the Roman
mind had already put this relation of dependence
into a definite form, with distinct rights and duties
on each side. The clients were thus a part of the
State, but in a diminished sense (*minuto jure*): they
could hold no office under the king; they could not
take the auspices; they could not marry into the
families of their *patroni*, and probably could not
share the advantage of the public land. They
were *in statu pupillari*, and could only, as it were,
be represented by a tutor. But they were protected as a matter of duty by their *patroni*. They
had at least a piece of garden ground given them
sufficient to live upon; they were admitted into
the *curiœ*—the earliest political division of the
State, — and it seems likely that they could in
these divisions answer Yes or No to such questions
as the king chose to lay before the whole people.

What was the origin of these clients is a question which does not concern us here. What does
concern us is to note how they came to form the
material of the later Roman State. If a patrician
family died out, the relationship between it and its
clients ceased to exist. There may have been other
ways in which the bond of dependence was relaxed,
but this is the only one which we can discern at all
clearly. These emancipated clients could not be
turned adrift, for they were already part of the
State; they remained so after their emancipation,
and were called by one of the many Latin words
which bid fair to be immortal. They became the

plebs, or multitude, retaining exactly the diminished
rights they had before, but being now quite independent of patrician authority.   In a certain sense,
indeed, they were in a worse position; they had to
stand on their rights for themselves, and could get no
help from patrician *patroni*. They had no organised
religion of their own, no legal *locus standi* in the
State; yet they were still a part of it, served in the
army of *curiæ*, and apparently, as we saw, voted in
the curiate assembly.   Steadily they increased in
numbers, and more and more they came to be felt
as an indispensable part of the State; but citizens
in the true sense they certainly were not.   They
were now free men, while as clients they had been
only half free; but their freedom was a negative
one, and brought no positive rights.   They were
wholly outside the sacred circle of the gentes; outside the groups of real or supposed kin in which all
cives optimo jure were comprised.

This plebs, the many as against the few, slowly
won for itself a definite and recognised position both
in social and political life.   Gradually they must
have come to be reckoned as *ingenui*, and as forming gentes of their own; and so they came also
to have their own popular worships like the Demos
in Attica in the sixth century.   How these steps
were one by one secured we can hardly do more
than guess; but it is the story of their admission
to political equality which concerns us now, and we
may leave the other questions to conjecture.

Up to the time of the later kings nothing had
been done to utilise and organise this population

as a part of the State. It could not indeed be
united in any real social union to the patrician
gentes, for it did not share in their religious com-
munion. But Servius Tullius, or some monarch of
genius (the name is of little moment), saw that it
could be turned to good account. It may be that
wars were at this time frequent, and that the king
was hard pressed; certainly the great city-wall
was built at this time,[1] and as surely was the new
organisation a military one. The city and its territory were divided into four regions or local tribes,
comprising all free men, whether patricians or
plebeians, who possessed and occupied a certain
amount of land (*assidui*). The object of this was
doubtless to get an administrative basis for military
and financial purposes. Following on this there
came a division of all those free men into five
summonings (*classes*); the first of these being the
largest in number, and comprising those who had
most land, and so downwards to the fifth. These
were again divided into bodies of a hundred (*centuriæ*), which formed the tactical unit of the newly-
constructed army. Thus the men of the plebs, or
all of them who were settled on the land as freeholders, found themselves part of a real working
organisation, comprising the whole community
(*populus*), and destined for military purposes.
They gained no political advantage; they had
no more to do with the *auspicia*[2] and the *imperium*

---

[1] For the Servian wall and its existing remains, see Professor
Middleton's *Rome in 1889*, ch. ii.

[2] For the *auspicia* and the right of taking them, see Mommsen,

than they had before. They were simply utilised and organised. But their relation to the State was made much more distinct; they were no longer merely attached to patrician gentes, no longer in an ambiguous position as regards citizenship; they were embodied in the State on the principle of settlement and locality, destined here, as everywhere else, slowly to obliterate the older principle of kinship. The revolution was of the same nature as that of Cleisthenes at Athens; all primitive divisions of the people were superseded, though not destroyed, by the new ones. The State is throwing off the dress of its infancy, and preparing to live the life of vigorous youth in a new form.

At this point, then, and under the same influences as in Greece, the State seems in a fair way to make progress towards democracy. The aristocratic society, of which, as I have pointed out before, the early monarchies were only the constitutional expression, has passed under the influence of a form of *tyrannis*, and the multitude has been brought forward as an essential factor in the State. But it is not given to every people to develop the art of governing itself; it would seem to need a peculiar type of character to produce this result as it was produced at Athens, —a type in which intellectual quickness is not too strongly tempered by reverence for ancient usage and for ancient social distinctions. Now the Roman, whether patrician or plebeian, had little

Staatsrecht (ed. 2) i. 73 foll. ; Willems, *Droit public Romain*, 232 foll.

intellectual quickness, but he had a marvellous capacity for discipline, and an unbounded veneration for the customs of his forefathers. It was natural, then, that at Rome, when the *tyrannis* came to an end, it should leave society and manners comparatively unchanged; and in fact we find that as soon as it disappears the aristocratic idea asserts itself as strongly as ever. The aristocracy, as we have already seen, adapted the kingly constitution to their own ends, and the State became aristocratic in form as well as in fact.

The patrician families alone could exercise the *imperium*; they alone knew the unwritten law; they alone knew the secrets of religion,—how to take the auspices, how to purify the State, how to conduct marriages and funerals in that traditional way which alone could find favour with the gods. On the other hand, the plebeian had his place in the army, and might fight side by side with the patrician, but he could never attain to high command. He might accumulate wealth, and add field to field, but if he had a quarrel with a patrician neighbour he had to submit it to a patrician magistrate, to be decided by rules of which he was wholly ignorant. If he borrowed stock or plant from his neighbour, he had to give his own land or person as security for the debt.[1] He could not marry into a patrician family without violating the most sacred prejudices. Thus the "men of the fathers" and

---

[1] On the Roman law of debt see Clark, *Early Roman Law*, p. 108 foll.; and article "Nexum" in the new edition of the *Dict. of Antiquities.*

O

the "men of the multitude" stood face to face in the same State; the former in exclusive possession of political power, and forming a solid aristocratic government of high-born and wealthy men; the latter giving their services to the State in the newly-organised army of centuries, but politically almost helpless, the machinery of government being wholly out of their reach.

But the innate political wisdom of the Roman people, the increase of the plebs by the absorption of conquered peoples, and the necessities of warfare in the period which followed the abolition of monarchy, combined in course of time to unite these two distinct bodies into one solid political whole. The process went on through two centuries, but was at last completed, and left no ill blood behind it. The patrician position was forced at all points; the fortresses of legal knowledge, of religious knowledge, of executive government, of social exclusiveness, were carried one after the other, and, according to the traditional accounts, with little violence and no bloodshed. Let us trace the story of this process of unification step by step, leaving to another chapter the question as to the form of government which was the result of it.

At the very outset of the Republic, according to the received tradition, the new form of the armed people—which we may believe to have been so far used, as it was originally intended, only for military and financial purposes—began to be now applied in the election of magistrates; the centuriate army became a centuriate assembly.

Thus the plebs at once gained a voice in the election of aristocratic magistrates. And more; to this centuriate assembly they could now appeal equally with patricians if a consul threatened them with capital punishment. The aristocracy, in securing their own liberties against the power of the executive, could not help going some way towards securing those of the plebs as well.

But this security was really of little value to the plebeian. Beyond doubt, the assembly of centuries was dominated by patrician influence. The mass of small plebeian freeholders had no resource if they were subjected to severe treatment, however legal. The laws or customary rules of debt, for example, were terribly hard; and all small agriculturists are liable to be driven to borrow by bad seasons or unlucky accidents.[1] The Servian census proves that the Romans were a people of farmers, and it also proves that their holdings differed greatly in size. Under such conditions it is almost inevitable that the small holder should borrow of the greater; and if he does so under such a law as the Roman law of debt, administered by magistrates over whom he has practically no control, it is inevitable that he should come under bondage to his creditor. The only resource the plebs could fall back upon was to unite in depriving the State of their services, to refuse the military service without which the State

[1] We have seen the effects at Athens of this inherent weakness of a society of small holders of land (see p. 130). It may be illustrated at the present day from India, Russia, Ireland, and even Switzerland.

could not resist its enemies, and, as their brethren had so often done in Greece, to leave the city and find a home elsewhere.

This must be what is indicated by the famous story of the Secession to the Sacred Mount. It was a *strike* on a grand scale, and in a State instead of a private undertaking. Such combinations to resist oppression, and to gain some control over the oppressing management, were not possible or needed in the same form as our strikes, which are the struggles of organised labour against organised private capital ; but they occur both in Greek and Roman history in the sense of practical protests of one class against the domination of another. The plebs marched out to the Anio after refusing their services at a levy, intending to found a new city on the banks of that river. Rome was at the mercy of her enemies, helpless and deprived of that middle class which is the source of all political strength. But the plebs were helpless too. Where was the genius to be found who could overcome for them the tremendous difficulties in which they were placed ? Cities could not be founded by any one who wished, without the aid of priests and religious lore, without the elements of cohesion in the form of king and gentes. Mutual perplexity brought mutual concession, as the story suggests ; and the plebs returned to Rome to fight again for the old city, and also to fight a long series of political battles under leaders now definitely recognised by the whole State.

Perhaps there is no such singular event in ancient history as the establishment of the tribunate

of the plebs in 494 B.C. ; certainly there is none of
which the results were so strange and far-reaching.
Nor is there any known fact which brings before us
so clearly the contrast of privileged and unprivileged
in a City-State, or the distinctness with which the
Romans conceived this contrast. We see here the
almost absolute separation of noble from ignoble, of
the members of the ancient clans from the population
which had grown up outside them. For these tribunes had nothing to do with the State as a whole ;
they were not magistrates of the State ; they had
no seat in the Senate ; they were not even *cives
optimo jure.* They had no direct hold upon the
policy of the executive and its council. They were
simply officers of the plebs, and, so far as we know,
their powers were limited to the protection of plebeians against the action of the State and its magistrates. And this protective power could only be
exercised within the city and a mile beyond its walls ;
against the *imperium militiæ*, the absolute power of
the consul in the field, they were quite powerless.
Within the walls, if a plebeian called upon them to
help him, the patrician magistrate must withdraw
his lictors ; but in this negative sense only could
they bring influence to bear upon the *imperium.*

But what guarantee could there be that the
magistrates would respect the interference of these
plebeian officers ? There must be some special bond
to secure this respect, for the nature of the office
suggested none of itself. The tribune was elected
without *auspicia*, and no religious sanction protected
him such as protected those who were responsible

for the State religion. The device invented for this purpose was a curious one, and well illustrates the peculiar character of the Roman political mind, which demanded the sanction of the gods for every step taken. The tribunes were, during their year of office, devoted to the gods (*sacrosancti*) ; the binding force of the religious idea was called in to protect them. De Coulanges, going perhaps too far, has called them a kind of living altars to which the oppressed could fly for refuge ; at any rate, any one who violated their sanctity was guilty of sacrilege. The act of legislation by which this was secured was itself a *lex sacrata*[1]—that is, a kind of treaty between two communities foreign to each other, whose relations need to be controlled by some special religious security. Soon afterwards the position of the tribunes was further strengthened by a law which forbade interference with any assembly of the plebs which a tribune had summoned, and perhaps also giving them some means of securing the punishment of any one who violated their sanctity or hindered their activity.

It is not necessary here to trace the steps by which these germs of authority grew gradually into a most formidable power, positive as well as negative. Let us keep to the Tribunate as it originally was, and note the stage it marks in the transitional period we are traversing. It is no advance towards a real political union that is here indicated. The aristocracy as yet shows no sign that it can entertain the

[1] For the meaning of these terms see Cicero, *pro Balbo*, ch. xiv. 32.

idea of a State uniting the multitude with the gentes in one body politic; the barrier between the two is even more distinctly marked here than it was under the kings. In the armed host alone the two appear as one, and so also in the form in which that host meets for political purposes (*comitia centuriata*). In all other respects the plebs appears now as a distinct corporation, with officers and a kind of charter of its own, enabling those officers to transact its business in a purely plebeian assembly, meeting in tribes.

But the very distinctness of this separation brought the plebs into a new prominence. The mass of unorganised humanity that seceded to the Sacred Mount had been given a form and a voice, and could now act and speak, imperfectly, perhaps, but efficiently. And as every motive which could call forth their speech or action was rooted in the inequality of their position in relation to the patrician executive, we are not surprised to find them using their new advantages to do away with that inequality. They have at last secured the means of doing this. They are no longer a mere rabble, like the followers of Jack Cade, or the Kentish masses who flocked to London with Wyatt in 1553. They are a compact and organised body, which has already gained its charter and its officers, and is about to use these advantages to obtain others still more effectual and permanent. Their claim is now for union and equality; union with the patrician City-State of which they have so far been, as it were, a mere annex or suburb, and equality with it in all its rights and honours and privileges, both social and political.

The first step they gained in this direction
was by securing what the Greeks called ἰσονο-
μία, or equality in the incidence of the law on all
classes of society. The law, as we have seen,
meant simply the rules of practice, in public and
private life alike, which had grown up as the State
grew, and formed the outward expression of the *imperium*. Up to this time the knowledge of these rules
had been a secret science, of which the patrician
families were the only craftsmen. All others were
still ignorant of the art of government, and unfit to
propitiate the gods, which was not the least important part of that art. To borrow another metaphor
from the modern world, the multitude was a multitude of *hands*, suited to fight and to till the ground,
but wholly ignorant of the science which could turn
their labour to account. But in 451 B.C. they
began to be initiated in the craft. In that year
the rules of practice were at last embodied in a
written code of ten tables, to which two others
were shortly added. This is the *fons aequi juris*
of Roman law; it is also the first unquestionable
fact in the history of the Republic, for many genuine
fragments of it still survive.[1]

It is interesting to note that this great result
was brought about by the same agency as in the
parallel revolution at Athens. The details of the
story are indeed quite worthless, but the fact is
beyond doubt that the new code was drawn up by

[1] For the fragments of the Twelve Tables see Wordsworth,
Fragments and Specimens of Early Latin, p. 254 foll. ; or Bruns,
Fontes juris Romani, p. 16 foll. (ed. 4).

a Board of Ten, having almost absolute power, while
Consulship and Tribunate were for the time sus-
pended. The position of this board thus resembles
that of Solon, and of the Greek arbiter; it is a
genuine example of the tendency to have recourse
to absolutism in settling internal troubles which
were the result of fermentation. But the Romans,
with their singular gift for legal definition, and their
political conception of collegiate power, placed this
new power on a constitutional footing, shared it
between ten members, gave it a definite task to do,
and called on it to resign when the task was accomplished.[1] The work was so well done that it lasted
the Roman State throughout the whole of its
political life. But the immediate result of it was
to give the plebs, through their tribunes, a real
controlling power over the patrician executive, and
so to supply exactly that political basis of action
which had been wanting so far. At this point it
may be said that politics really begin—that is, the
reciprocal action of parties and interests in a
single State as distinguished from negotiations
between two distinct communities. The whole
State has now a common code to refer to in
all legal difficulties. Consuls and tribunes are
now officers of the same State, and the tribunes
can take measures, now they know the secrets of

---

[1] The same formality is well seen in the method of appointing
a Dictator. The Dictatorship affords another example of recur-
rence to the monarchical principle ; but its holder was, strictly
speaking, only the *collega major* of the consuls, and was limited
both in respect of the work he had to do, and of the time he was
to do it in.

the *imperium*, to gain a positive control over the executive which exercised it.

That the battle had been already practically won, even before the last two tables had been completed, is made clear by the annalists. The list of the second Board of Ten comprises some names which are almost beyond doubt plebeian; and this is the first example we meet with of plebeians actually sharing the executive power. And now the victorious side begins rapidly to press its advantage. In 449 the consuls Valerius and Horatius passed a law giving the plebeian assembly over which the tribunes presided a real sovereign power in legislation, binding the whole State under certain conditions which we cannot now recover. Up to this time such resolutions as the plebs had passed (*plebiscita*) had been binding only on the plebs itself; they were no more laws of the State than the tribunes were magistrates of the State. This Lex Valeria-Horatia marks the beginning of an entirely new status for this plebeian assembly. Step by step it gained a legislative power for the whole State concurrent with that of the patricio-plebeian assembly of centuries. The latter was never done away or dropped, for reasons which can only be thoroughly understood by those who have studied the Roman mind and character in its institutions; but it was gradually to a great extent superseded.

Henceforward we have the strange spectacle of two sovereign assemblies side by side—the *populus*, or host of the entire people, presided over by

consuls (*comitia centuriata*), and the plebs meeting
in tribes and presided over by tribunes (*concilia
plebis*). And this means, to put it briefly, that
the plebs is now in the fullest sense part of the
State, and that their tribunes are now State
magistrates.

Four years later the process of social union, as
distinct from political, which had no doubt been
long going on without legal sanction, is marked by
a law enabling patricians and plebeians to inter-
marry, and so to form one *species* where there had
been two before. Doubtless there were great
searchings of heart over a measure which must
have hurt many ancient prejudices, and Livy has
reproduced these misgivings with all his rhetorical
skill.[1] The gentes were losing their religious
exclusiveness ; the crowd was pushing profanely
into the sacred ground of high descent. But this
must have been going on for at least a generation
before any one could have been audacious enough
to propose to legalise it ; and we may take this
Lex Canuleia as the best possible proof that there
was now a growing tendency on both sides to look
upon the State as one complete whole, with common
interests and common duties. The State has won
its final victory over the gens.

And in the same year we meet with yet another
step forward, which is attributed to the same
Canuleius. The question had been already raised
why plebeians should be excluded any longer from
that supreme executive which had now been placed

[1] Livy, iv. 1 foll.

under the restriction of written laws. There had been plebeian decemvirs, and there were undoubtedly rich plebeians attaining to eminence in the army, the conduct of which was at this time of constant warfare the special duty of the Consul. Why should not such men be entrusted with the highest command ? This question was now answered by a law which made it possible in any year for the Senate to decide on the election of six military tribunes (officers of the highest rank in the legion), invested with consular *imperium* like the decemvirs, and taking the place of consuls. In other words, if there were eminent plebeian officers their services might now be utilised by the State as supreme commanders without admitting them to the patrician privileges of curule chair and purple-edged toga. According to the annalists and the Fasti, it was indeed forty-five years before the ability of any plebeian was thus actually called into play ; but if the law be rightly dated, the inference is that the idea of service done for the State, which itself implied a certain amount of wealth, was beginning to override the idea of gentile exclusiveness.

From this point follows a long period in which we have no landmark of political advance. Though the records of it are purely traditional, it was beyond doubt a period of continued wars with the neighbouring Æquians and Volscians, and with the Etruscan city of Veii, resulting in a great extension of Roman territory, and a great increase in the number of plebeian citizens. The terrible Gallic invasion of 390 B.C. united all in the common

defence, and brought out their best qualities. Such
a period of wars must have wrought slowly but
surely a great social revolution which prepared the
way for the completion of the political one. Individuals among the plebs must have become noted
for their prowess and for their wealth. Patrician
families may have died out under the stress of war.
The great holders of land, increasing in number as
the territory increased, were now plebeian as much
as patrician, and they came thus to have an identical interest, and the same way of looking at public
questions. More and more it became visible that
the real material of the State was plebeian, and that
the old families could no longer be thought of as
the only true-born *cives*. New worships began to
gain ground associated chiefly with the plebs. When
the Gauls had retired, and the State was once more
free from immediate danger, it became obvious that
the time was at hand when this slow revolution in
ideas must take shape in a final victory of the
plebs.

In the year 367, after a struggle of ten years,
this final victory was won. There was no revolution, no bloodshed, only persistent attack on the one
side and obstinate resistance on the other. The
Tribunate, in later times the instrument of passion
and violence, here served the State well, and at last
secured the necessary constitutional reform by
reducing the machinery of the constitution to a
deadlock. The tribunes Licinius and Sextius in
this year passed a law restoring the Consulship in
place of the military Tribunate, and enacting that

henceforward one consul must necessarily be a plebeian.[1]

The work of these two tribunes may be looked on as the second of the three most conspicuous landmarks in the political development of Rome. The first was the reform attributed to Servius Tullius; the third was to wait for nearly three centuries. The ordinances of Servius first organised the plebs, and by giving it duties to perform for the State made it and its services indispensable. After an interval of at least a century and a half the Licinio-Sextian laws, passed by the plebs itself as a sovereign legislative body, secured for it a permanent share in the executive government of the whole State. The outward political form of Rome as a City-State was now complete, and no further striking change took place, until once more a new population claimed admission to the State and its government, and in enforcing their claim initiated a vital change in the very nature of the Roman polity.

It is worth noting that these leading events in the history of Rome, as well as the more subordinate ones we have also mentioned, are not connected with the names of any individuals whose personality has struck root in human memory. The laws bore the names of their authors, but these are names and little more. In Athenian history it is just the

[1] This law was not at first faithfully adhered to by the patricians. But the Licinian law was re-enacted in B.C. 342, and in the same year it was further enacted that both consuls *might* henceforward be plebeians.

opposite. There the collective wisdom of the community seems reflected in the virtue or the ambition
of Solon and Cleisthenes, Themistocles and Pericles.
The earlier heroes of Roman tradition, Coriolanus,
for example, or Camillus, were patrician and conservative ; the leaders of progress either were not
suffered to survive as heroes, or, as may very well
have been the case, had nothing heroic about them.
But if they did not leave their features graven on
the stone, these Roman builders at least understood
their trade ; and this is more especially true of the
Licinius and Sextius who completed the equalisation
of the patrician and plebeian orders.

The work of these two tribunes was as completely
rounded off as that of Solon himself. Like Solon,
they seem to have understood that political advantages are comparatively useless except in the hands
of men who are socially and economically *comfortable*; that agitation is for men who seek comfort,
while government is for men whose discomfort is
already alleviated. Thus with their great political
law they combined others which were meant to
maintain the well-being and numbers of the Roman
middle class of freeholders; and for this combination
they struggled hard for years, even in spite of the
sluggishness of the very class for which they were
fighting. They aimed directly at reducing to a
minimum the two chronic evils of the Roman
economy—large private estates, and the slave-
labour employed in their cultivation ; so that the
smaller holders, now admitted to a full share in the
government, might retain their land, or at least find

employment on the estates of their richer neighbours. Their motives in this struggle may have
been less pure than Solon's,[1] but their efforts were
plainly directed to the same end as his.

Their work marks, indeed, a stage of development
in some sense even nearer to democracy than that
of Solon. The highest executive office was now open
to all citizens; the popular legislative assemblies
were sovereign in the constitution; and if these laws
were faithfully carried out there would be a fairly
even distribution of wealth throughout the community, such as would enable all to take a reasonable
amount of interest in the government, propor-
tionate to their own share in the general wellbeing.
On the face of things there was no reason why
genuine democratic institutions should not have
taken root and grown, and there are some signs in
the annals a generation or two later that such a
growth was actually beginning.[2] But true democracy
is a plant of very great rarity, which will not grow
on every soil. Why it withered at Rome—why
after all, the Romans never learnt to govern themselves like the Athenians—will be explained in
another chapter.

[1] It is likely enough, as Mommsen suggests, that they represented the claims of the richer plebeians in their efforts to throw
open the consulship. Sextius was himself the first plebeian consul
in the year 366 B.C.

[2] Livy, ix. ch. 46, x. 7. For the action of Appius, the
censor of 312 B.C., in allowing landless citizens to be enrolled in
any tribe, see Appendix to the first volume of Mommsen's *Roman
History*, p. 498 foll. There are undoubtedly some signs in the
story both of a tyrannic and of a democratic tendency to deal reck-
lessly with ancient custom, which is exceedingly rare at Rome.

Let us turn for a moment, before we leave these earlier stages of Roman progress, to another aspect of Rome's development as a City-State, which has been of much greater interest to the world than even the growth of her constitution. The genius of the Roman people was to leave one valuable legacy to modern civilisation; but it was not to be the memory of a gifted democracy, like the Athenian, the nursing mother of poets, orators, sculptors, and philosophers. It was to be a legacy of legal ideas and practice; a systematisation of the rights and duties of men to each other and to the State, and of the procedure and the sanctions necessary to secure them, which preserved the conceptions of legal justice and equity throughout all the chaos and confusion of the Middle Ages. Though hard to realise, and especially so for Englishmen, it is true that modern Europe owes to the Romans its ancient inherited sense of the sacredness of a free man's person and property, and its knowledge of the simplest and most rational methods by which person and property may be secured with least inconvenience to the whole community. The nations to come after Rome were saved the trouble of finding out all this for themselves; and it may be doubted whether any of them had the requisite genius. We in England, for example, owe the peculiar cumbrousness of our legal system to the absence of those direct Roman influences, which, on the continent, have simplified and illuminated the native legal material.

The beginnings of Roman law are to be found in the period we have just been traversing; here began that work of systematisation which was to form a framework for the loose threads of our ideas of legal justice and equity. It was not, indeed, as the law of the City-State of Rome that this systematisation was to dominate the world; but it was in the City-State that its roots were firmly fixed. The *jus civile*, or law of the *cives Romani*, was first formulated in the Twelve Tables drawn up by decemvirs in 451 B.C. and the following year; and we have sufficient fragments of these to gather something both of their contents and their method. The political advance which they indicate is very great. We here see the State for the first time definitely formulating the rules which were to govern the relations of men,—of privileged and unprivileged alike, —in regard to person and property; rules hitherto traditional in family or *gens*, or administered by the magistrate under no security for the consistency of his action. To these were probably added new ones adapted from the codes of other States, and especially from that of Solon. Custom, thus at once solidified and extended, became what we may justly call law. Law is a natural product of the true City-State, which demands something to give security to the life and dealings of all its members, — something which neither the savage, nor the member of a village community, nor even the *gentilis* within the infant State, has ever yet possessed in a formal and, so to speak, scientific shape; and this product of State-life the Romans were now developing with characteristic exactness. We see also that the rules laid down in these Tables

are characterised by a peculiarly rigid formality,—
that is, that the rigid formality of pre-existing
Roman practice is to characterise also the written
law. As in politics the Romans thought clearly
and logically, and expressed their thoughts in pregnant technical terms, so also in the region of law.

The Tables were regarded for centuries with
profound veneration, and throughout Roman history
continued to form the nucleus of the *jus civile* (law
of the City-State), which was expanded to meet
further needs almost entirely by interpreting and
adjusting them. This veneration for prescribed
rules and forms is perhaps the most striking feature
in the Roman character; it passed from their practice in religious ritual into their practice in legal
procedure, and gave their conception of law a distinctness and certainty never realised by any
other people. The conservative instinct inherent
in human nature, the spirit that shrinks from losing
one jot of what laborious forefathers have stored up
with infinite pains—this spirit was far stronger in
the Roman than the Greek, and it is one great secret
of the extraordinary solidity of the legal structure
which he raised. It was in this way that the
Romans realised "the good life"; not, like the
Greek, by rising from the κώμη to new vigour of
intellect in poetry and art, but in perceiving with a
vision so direct how justice could best be secured
between citizen and citizen, and in holding to the
formulated result with a veneration so deep and so
lasting. They never entirely ignored anything that
they had once discovered and prized.

They never, indeed, wholly ignored it; but they had also the true legal instinct of adapting their forms and methods to new circumstances, or of inventing new ones while they still retained the old. This is the other secret of the stability of their legal masonry. The *jus civile*, as expressed in the Twelve Tables, and even as expanded by their interpretation, could hardly have been made to suit the needs of the empire that the Romans were to acquire in the next three centuries and a half; even to have made the attempt would have violated their legal sensitiveness, and broken the traditions of the City-State. But they were not at a loss; they had now in the Twelve Tables the means of rudimentary legal training, and they had constant practice in adjustment and interpretation; and these, together with their clear conception of magisterial power, carried them in due time safely over the difficulty. We shall return to this subject at the end of the next chapter; this further development of the Roman legal instinct was the work of the two centuries which followed the equalisation of the orders, and the result of the wholly new conditions of life under which the State was brought by ever-increasing conquest and commerce.

CHAPTER VIII

BY the year 300 B.C. the first great revolution in
Roman history is completed. The men of the multitude have forced their way into the sacred ground
which patrician exclusiveness regarded as the only
true State ; at point after point the defences have
been broken down, and the crowd mingles freely
and on equal terms with the aristocratic garrison,
sharing with them all privileges and all duties
which the State bestows or demands.

This great change, it should be noted, had been
brought about chiefly by the sheer necessities of the
government in the long series of wars in which Rome
had for two centuries been engaged. It was no more
possible for an army of patricians and their clients
to survive defeat, or reap the fruits of conquest,
than for the feudal army of our own earliest kings
to maintain dominion in France and successfully
attack Wales and Scotland. In each case the people
came to be recognised as the essential material of

the State and its armies, and in each case this led to a further recognition of the right of the people to have its voice heard in matters of government. The parallel must not be pushed too far ; but this at least is clear, that had Roman aristocracy and English kingship been able to live and rule in peace, studying simply the comfort of their subjects and the maintenance of existing conditions of society, neither would so soon have found itself face to face with the people, and obliged to make terms with them or renounce a career of conquest. No historian should allow his sense of the iniquity or the fruitlessness of war to hinder him from paying due attention to the vital struggles of a great State ; for it is in war that the real fibre and mettle of the masses of population are seen at their best, and win acknowledgment most effectually. Less, indeed, than economic history, but still to be reckoned along with it, military history is the exponent of the strength and vitality of a nation ; constitutional history, after all, does but sum up the changes in the outward form of government to which the vicissitudes of war, commerce, and agriculture slowly and painfully give birth. In the present chapter we shall have special reason to bear this in mind ; for once more we shall note the constitutional results of a long period of war and conquest—results so surprising as to seem almost paradoxical.

If we take our stand at the year 300 B.C., or better, perhaps, at 287 B.C.,[1] and read carefully the

---

[1] This is the date of the Lex Hortensia, the third of the three

last two or three books of Livy's first decade, we shall see no apparent reason why the Roman constitution should not develop in the direction of democracy. All the preliminary steps seem to have been taken. The old idea of the prestige of patrician kinship is gone past recall, and every department of government is open to plebeians. If any class is under disabilities, it is the patrician.[1] The plebeian assembly is becoming the chief legislative body, and has also no small judicial power. The executive seems to be under the control of the people, for a form of popular trial has come into vogue, by which the tribunes frequently impeach an ex - magistrate, examining the case at informal meetings in the forum, and calling for a final condemnation in the assembly of centuries. In this assembly, which also elects the chief magistrates, it is not birth, but property, that preponderates in the voting; and the acquisition of property, landed or other, has long been as much open to plebeians as to patricians. The territory of the State has been immensely enlarged, new tribes have been added, new communities received into citizenship; and thus the plebs has continually been strengthened by absorption, while the patrician body must have as steadily dwindled in number. Patrician families, in order to survive, strengthen themselves by plebeian mar-

laws which changed the assembly of the plebs into a sovereign legislative body.

[1] *E.g.* one consul *must* be (Lex Licinia, 367 B.C.), both consuls might be, plebeian (law of 342 B.C.). So, too one censor must be plebeian. A patrician, too, was of course ineligible for the Tribunate of the plebs.

riages, and the old prejudice against such alliances lives on only among a few, or in the hearts of patrician matrons.[1]

To sum up : the old social and political inequality has vanished ; the laws press equally on all, and can be read by all ; the people is clearly sovereign in the legislative assembly of tribes, presided over by the tribunes of the plebs ; the executive is under control, each magistrate being liable to impeachment and popular trial after his year of office. This is not, indeed, democracy in the Athenian sense, for the people does not itself do the actual work of government, though its decision is paramount whenever it is called on to legislate, to give sentence, or to decide on peace and war. But it answers fairly well to Aristotle's conception of a *moderate* democracy, and rests, in fact, upon much the same social conditions which he postulated for that kind of constitution. Aristotle points out that the characteristic drawbacks of democracy are not likely to be present where the mass of the people is occupied with agriculture ; for their work in the fields will keep them away from the city, except on certain occasions, and they will thus escape becoming too *political*—too much interested, that is, in matters which they cannot understand. They may elect their magistrates, and ex-

[1] Read Livy, x. 23, which contains a characteristic story of this age, illustrating both the survival of patrician prejudice among the ladies of high family, and the renunciation of it by the more daring. A patrician matron, married to a plebeian, erects an altar to *Pudicitia plebeia.*

ercise judgment on them after their time of office;
but in such a democracy the actual government will
be left to those whose wealth, position, virtue, and
renown, make them competent to discharge such
duties.[1]   At Rome, at the period we have reached,
these conditions of a moderate democracy were present; the population was mainly agricultural, and
came into the city only to vote in elections, or now
and then to decide questions legislative and judicial.
The government was left to those who were capable
of it; the Roman people itself tilled the ground
and served in the army, but did not govern; it
was sovereign, but it did not rule.   Such a constitution was admirably suited to the Roman State
and character, which was as different from the
Athenian as an English labourer is from an Irish-
man.   But Rome was already started on a career
which was to bring her under conditions of political
life unknown in Aristotle's philosophy; and how
would her constitution fit itself to these?   Was it
to go forward in what might seem its natural course,
towards a complete democracy like the Athenian?
Or was the character of this δῆμος γεωργικός unsuited for the detailed work of self-government, for
the organisation of conquests already won, and for
the conduct of long struggles against enemies which
were at this very time beginning to threaten?

Instead of pursuing the course of Roman history
step by step, let us at once look forward a century
and a half, and, taking a fresh stand about the year
150 B.C., let us take note of the constitution as we

[1] This is the general sense of *Pol.* (1318 B).

find it at that point. There was living then in Rome
a Greek of ability, who had ample means of observing
the working of the Roman constitution, and whose
record of it has most fortunately come down to us.[1]
Polybius' account is not, indeed, to be accepted
without reserve ; it was coloured by his unbounded
admiration for Rome and her great deeds, as well as
by the peculiar philosophical bent of his own mind,
which was apt to deal with political institutions in
the abstract, without taking sufficient account of the
social and economical forces which are continually
acting upon them. But we are not without the
means of criticising and verifying Polybius. Livy's
history, based, in these last books which have survived from his vast undertaking, on records for the
most part of undoubted value, brings us down to
within a few years of 150 B.C. Looking on, too, we
have materials for a consistent view of the constitution from the tribunate of Tiberius Gracchus in
133 B.C., in Appian's *Civil Wars*, in Plutarch's *Lives
of the Gracchi*, and in many other writers of whom
Cicero is the most copious. Livy gives us a picture
of a constitution in the highest state of efficiency, performing its work admirably, and almost
without a hitch ; Appian and the later writers show
us this same constitution rapidly getting out of gear,
and sustaining formidable attacks with difficulty ;
and between the two we have Polybius, studying it
calmly as a foreigner, admiring its perfect balance

---

[1] Polybius, book vi. 10 foll. It is probable that these chapters
were written about 140 B.C. ; certainly before the Tribunate of
Tiberius Gracchus.

of parts, and apparently quite unconscious either of weakness inherent in it, or danger about to beset it. Our materials are therefore sufficient; we can make no serious mistake about this constitution.

And what then was it? The answer may well be startling and even paradoxical to those who have not yet studied the Roman character, or learnt to recognise the sternly tenacious conservatism of the Roman political mind. Though the conditions of the Roman City - State have entirely changed, though she has already become an imperial State, and though her sway now extends from Macedonia to Spain, the constitution remains *in outward form* precisely what it was a hundred and fifty years earlier. It is still democratic—not indeed in the Athenian sense, but in a sense in which we often use the word now. The people are sovereign in legislation, and in the most important judicial cases; they decide on peace and war; they elect their magistrates yearly. They are sovereign whenever they are called on to act, and they must of necessity be called on frequently. "One might reasonably conclude," says Polybius, describing the position of the Demos at Rome, "that it has the greatest share of power, and that the constitution is of the most pronounced democratic type."

But this constitution, as it was actually worked in practice, was no more a democracy than the British constitution is a monarchy. It was not even what Polybius pronounced it to be, after surveying its several parts,—a constitution in which the elements of monarchy, aristocracy, and democracy were all to be found, acting and reacting on each other in a perfectly happy and harmonious combination. Nor again was it, as Cicero, looking back on it a century later through the rosy medium of his own imagination, vainly pictured it to Roman jurymen, a constitution in which the duties and honours of government were open to every citizen whose capability and industry could give him a claim to them.[1]   As we see it in Livy's later books, and as we see it put to the test in the history of its fall, it was neither a democracy, nor a mixed constitution, nor a government of the best men in the State, but an *oligarchy*—the most compact and powerful oligarchy that the world has ever yet seen.   As Athens realised the most perfect form of democracy of which the City-State was capable, so did Rome realise the most perfect form of oligarchy.

The rest of this chapter must be occupied (1) with showing that this was the true character of the constitution in its actual practice, whatever may have been its apparent or legal form, and (2) with explaining how this strange result had come about. The constitution of the Roman republic is indeed an exceedingly difficult one to handle, more especially in a limited space.   But it amply repays the careful student, for it brings him face to face with one of the most curious and puzzling problems of political science.   How can a constitution be one

---

[1] Cicero, *pro Sestio*, ch. 65 : "Ita magistratus annuos creaverunt, ut consilium senatus reipublicæ præponerent sempiternum, deligerentur autem in id consilium ab universo populo, aditusque in illum summum ordinem civium industriæ ac virtuti pateret."

thing in theory and another in fact? How is it possible to retain the form of a democracy while the government is actually in the hands of a few or of one? Even such an elementary account of the Roman system of government as I can find space for in the following pages may possibly throw some light on these questions.

And first let us see what the Roman constitution was in its working form at any year in the period covered by the last books of Livy—say between 200 and 167 B.C. The first point to notice is that the essential mark of an oligarchy is to be found in the *executive*; the great magistracies are in the hands of a comparatively small number of families. We see, in fact, a reversion to the character of the earlier aristocratic period, as in organic nature we often meet with a "throwing back" to the features of a primitive form. As formerly the consulship could be held only by the limited number of old patrician families, so now, if we look through the consular fasti[1] for the period 300-150 B.C., we shall find the same names constantly recurring. There are now, of course, plebeians also in the list; but the plebeian names also appear again and again, and new names are of comparatively rare occurrence. It is plain that these families, patrician and plebeian alike, have acquired a kind of hereditary right to hold the consulship. The people, it is true, can elect exactly whom they please; but they evidently prefer to

---

[1] *Corpus Inscr. Lat.* vol. i. 483 foll. Cf. also the short table in the second volume of Mommsen's *History*, ch. xi. p. 325, note.

entrust those persons with power whose ancestors
have already held it. We see here, in fact, a new
hereditary nobility—not a nobility of patrician
descent, though the spirit of patricianism is
evidently not extinct, but a nobility resting its
claims chiefly on *service done to the State.* The
patrician Cornelii, Valerii, Claudii, and others, and
the plebeian Licinii, Fulvii, or Junii, have done
good service to the State in former generations, and
it may be expected that they will continue to do
it ; for the traditions of wisdom and valour are in
these families, as the images of their ancestors are
in their halls.[1] The old instinct of respect for
noble descent has transferred itself to this new
nobility ; the Roman people, always true to its
veneration for a certain type of civic excellence, in
which marked individuality was not prominent,
believed that this type could best be secured in its
leaders by seeking it where it had already been
found. And so it came about that a " new man,"
one whose family had never yet been prominent in
public life, rarely found his way to high office. If
he did so, it was only as the result of pre-eminent
military services, or by the aid of some influential
noble in persuading the people of the validity of his
claim. At a later date the art of oratory came also
to be reckoned as one of the aids of a *novus homo* ;

---

[1] The *jus imaginum*, or right to keep in the house the images
of ancestors who had held a curule office, and to have them carried
in funeral processions, is a most characteristic feature of this
nobility. Read Polybius, vi. 53 ; Cic. *ad Fam.* ix. 21 ; Mommsen. *Staatsrecht*, i. 426 foll.

for in defending great men who were attacked in the law-courts, the young orator could not fail to improve his own chance of rising to greatness.

To illustrate the paramount social influence of this new nobility, which thus secured for it as a class the almost exclusive possession of the executive in the State, we need only glance at the circumstances of the three most famous "new men" who reached the consulship between 200 and 60 B.C. The first of these was M. Porcius Cato (Cato the elder), consul 195, a farmer at Tusculum, who entered public life through the influence of a friend and neighbour belonging to the renowned family of the Valerii Flacci.[1] The second was Gaius Marius, of an obscure family of Arpinum. This man, who reached the consulship in 105 comparatively late in life, was first noticed by the younger Scipio in the Numantian war as a young officer of ability, and obtained the tribunate of the plebs in 119 B.C. with the help of L. Cæcilius Metellus, with whose family the Marii had long been in some way connected as adherents.[2] The third, M. Tullius Cicero, also a native of Arpinum, owed his rise chiefly to his own ability as a pleader, but also in no small measure to the notice taken of his father and himself by men of family and influence in the time of his boyhood.[3] And indeed when Cicero became a

---

[1] Plutarch, *Cato major* 3. C. Lælius, cos. 190, probably owed his success to his friend Scipio Africanus : Mommsen, *Hist.* ii. 325.

[2] Plutarch, *Marius*, 3 and 4.

[3] Cic. *De Oratore*, ii. 1.

candidate for the consulship, at a time when the power of the nobility had long been waning, he felt the disadvantage of his *novitas* most keenly. Quintus Cicero, in the short " Handbook of Electioneering " which he drew up for his brother's use, starts with an emphatic warning on this point—" Every day, when you go down to the Forum to canvass, say to yourself these words : I am a new man ; I am a candidate for the consulship ; and this is Rome." [1] And though Cicero was elected, the unwillingness of the nobility to act with this newcomer as with one of themselves had a permanent and disastrous influence on his declining years.

The overwhelming social prestige of the families already ennobled by State service, giving them a strong moral claim to retain within their own circle the honours and duties of executive government, is the first fact which must be grasped if we are to understand the constitution of this period. But there is another fact still more important and less easy to explain. If we turn again to our authorities—if, for example, we open the third, fourth, or fifth decades of Livy—we shall very soon find that it is not with the executive magistracy that the real conduct of the State resides. The consul is in office for a year only, and during that year he is constantly away from Rome in command of an army. He may initiate a policy, but he cannot secure its permanence ; he is liable to be hindered by the voice of his colleague, or by the veto of the tribune of the plebs. He is a functionary without

[1] Quintus Cicero, *Commentariolum petitionis*, ch. 1.

whom the State cannot be governed; no kind of
public business can be transacted without him, or
without the magistrates below him in rank; yet it is
not his hand that is on the helm. Nothing can be
done without his initiation, yet he is not the guiding
spirit of the State. It is the great Council over
which he presides, and whose advice an almost
unbroken tradition enjoins him not only to ask, but
to take, in whose hands are really the destinies of
Rome, her empire, and the world.[1]   What, then, was
this Council? in what manner selected, and entrusted
with what duties? Do we find here, as in the
executive, the characteristic marks of an oligarchy?

Let us see in the first place how the Senate was
filled up, and who were the persons who sat in it.
Every five years the list of its members, three
hundred in number, was revised; and the revision,
once the duty of the consul, as of the king before
him, was now entrusted to two censors. These
censors must have previously held the consulship;
they were therefore men of experience, advanced in
life, and members of the hereditary nobility.[2]   The
principles on which they were to select the senators
were clearly understood, and even defined by statute

[1] The following chapters of Livy may be selected as examples to
illustrate the statements in the text:—xxxi. 6; xxxiv. 55 and 56;
xxxv. 20 (where the consul is forbidden to leave the city); xxxvi.
40 (where a tribunician veto is overcome by the Senate; cf., however, xxxiii. 25); xlv. 21.   An excellent example of senatorial
authority in combination with tact will be found in xxxix. 39.

[2] Cato the elder is again a signal exception: read Livy, xxxix.
40, and Plutarch, *Cato* 16. He was in actual antagonism to the
nobilitas; but he had still the support of Valerius Flaccus, who
was elected as his colleague.

—they were to choose, up to the number of three hundred or thereabout, "every most excellent citizen of any rank" (*optimum quemque ex omni ordine*).[1] But by what standard were they to measure this excellence? Whatever was the precise intention of the words just quoted,—if indeed they were the actual words of the statute,— there is no doubt at all as to the way in which the censors interpreted them. In a community like the Roman, where the virtues of the private man could not expect to attract notice, they had practically no choice. The only available measure of excellence was the performance of public duty. They first of all put upon the roll all who had in any year held a curule office, *i.e.* who had been consul, prætor, or curule ædile. All of these had already sat in the Senate ever since their year of office, and were well acquainted with senatorial procedure and the manner of conducting business; those who had held office since the last revision now became for the first time full senators, though they had been allowed hitherto to retain the seats they had acquired as magistrates. Next the censors added all who had been non-curule magistrates, *i.e.* all ex-ædiles of the plebs, ex-tribunes of the plebs, and ex-quæstors. It has been calculated that, without going further, the list of three

---

[1] The only information we have about this important law is in Festus' abridgment of Verrius Flaccus, the antiquary of the Augustan age : ed. Muller, p. 246, s. v. *prœteriti senatores.* A full discussion of it in Willems' *Sénat,* i. 153 foll. Cf. Mommsen, *Staatsrecht.* ii. 413 ; iii. 873.

hundred might in some years have been thus completed.[1] But if any more names were needed, as might happen after severe loss in war, or if the censors, as they were entitled to do, struck off any names from the list drawn up by their predecessors, the persons nominated in addition would be such as had specially distinguished themselves in the field, or had in some way gained themselves public credit; and these were no doubt usually the sons or relations of men who were or had been senators.[2]

Thus the Senate was at this time almost entirely made up of men who had held office and done the State good service; and no small proportion of these had actually reached the consulship, or at least the prætorship. They had therefore been several times elected to office by the votes of the people, and it may indeed be said, with every appearance of truth, that the Senate represented the popular choice. But we have already seen that the people almost invariably chose for these higher magistracies members of the families of old repute and standing; and thus, though the Senate was in a sense representative of the popular will, it is also true that it was *fed by the hereditary nobility*.

And we must also notice that in the actual

---

[1] It will be worth the reader's while to examine at this point the hypothetical list of the Senate as revised by the censors of 179 B.C., drawn up at great pains by Willems (*Sénat*, i. 308 foll.).

[2] Read the account, in Livy xxiii. 23, of the *lectio senatus* of 216 B.C., after the terrible losses at Cannæ. It ends thus : "Tum ex iis qui magistratus non cepissent, qui spolia ex hoste fixa domi haberent, aut civicam coronam accepissent."

conduct of business in the Senate this nobility had everything their own way. Among the ex-tribunes and ex-quæstors there might be many men of *new* families outside of the hereditary nobility, but these men would not easily make themselves heard. When a consul or prætor summoned the Senate to seek its advice, he began by placing before it the question to be decided, and then proceeded to ask the opinions, in a regular order, of the leading senators. He began with the consuls-elect, and went on to the consulares (ex-consuls). Long before he reached any lower rank it is probable that in the age of which we are speaking the debate had usually terminated. The tribunes, as magistrates armed with a veto, would occasionally interfere; but at this time even they were rarely disloyal to the prestige of the nobility.[1]

This great council, then, was not only composed to a large extent of members of the hereditary nobility, but these, as men who had seen the longest service, and best understood the conduct of business, were by far the most influential men who sat in it, and could easily influence the votes of any who were outside the pale. It is a true oligarchical council; not, like the Athenian Boulê, merely a large committee of the popular assembly. Almost every member of it has submitted himself once, or oftener, to the vote of the people in their elective

---

[1] The Senate was in this period, as a rule, on the best of terms with the Tribunate; read Livy, xxxvi. 40, xxxviii. 47, where the latter is influenced by the Senate; and xxxiii. 25, and xlii. 21, where the tribunes urge the Senate to a certain line of action.

assembly; but as a consequence of the popular veneration for families of tried worth, the really powerful senators almost always belong to a limited social oligarchy. In the Senate is gathered all the wisdom and experience of the State; but this wisdom and experience is not to be looked for outside of a certain boundary line of society. This is oligarchy, and oligarchical machinery, of the most admirable and effective kind. The executive and its advising council form together a compact and narrow body of *identical interest*; a government of the capable minority such as no other constitution has ever developed. The English Whig oligarchy of the eighteenth century was powerful enough, but it was far from being as compact, or as capable, as the Roman senatorial oligarchy. Perhaps the only modern State to which we can look for a parallel is mediæval Venice, whose Grand Council, administering a great empire, reminds us in some ways of the Senate in its best days.[1]

Let us now turn to consider how the oligarchy, thus constituted on the basis of a hereditary claim to govern, actually secured and exercised power in a State legally and theoretically democratic. For it must be clearly understood that the Senate, the essential organ of the oligarchic families, had in constitutional law no independent power of its own; it was merely the advising council of the king, and afterwards of the consul. It could not meet unless

---

[1] Read the valuable comparison of the Venetian Grand Council and the Roman Senate in the late Professor Freeman's *Historical Essays*, vol. iv. pp. 410 foll.

summoned by a magistrate; it could not command the magistrate to take any course of action. Nor could it necessarily control the assemblies of the people; for the magistrate, when proposing a law, was not legally bound to consult the Senate on the subject. Whoever studies even cursorily the constitution of the Roman Republic will soon find that the magistrate had the sole initiative, and that the ultimate sovereign power lay with the people. How then was it possible that the Senate should become the instrument of the dominating power of a close oligarchy?

The explanation of this strange phenomenon is to be found (1) in the moral force exercised by an assembly of ex-magistrates; (2) in the nature of the business which the Roman government had to transact as the State increased in power and importance; (3) in the character, lacking culture and initiative, of the Roman people itself. A few remarks on each of these points must suffice in this chapter; but to understand the problem thoroughly an accurate knowledge is needed not only of the constitution, but of the economy, the literature, and the external history of the Republic.

1. The magistrate, as we have seen (p. 108), was under no legal obligation to obey the decrees of the Senate. But he was morally bound to consult it; for it was a principle of the constitution from the earliest times to the latest,—one of the εἰωθότα νοήματα of the Roman mind,—that one in authority should fortify himself by the advice of a consilium.[1]

---

[1] See above, p. 77.

And his own natural instinct must have prompted him not only to seek this advice, but to follow it when given ; for the Roman, habitually conservative, was only too apt to guide himself by the custom of his ancestors (*mos majorum*), and to avoid untrodden paths.

Now consider how this instinct of his would be strengthened by the overwhelming prestige of such a council as the Senate. The consul had before him in the Senate every living man who had already held the consulship, as well as all who had learnt experience in any department of public administration. He was but one among many who were older and more experienced than himself; the duties he was now for the first time learning they had already discharged with credit. If his council of war consisted largely of ex-commanders-in-chief, what general would be able to resist the force of their authority ? The united voice of such a body as the Senate, in which was gathered all the wisdom and experience of the State, was not to be defied or even neglected by men of the steady and loyal type which the Roman people preferred at this period to entrust with magisterial power.

Thus it is not hard to see how the consul, though always revered as the impersonation of the majesty of the Roman State, and though he summoned the Senate, presided over it, and technically initiated all its business, should have gradually slipped into the position of the *servant* of such a council of sages. Even the tribunes, young men often and inexperienced, came to feel the same irresistible authority, and hardly ever ventured in this

period to dispense with the Senate's sanction for
their legislative designs. And though the process
was a gradual one—for the Senate's prestige had
itself grown with the growing State,—the impression
made on the Roman mind was never wholly ob-
literated. Cicero expresses it exactly when, in the
outburst of republican enthusiasm which has already
been quoted, he speaks of the magistrates as "the
agents of the weighty designs of the Senate." He
does not describe them seeking its advice, as men
who might follow it or not as they pleased: that
was indeed the strictly legal view of their powers,
on which, in Cicero's own time, and to his infinite
disgust, his political enemies occasionally acted.
The view he so eloquently enforces represented the
practice of the constitution in its best days, when
the Senate's commanding wisdom was still un-
questioned; the magistrate must obey the great
council of ex-magistrates, and be the loyal agent of
its most weighty designs.

2. This startling change in the working of the
constitution might, however, have never taken place,
if Rome had enjoyed the comparatively untroubled
youth of most of the City-States of antiquity. But
Rome, as Virgil sang of her, and as Dante wrote of
her long afterwards from a very different point of
view,[1] seemed destined from her infancy to conquer
and to rule. Even by the time when the political
equalisation of patricians and plebeians was complete, she had won a dominion in Italy such as had

[1] In the De Monarchia, Bk. ii. ; cf. Paradiso, canto vi. ; Virgil,
Æn. vi. 756 foll.

been achieved by no Greek city—neither by Athens nor Sparta. From every disaster, like England in the eighteenth century, she rose with renewed strength to fresh expansion. The Latins of the Campagna lost their ancient equality with her, and had to become Roman citizens, for the most part on an inferior scale of privilege. The dwellers on the hills round about Latium had already submitted to her; and by the year 290 B.C. the Sabine popula- tions of central Italy, the hardiest of all Italians, had ceased to struggle against the inevitable. The Etruscans to the north were less stubborn, and Rome already dominated the peninsula. In 281 B.C. Pyrrhus of Epirus seemed likely for a time to put an end to her career; but Rome at last forced him to depart, and all Italy acknowledged her as mistress. Next came the collision with Carthage, and the long struggle in Sicily ending in the acquisi- tion of new provinces of government beyond the sea; and then more conquest to the north, among the Gauls of the great plain of the Po. Again for fourteen years she struggled for life with Carthage, when Hannibal brought his army to her very gates, and stripped her for the time of almost all the dominion she had won. But even such a war as this only ended in a fresh series of conquests; Carthage made humiliating terms, and lost all her dominion in Spain. Hannibal, intriguing as a last resource with the Macedonian king, turned Rome's attention eastwards, and in the course of another half-century both Macedonia and Greece were under the rule of Roman magistrates.

We need not now pursue this wonderful story further, for it is not with the conquests themselves that we are concerned, but with their reaction on the constitution. In reading the history of conquering States, we are apt to dwell too little on the immense amount of energy and brain-power which such States have to expend. The levying and equipment of armies, the building of vast fleets, the adequate organisation of finance, the choice and control of commanders, and above all, the settlement of conquered territories and the vigilance needed to secure their obedience—all these demand such a strenuous industry in the conquerors as in these days we can hardly realise. To us Englishmen, with our peaceful and commercial instincts, a single little war seems a matter of difficulty and moment; the defeat of a single battalion seems a serious disaster. We have to go back to the days of Pitt to understand how great a strain on the energies and resources of a nation is a fierce and widespread war which lasts for many years with varying result. But he who would really grasp the meaning of the senatorial government at Rome must try and realise the business which that government had to get through. It was business which called for experience and knowledge, as well as industry; it could not be done by *amateurs*. It needed the cool-headedness of men of age and standing; the steady perseverance of men who had been trained in business from their youth; the reasonableness in command of men accustomed to obey. It called for unsparing attention to detail, and that exact adaptation of means to ends to which no novice in statesmanship can readily attain.   And lastly, this task of conquest and organisation could not be fulfilled without sobriety in debate, unity in action, and that good sense and self-restraint which alone can make a State orderly, and allow it to put forth its full strength whenever it strikes a blow.

All these rare gifts were to be found in the Roman Senate of this period; not high intellectual gifts, but perseverance, industry, honesty, orderliness, and good sense.   Probably no body of men has ever sat together for consultation so richly endowed with these unpretentious qualities; and the reason lay not only in the Roman character (of which I have a word to say directly), but in the traditions of those noble families of whose scions the Senate was composed.   To those men office meant really work, and work meant distinction and honour; all had served the State from their youth, and most of them had learnt how to serve it from their fathers.   If they had only been called on to transact the ordinary duties of a Greek πολίτης, these traditions might have had less force, and the peculiar capacity of the Roman senator might never have been developed; but, drawn on as she was from war to war, Rome produced exactly the kind of Statesmanship she most needed, and produced it also in abundance. We need, then, feel no surprise that in all departments of government the Senate, in which was gathered all the wisdom and experience of the State, should have gradually drawn the actual conduct of business into its own hands.   And we have only to read a

few chapters of Livy's later books to convince ourselves that this was so. The people pass laws, but
at the instance of the Senate ; and it is the decrees
of the Senate which the magistrate executes. The
Senate is foreign minister, financial minister, war
minister ; and the Senate is responsible to no other
person or assembly. Here is an oligarchic organ in
the highest state of adequacy to which necessity and
use can develop it.

3. At Athens, as we have seen, the work of
government in all its details was done by the people
themselves. A novice in Roman history might not
unnaturally ask why the Roman people was incapable of such work, or let it pass without remon-
strance into the hands of a few. To account for
this merely by reference to the composition of the
Senate, and the long series of wars through which
the Senate steered the State, is hardly going far
enough, it might be said ; the people, as really and
ultimately sovereign, was itself responsible for these
tendencies, and might have substituted for them a
peaceful development towards real democracy.

It is to the Roman character and public economy
that we must look for an explanation of this
difficulty. The very first thing a student of the
Republican period should set himself to do is to
make it clear to himself what manner of people
the Romans were, and what was their daily life and
occupation. In the Latin literature he ordinarily
reads, in Virgil and Horace, for example, he will
find some indication of the way in which the later
Romans believed their ancestors to have lived. But

let him open the earliest Latin prose work which we possess, and if he reads no further than the very first chapter, he will find a sentence or two which should give him a clue never to be lost sight of. Cato wrote his work on agriculture at the close of the period I have been speaking of, when serious changes, both in character and economy, had begun to tell upon the Roman people; but he had the tradition in his mind of an older and better state of things, and acted upon it himself to the best of his ability.   Here are two sentences from his brief preface. "When our forefathers would praise a worthy man, they praised him as a good husband-man, and a good landlord; and they believed that praise could go no further."   And again: "Hus-bandmen make the strongest men, and the bravest soldiers; their gain is far less selfish, less uncertain, less open to envy (than that of the merchant ")[1].

Cato's evidence is borne out by all we know from other sources.   The older Roman and Latin population had two occupations, agriculture and war, a fact which is reflected in their conception of their great deity Mars, who was essentially the god of the husbandman, yet had from the first charac-teristics which could easily transform him into a god of war.   These farmer-warriors made up that true middle class of which I spoke in the last chapter.   They were not densely packed within the walls of a city, but spent their time on their farms, and only came into Rome for marketing or occa-sional voting in Comitia.   They had the virtues of

[1] Cato. *De Re Rustica*. 1.

an agricultural class, as Cato knew; but to an
Athenian their shortcomings would have been more
obvious. They were not *political* men; the real
end and aim of all their political struggles had so
far been economical reform, the recovery of their
land and status, the limitation of large estates.
Constitutional reform had been a means, not an
end, and had been left in the hands of their more
wealthy leaders. They belonged to the type which
the Spartans represented in Greece; they were not
men of keen intellect or ready speech, nor were
they eager for new things, or seekers after truth.
They knew their own wants, and did their work
well; they had a strict sense of duty to the State,
to their families, and to the gods, which made
them excellent soldiers, fathers, and citizens. ·They
had clear notions, as we have seen, of constituted
authority, and of the reasonable limits which may
be set upon it; and they had very precise conceptions of the nature and use of legal transactions.
But they were not men of the world, or men of
affairs, nor had they the acuteness or the leisure of
the Athenian. It is plain that they were not the
men to govern themselves; government they could
leave to their betters, who understood the traditions
of the art. They were not fitted to guide, but they
were always ready to obey; by their obedience they
conquered the world, but left it to their leaders to
make the best use of their conquests.

Democracy, then, in the Athenian sense of the
word, could never have been realised at Rome.
The people had neither wish nor ability to govern

themselves, but were perfectly content to elect their
magistrates, and to express their opinion occasionally
on projects of legislation, of which perhaps they
only half understood the import. They put entire
trust in the governing class, and their loyalty made
the Senate an object of awe for all the peoples of
the Mediterranean. It was long before that loyalty
gave way,—not till it became perfectly clear that
their natural interests were no longer in harmony
with those of their rulers; not till the trusteeship
of the oligarchy had been grossly and irretrievably
abused. And by that time they were themselves
ruined, both morally and materially; their part in
the history of the world was played out, and they
rapidly disappeared. By that time, too, the whole
face of the civilised world was changed; the City-
State was no more, and a new political system was
beginning slowly to appear.

Before we leave the Roman oligarchy and its
work of conquest and government, let us turn for
a moment to another side of its indefatigable activity, to which I have had no opportunity as yet of
alluding. At the end of the last chapter it was
pointed out that in the period of the equalisation of
the Orders was laid the foundation-stone of that
system of legal rules which was to become Rome's
most valuable legacy to modern civilisation. The
Twelve Tables, however harsh and rude they may
appear to us, provided a sufficient legal basis for
the mutual transactions of Roman citizens. But
this code was meant for Roman citizens only; it

expressed the *jus civile*, that is, the law which bound *cives Romani* and no others. Now in the oligarchical period just surveyed, in which Rome came into contact with and conquered a great number of other peoples, Italians, Greeks, Carthaginians, Spaniards, her commercial transactions increased to an extraordinary extent, and the city became the chief centre of business for the whole Mediterranean. In the earlier part of this period a serious legal difficulty arose out of this great commercial development. Each foreigner who came on business to Rome was accustomed to the law of his own State, but at Rome that law had, of course, no force, nor could the Roman *jus civile* be of any avail for him, unless the use of it were specially secured him by treaty, which was very rarely the case.[1] If he wanted to borrow on equitable terms, or to recover a debt, or to prove his right to a property he had bought, he had no legal force to fall back on ; all his transactions were carried on at a risk, and had no more legal security than the barter of savages.

About the end of the first war with Carthage, it became plain that if Rome was to rival or to outdo the great trading city of the west, her government must find some method of giving a legal sanction to the transactions of foreigners with Romans, or among themselves on her own soil. It does not seem to have occurred to them to apply the *jus civile* in this way, for the spirit of the City-State

---

[1] Such a provision is to be found in the second treaty with Carthage, preserved in Polybius, iii. 24. Reciprocal advantages were secured to Romans trading at Carthage.

was still strong in them in spite of its wonderful expansion, and the law of the Tables was a sacred heirloom of the *cives Romani*, whose paramount importance in the world was increasing every year. The dignity of the Roman could not brook the use of his most precious possession for the benefit of foreigners.

This exclusive spirit forced the Romans to a step by which a permanent solution of the difficulty was found; at the same time it opened a new period of development for their system of law, and widened their appreciation of all legal principles, which had hitherto been as narrow as they were clear and strong. They fell back now on that distinct conception of magisterial power to which I have already several times alluded. They had already, at the time of the reforms of Licinius and Sextius, handed over the civil jurisdiction of the consul to a prætor, a new magistrate with an *imperium*, like that of the consul, sufficient to enforce his commands and rulings, though he was inferior to the consul in precedence and dignity. In 243 B.C. they added another prætor, whose business it was to be to decide all suits between Romans and foreigners, or between foreigners themselves; and henceforward the prætor urbanus administered the *jus civile*, while the prætor peregrinus was to do the best he could with another kind of *jus*, in which the solution of the growing difficulty was to be found.

What was the *jus* which the prætor peregrinus was to administer ? It existed in no code, like the Twelve Tables; it was not law in any true sense of the

R

word.   It consisted of the practices and customs of the various peoples, chiefly Italian and Greek, who came in that age to Rome on business, and needed a legal basis for their transactions ; taken together, no doubt, with those principles of the *jus civile* in which the prætor himself had been trained, and from which he could not escape, especially in dealings between foreigners and Romans.   This *jus* came to be called the *jus gentium*, or law of all peoples, when lawyers began to reason upon it and to endeavour to explain it scientifically ; at first, however, it was no more than a series of rulings of which the force depended simply on the *imperium* of the prætor, entrusted to him for this purpose by the Roman people.   Thus their clear idea of magisterial power came to the rescue of the Romans when their legal sense was puzzled by the new conditions under which they found themselves ; and it combined with their strong practical common sense to build up a system of equity outside the narrow law of their own State.

From the close of the first Punic war and onwards, the rulings of the prætor peregrinus continued to accumulate, and to form a body of legal principles applicable to almost all difficulties that might arise.   They were recorded year by year in the edict which each prætor issued at the beginning of his year of office, by virtue of the *jus edicendi* which all the higher Roman magistrates possessed. Here the conservative spirit of the Romans, and their instinct for order and precedent in public transactions, saved them from a contingency which might have ruined the new system, and disordered the relations between themselves and their subjects and neighbours. Every prætor issued a fresh edict on entering office, and it was in his power, if he chose, to drop all the rulings of his predecessors. Had he done this, the legal sanction of his juris-diction would have had no fixity or credit. What he did was to adopt the edict of his predecessor in its entirety, expunging perhaps only such rulings as had been clearly inexpedient, and adding such others as his own good sense or his predecessor's experience suggested. Thus was formed by slow degrees a solid body of precedent, which had the force of law as issuing from the *imperium*. It was not law in the sense in which the Twelve Tables were law, but it was infinitely more valuable to mankind, and it was capable of almost endless expansion. It even came to be considered, in Sir H. Maine's words, " as a great, though imperfectly developed model, to which all law ought, as far as possible, to conform." And it was the immediate fruit of that love of work and attention to detail of which the oligarchy gave such splendid proofs in other departments of government; and when we blame them for hardness and materialism, for rapacity and cruelty, it is as well to remember that they made at least one discovery which was of great and lasting value. They found out that the law of the City-State was not equal to the needs of mankind in an age of increasing human intercourse ; and that such intercourse could be governed by rules drawn from a wider range of

life than that of a single πόλις, if these were
sanctioned by the irresistible force of the *imperium*
of the Roman magistrate.[1]

[1] On the subject of the *jus gentium* and the prætor's edict read
Gaius, i. 1 ; Maine, *Ancient Law*, chs. iii. and iv. ; Sohm's *Institutes of Roman Law* (translated by Ledlie), pp. 38-58. Cf. also
Mommsen, *Staatsrecht*, iii. 590 foll., who embodies the researches
of Professor Nettleship into the meaning and history of the phrase
jus gentium.

CHAPTER IX

So far we have been chiefly following the development
of those two famous City-States of antiquity which
have left us a richer inheritance than any others
It would be a long tale to reckon up the various
causes to which the pre-eminence of Athens and
Rome may be ascribed ; but from what has already
been said in these pages, one at least, and that a
leading one, should have become tolerably clear.
These two States, after passing through the
normal stages of early growth, succeeded in overcoming the most serious dangers which those stages
brought with them, and above all, the disunion
caused by the struggles of the unprivileged many
to prove themselves a genuine part of the State,
and to share in its government equally with the
privileged few. In other words, when the principle
of *locality* came into collision with the older
principle of *kinship*, these two States took no
serious or permanent damage from the ensuing
strife of interests. So far from being crippled in

this critical period of their existence, they emerged
from it stronger and healthier, as from a fever
which has purged away all unwholesome tendencies ;
for they gained vigour by gaining union—by an
almost complete fusion of all conflicting elements.
In each case the few were reasonable enough to
refrain from violence in the contest, and to acknow-
ledge in course of time that their commanding
position had been wrested from them ; and in each
case, too, the many were rational enough to make a
moderate use of their victory. It was a struggle,
both at Rome and Athens, of reasonableness against
ancient prejudice ; and in each case the victory of
good sense was followed by a long period of unity
and prosperity. Athens, pursuing a course natural
to the quick intelligence of her citizens, developed
the most complete democracy that the world has
ever yet seen ; and at Rome there grew up an
oligarchy, founded on the reverence of the Romans
for tried practical wisdom, whose extraordinary
aptitude for government changed the whole face of
the civilised world.

But many, and perhaps most, other States could
hardly have been equally fortunate. Tyranny, as we
have seen, was mild at Athens and almost absent
at Rome, and in both States it helped rather than
hindered the ultimate fusion of interests. But in
some States, at least, tyranny must have left the
jarring elements of society unharmonised and out
of tune. After the earlier tyrannies had passed
away, about the beginning of the fifth century B.C.,
we begin to hear constantly of discord within the

cities—discord that in some instances reaches to a terrible pitch of recklessness, and points to a complete absence of the spirit of compromise and reason which we have met with at Athens and Rome. In all such cases the phenomena are much the same; the few, the comfortable, the rich, the well-born, the good and honourable, as they were variously called, are at feud with the many, or, as their enemies called them, the base, the bad, the low-born. In these States it is plain that no union of hearts has been achieved, and that the government must necessarily be in the hands of one party or the other, and that the party in power will deal harshly with its opponents. And, in fact, throughout the fifth century almost every City-State is either a decided oligarchy or a decided democracy, and as the oligarchies have the stronger tradition and greater experience to help them, they for the most part are found to have the government in their hands. They sometimes even succeed in getting rid altogether of the most dangerous portion of the many, who leave the city in a body, not to return as did the plebs at Rome; and sometimes it is the many who turn the few out of house and home, as the only way of securing themselves against political intrigues and conspiracies.

Instances of this uncompromising and fatal spirit are to be found in abundance both in Herodotus and Thucydides, who often relate them with apparent indifference, as though they were too common to call for special emphasis. But let us take two or three notable cases by way of illustration; cases of which we have some definite information, and which will fix themselves on the memory as we become sensible of the disastrous results which each of them brought incidentally upon the whole of Hellas.

At the end of the sixth century Naxos was one of the most flourishing States in the Ægean Sea; it lay in a most favourable position, not too near the coast to be in danger of conquest by the Persian, and was the largest of the islands which the Greeks knew as the Cyclades. It was reported to be able to muster 8000 armed men, and to equip a large fleet of warships. It was also said to be rich both in money and slaves. But Naxos was divided against itself. In the year 501 B.C. a number of its oligarchical party (of the "fat," or comfortable, as Herodotus calls them) were sent into exile by the Demos, or fled of their own accord before violence. They chose to go to Miletus, then the most powerful Greek city in Ionia. Miletus had also suffered from internal discord, but had called in the Parians to cure the disease, and was now prospering greatly under the strong rule of a leading citizen, Aristagoras. To this man the Naxian oligarchs applied for help. Aristagoras did not refuse it, but for reasons of his own he made it a bargain that he should himself ask aid for the undertaking from his friend Artaphernes, the Persian satrap of Western Asia. This is a story which is constantly repeated in various forms during the two following centuries; Greeks, quarrelling among

themselves, allow the common enemy to be called
in. In this case, indeed, the Naxian democracy
were for the present let alone, nor do we know
what became of the exiled oligarchs; for Aristagoras and Artaphernes fell out, and the former,
fearing the consequences, and hoping as leader of
the Greeks to make himself " king," *i.e.* tyrant of Miletus, stirred up the Greek cities in Asia Minor to
attack Persia, and thereby ultimately brought upon
all Hellas the fearful perils of Persian invasion.
In this invasion Naxos herself was one of the first
to suffer; her city and its temples were burned, and
a part of her population enslaved. Among the
contingents of which the Greek fleet at Salamis was
composed, there were but four ships from Naxos;
and these, which had been sent by the democracy
to join, not the Greek, but the Persian fleet, only
escaped the disgrace of other islanders by disregard-
ing the orders of their too submissive government.
Naxos had fallen low, and never really lifted up
her head again.[1]

The other great war which did most to sap the
vitality of the Greeks was also immediately brought
about by one of these violent intestine feuds. The
story, familiar as it is, is worth careful study in
Thucydides's own words, for it shows how easily
the internal dissensions of a single city could awaken
old jealousies between other cities, and kindle them
into fresh animosities, leading at last to a general

---

[1] For this story, read Herodotus, v. 28 foll., and cf. vi. 96, and
viii. 46. Cf. Thucyd. i. 98 for the later revolt of Naxos from
Athens : after which the island is seldom mentioned.

conflagration in which the life and strength of all
that was best in Hellas was withered. Thucydides
shall tell the tale for himself of the first beginning
of this momentous war.

"The city of Epidamnus is situated on the right hand as
you sail up the Ionian gulf. Near it dwelt the Taulantians,
a barbarian tribe of the Illyrian race. The place was
colonised by the Corcyræans, but under the leadership of a
Corinthian ; . . . he was invited, according to ancient custom,
from the mother city, and Corinthians and other Dorians
joined in the colony. In process of time Epidamnus became
great and populous, but there followed a long period of civil
commotion, and the city is said to have been brought low in
a war against the neighbouring barbarians, and to have lost
her ancient power. At last, shortly before the Peloponnesian
war, *the notables* (i.e. *oligarchs*) *were driven out by the people ,
the exiles went over to the barbarians, and, uniting with them,
plundered the remaining inhabitants both by sea and land.* These,
finding themselves hard pressed, sent an embassy to the
mother city, Corcyra, begging the Corcyræans not to leave
them to their fate, but to reconcile them to the exiles and
put down their barbarian enemies. The ambassadors came,
and sitting as suppliants in the temple of Herê, preferred
their request ; but the Corcyræans would not listen to them,
and they returned without success," etc.[1]

Here we must note, not only the struggle of fac-
tions, and the expulsion of the oligarchs, but once
more the significant fact that these are ready to
take part with non-Hellenic peoples in order to get
the better of their own fellow-citizens. And worse
still, when the cry comes up to Corcyra of the besieged Epidamnians asking for friendly intervention
and aid against barbarian attack, the mother city will
not listen ; she prefers to sit still and see the up-

[1] Thucyd. i. 24 (Jowett's translation).

start Epidamnus destroyed. A policy so selfish and
suicidal in itself was also full of mischief for Greece.
Epidamnus called for aid from Corinth, the mother
city of Corcyra; this brought Corinth and Corcyra
into collision, in accordance with an old and
smouldering ill-will; Corcyra left the Peloponnesian league and joined the Athenian, and thus
by exaggerating the tension which had long existed
between Athens and Sparta, brought about the
war in which the best energies of Greece were
wasted. Corcyra herself, like Naxos, paid dearly
for her folly and selfishness. Five years later she
was herself the victim of one of these outbreaks
of faction, the direct inheritance of her former
misdoings; and this outbreak, to which I shall
shortly again refer, was perhaps the most savage
and the most paralysing of any of which we have
record.[1]

I shall mention one more example of this epidemic disease, not because it was very serious in
itself or its consequences, but as a negative instance,
showing that where a State had once fairly overcome the difficulties of disunion, any attempt of a
weaker party to overthrow a stronger was not likely
to cause permanent ruin or weakness.   In 411 B.C.
the oligarchical party at Athens, which had always
continued to exist, and to carry on a policy of
reasonable opposition to the leaders of the democracy,
succeeded for a short time in getting the government into its own hands.   The story of this
singular episode in Athenian history, as told by

[1] Thucyd. iii. 70.

Thucydides,[1] is of very great value, and should be studied with the utmost care; for it shows admirably, not only the strength of the safeguards of the democracy (see p. 170), but also the advantages possessed by a State whose noblest traditions were traditions of the union of all interests in self-improvement or in self-defence. I may not describe it here at length; but the reader of Thucydides's account should note accurately the following points in it. First, he should examine the circumstances under which this revolution came about, and observe that it was only under the severest possible pressure, and with the hope of bringing back by this means to Athens the only man whose abilities and resources would bo likely to save her. Secondly, passing in review the details of the revolution, he should see how, without any open violence, the constitution was changed *by a show of constitutional means*, the Demos being induced by its own orators to resign its own sovereignty, and to entrust it to a Board of 500; and how even then it was deemed necessary to keep up the phantom of a democracy, in the shape of a body of 5000, which perhaps never really met. And lastly, he should pursue the story to its sequel, till he finds the oligarchy of 500 done away with the very next year, and the democratic constitution revived in its entirety without needless violence.

This disease of internal feud, of which the Athenian revolution was so mild an example, was epidemic in Greece during the fifth century, and especially during the Peloponnesian war. That

[1] Thucyd. viii. 53-70.

war may in fact be called a war of oligarchies and
democracies; it could not have lasted so long, or
been maintained with such persistent determination,
if in all the cities that took part in it there had
not been some feeling of self-interest or fear, some
desire of revenge upon enemies at home as well as
abroad.   In almost every city the few were for
Sparta, and the many for Athens,[1] and the party in
power knew that its only hope of safety either for
person or property lay in the retention of that
power at all costs, and in aiding to the utmost the
confederates on their own side.   In the course of the
war both leading States forcibly changed the constitutions of many cities; and when it was over, Sparta
used her victory to oligarchise them all.   These
facts speak plainly of the universality and the
bitterness of the strife of interests in the narrow
world of the City-State.

And it is to this that we must look for the best
explanation of the inward decay of this form of
State.   All States, like all individuals, are liable to
certain diseases, and doubtless there were many, of
which we can gain no accurate diagnosis, which
attacked the City-State of Greece and Italy.   We
have already had to deal with one—the Tyrannis;
and we found that its effects were as often good as
bad.   But from this other we can trace only evil
consequences.   The best test of healthiness in a
State is union of interests for the common good, or
at the least, the reciprocal action of opposing parties
in a reasonable spirit.   The tyrannis tended to

[1] Thucyd. iii. 47, 2 ; iii. 82, 1.

crush out the bitterness of party feeling, and to open men's eyes to wider interests than those which the " Few " and the " Many " respectively represented ; but this new disease was simply the re-assertion of the old spirit of disunion,—the breaking out of the old Adam, of the inbred sin of the City-State, in a form much less natural and far more dangerous than that which was healed at Athens by Solon, and at Rome by a gradual process of compromise. It meant, not so much the healthy self-assertion of the people, and the natural resistance of the old clans,—that inevitable struggle was over in most States ; but a struggle of reckless poverty against selfish wealth. The old parties are still there, and they bear the same names ; but each seems to have degenerated and to be losing self-control.

The name which the Greeks gave to this fell disease was *Stasis*,[1] *i.e.* a standing, or taking up a distinct position in the State, with malicious intent towards another party. During the Peloponnesian war it aroused grave anxiety in the mind of the philosophic historian of that day, and in commenting on one particular and most malignant outbreak, he has spoken in language so intense, so weighty, and withal so difficult, that he seems to importune us for our attention by the very earnestness of his endeavour to express himself. It will be well worth

---

[1] Cf. the Latin *seditio*. The malicious intent implied in *stasis* is well illustrated in the oligarchic oath quoted by Aristotle (*Pol.* 1310 A)—" I will hate the Demos, and do it all the harm in my power."

our while to see what it is that Thucydides is so seriously trying to impress on his countrymen.[1]

Stasis is common to mankind, he says, *i.e.* to mankind living in the only form of community which he recognised for civilised society; but it differs in intensity according to circumstances, and especially is it accentuated by war. For war is a severe schoolmaster, who makes men discontented and angry; the rich man's property is heavily taxed, the poor man is forced to serve in the field, and thus the capital which each possesses may be wasted and destroyed. After this preliminary remark, which had a special meaning for his own age, he goes on to point out the moral and political effects of *stasis*. The virtues, he says, seemed to lose their value, and to change into something foreign to their true nature. What in ordinary times would be called defects of character, laid claim now to be considered excellences. " Reckless daring was held to be loyal courage; prudent delay was the excuse of a coward; moderation was the disguise of unmanly weakness; to know everything was to do nothing. The lover of violence was always trusted, and his opponent suspected. . . . The tie of party was stronger than that of blood, because a partisan was more ready to dare without asking why." [2]

A society of clubs and coteries took the place of family life and family affection, a sure sign of internal decay in States that had been built up on the foundation of the family and the clan. Sim-

---

[1] Thucyd. ii. 82, 83.

[2] Jowett, *Thucydides*, vol. i. p. 222.

plicity and straightforward dealing were laughed
at, which means that the weakest points in the
Greek character were now coming to the front.
And lastly, turning to matters more strictly political,
Thucydides notes the corruption of party principles,
and the destruction of the life-giving middle classes.
He shall speak again in his own words :—

"The cause of all these evils was the love of power,
originating in avarice and ambition, and the party-spirit
which is engendered in them when men are fairly embarked
in a contest. For the leaders on either side used specious
names ; the one party professing to uphold the constitutional
equality of the many, the other the wisdom of an aristocracy,
while they made the public interests, to which in name only
they were devoted, in reality their prize. Striving in every
way to overcome each other, they committed the most mon-
strous crimes ; yet even these were surpassed by the magni-
tude of their revenges, which they pursued to the very
uttermost, neither party observing any definite limits either
of justice or public expediency, but both alike making the
caprice of the moment their law. Either by the help of an
unrighteous sentence, or grasping power with the strong
hand, they were eager to satiate the impatience of party-
spirit. . . . *And the citizens who were of neither party fell a
prey to both ;* either they were disliked because they held
aloof, or men were jealous of their surviving." [1]

It may be said that this language is exaggerated,
that Thucydides is sophistically making the most of
his point, and is carried away by the very magic
of the marvellous language which he is here forcing
into his service. But making all allowance for the
literary characteristics of his age, I cannot but
believe that in writing this he was conscious of a
great truth,—of a serious unnoticed evil,—and that

[1] Jowett, *Thucydides*, vol. i. p. 223.

it is his earnest conviction, and not only his
rhetorical art, which has led him into these crabbed
constructions and antithetical obscurities. He sees
evil days coming upon Greece, and he marks the
cause as being not so much the deadly war in which
almost all Greek cities were engaged, as the internal
tendency to disease on which that war acted with
fatal result. The life-blood of the City-State, he
believed, was poisoned and fevered; the true end
of this form of social life was no longer pursued;
every organ lost its natural and healthy action.
And we are justified in believing that Thucydides
was right; for the Greek cities never wholly recovered their *tone* after the war which had so sadly
exaggerated their chief inherent weakness. Corcyra,
for example, whose misfortunes suggested these
remarks to the historian, was a powerful State
before the war and its attendant *stasis*, but from
that time forward ceased to exercise any influence
in Greece.[1] She continued to exist, and later inscriptions testify to the working of her council and
her assembly, but her growth was apparently
stunted and her strength sapped by the disease.
And with loss of sanity and unity came loss also of
that spirit of youth and independence which in the
sixth and fifth centuries had borne such ripe fruit
in art and poetry. As we pursue Greek history

[1] Once, long afterwards, her name was heard in Greece again ;
but it was as the prize of a Sicilian tyrant, Agathocles.   This
obscure corner of Greek history has been lighted up by the late
Professor Freeman in a part of his history of Sicily as yet unpub-
lished.   See his smaller *History of Sicily* ("Story of the Nations"
series), p. 258.

into the fourth century, we feel that we have already enjoyed the best that Greece could give us; that in the heavier atmosphere of those later times, the "white violets" of Sappho, and all such delicate blooms of art and literature, could no longer blow in quite their old perfection.

Not, indeed, that the decay that set in was wholly the result of *stasis*. To reckon up all the concurrent causes, it would be necessary to do what is no longer possible, — to write the social and economical history of the Greek cities, as well as their external history and their internecine feuds. But I have followed Thucydides in selecting this phenomenon of *stasis* as the one cause most likely to let us into the secrets of decay, and the one cause of which we have any knowledge that can be called accurate; and I am now further going to call Aristotle as witness, though I have only space to allude briefly to his evidence.

Aristotle, writing some sixty or seventy years after Thucydides, was so deeply impressed with the universality and the virulence of this disease, that he devoted a whole book of his *Politics* to the analysis of it; a book which has aptly been called a treatise on the pathology of Greek society.[1] He deals with it in his own cool and scientific fashion, starting with a general declaration of its nature, and proceeding to analyse it as it appeared in the several forms of constitution (especially oligarchy and democracy), and to offer suggestions in each case

[1] Book v. in most editions; book viii. in Congreve's.   P. 1301 foll.

as to the best methods by which it could be anticipated. I can only say a word here of the way in
which he explains it in general, leaving the reader
to study it in detail, and to refer to it as he goes
on his way through Greek history ; but I shall also
note the two chief preventives for the disease
suggested by the *Politics* as a whole, as they presented themselves to Aristotle in the light of all
Greek experience up to his own time.

The real origin and fountain-head of all *stasis*,
says Aristotle, is to be found in a want of proportion in the respective claims of the two great
interests by which most States are divided. In
other words, it was an imperfect sense of political
justice that sowed the seeds of the disease. Where
the many, for example, are equal in one thing, *i.e.*
are all equally free and privileged under the law,
they will think themselves equal in all other respects ;
they will claim to be equal in ability, in virtue, in
dignity, and in wealth. Hence a want of justice
and proportion in their aims, leading to contempt of
moral goodness and of intellectual worth, or more
often perhaps to harsh treatment of old families and
confiscation of their property. This is naturally
resented, and *stasis* follows. And in the same way
the few, being unequal to the rest in one thing, *i.e.*
most often in wealth, think themselves entitled to
be superior in all things ; they believe that they
alone are the good, the noble, the valiant. Here,
again, we have the sense of justice warped, followed
by unfair dealing towards the many ; and the resent-
ment against this injustice will surely lead to *stasis*.

No doubt, Aristotle adds, we are all agreed that the fair claims of all ought to be respected, and that justice lies in the observance of such claims ; but after all it is over these very claims that the quarrels arise, and who is to enforce the necessary compromise ? [1]

These remarks, apparently so trite, have yet a value for all time, and for all states of society, for they are based upon facts of human nature which do not often find such clear expression. And when we apply them to that form of State which Aristotle was analysing, we feel their force yet more strongly. In our large modern State parties and interests are not brought into direct and (so to speak) personal collision ; or the heat of conflict in great cities is tempered by the comparative coolness of the numerous rural population. But in the small Greek city the conflicting interests were always in immediate contact with each other ; the rich man daily met the poor man and scorned him ; the poor man daily saw the rich man and hated him. In each the sense of justice and proportion was continually being injured by those little annoyances which are so apt to spoil the best natures, just as an organ of sight or hearing may become dulled by being constantly brought to bear on something which irritates it. No wonder that the fine sense of the Greeks for order and proportion should in this world of politics have lost its keenness ; no wonder that the reasonableness of Solon and the Athenians, and that the practical good sense of

[1] *Politics.* 1301 A and B.

the early Romans, should have carried their cities safely through successive attacks of the disease, and have proved them in all respects the fittest to survive.

But before we leave Aristotle, let us consider for a moment the remedies which he proposes for *stasis*, or rather, for he speaks like a wise and scientific physician, the two ways by which these outbreaks may best be anticipated or modified. The first of these has already been touched on in these pages, and referred to as a leading cause of the strength and prosperity both of Athens and Rome.   Of the second I have as yet said nothing ; and it is time that an opportunity should be found for some notice of it, however brief and inadequate.

Aristotle touches, indeed, to start with, on several maxims which he recommends as practically useful for securing stability in a State ; but ere long he recurs to the main principle which he has enunciated before—his favourite principle of the *mean*.[1]   It is in the middle stratum of society, he says, that salvation is to be found.   Real equality is only to be found in this stratum ; and as it is inequality which causes *stasis*, the encouragement or increase of this middle class should be the most valuable means of averting it.   " Every State would, if it could, be composed of men who are equal ; " this is the natural instinct of the State, and it is best realised where the middle class is strong.   And this instinct is indeed a natural one ; for a total loss of proportion in the distribution of wealth is at once recog-

[1] *Politics,* 1309 B : cf. 1296 A.

nised as unnatural. Where capital and labour face
each other menacingly, there can be no stability;
where wealth is evenly distributed there will be no
cause of quarrel, no desire to upset existing institutions.[1] Aristotle's preventive, it will be noticed, is
much the same as that of the modern Socialist,
whose theory is simply built upon this instinct for
proportion; but there is a difference both in the
object and in the method. Aristotle's object is to
preserve the State and its constitution, while that
of the Socialist (in spite of his name) is to make
the individual more comfortable. With the one the
State is the chief end, with the other it is only a
means. And again, Aristotle, always true to the
facts of life, not forcing them by indulging in ideals,
recommends a reasonable and practicable *policy*
which was within the reach of any Greek statesman; while Socialistic writers, exaggerating both
the evil and its remedy, are often apt to forget that
what can be done must be done by statesmen, and
that no statesman will ever be found to risk his
reputation on an ideal.[2]

The other chief remedy which Aristotle suggests
is Education; this he considered so important that
he devoted a whole book to it, of which, unfortunately, only a portion has come down to us.[3]
From this fragment, however, as well as from what
he says elsewhere, we can see that his idea of
education differed essentially from ours; and it is

[1] Compare Thucyd. iii. 82, 19; quoted above, p. 256.

[2] Cf. Sir T. More's *Utopia*, last words.

[3] *Politics*, book viii. (v. in Congreve's edition), p. 1337 A foll.

important to note this carefully. As in his
doctrine of the middle class, it is not the benefit
of the individual as such that is in his mind
when he deals with education, but the benefit of
the State, as the only means whereby the individual can reach his full mental stature. This is
quite in keeping with his view of the State as a
whole, and that view was founded upon the essential
facts of Greek life. Preserve the State, and you
will keep the conditions under which man can best
develop himself; and to preserve each State, you
must keep up the institutions which have grown
with it and are most natural to it. Education,
then, must be subordinated to the character (ηθος)
of the State; the citizen must be brought up, not
by a code abstractedly good for human nature, but by
one which is based on the traditions and feeling of
his forefathers. And this is how Aristotle comes to
be able to claim education as one great and direct
preventive of *stasis*. He does not look on it so
much as a process which makes virtuous and
sensible *men*, but as one which creates in the
oligarch or democrat the true spirit of the best
oligarchy and democracy of which his city is
capable. He might have used the pregnant expression of Herodotus to which I have so often referred,
and have said that while no citizen has a right to
step outside his εἰωθότα νοήματα, he should have
every opportunity of making the best of himself
within those traditional limits. Education, in his
view, should produce rhythm and order in the
State, by tending to subordinate all citizens to the

same end in life—the fulfilment of the "good life" of the State.[1]

These, then, are Aristotle's two prescriptions for *stasis*; the mean in the distribution of wealth, and education directed to the true end of the State. It would be tempting to go one step further, and to compare these maxims with the actual facts of Greek life; but my object is not so much to set out on a task of this kind as to suggest that it should be attempted. Every student of Greek or Roman history who will bear in mind these Aristotelian principles, and apply them as *criteria* as he advances in his study, will not only find his work become more interesting and instructive, but will gain a deeper insight into the problems of social and national life, at all times and in every kind of State. I will content myself by taking a single State, and that the greatest of all City-States, and briefly testing it by these *criteria* in the days when it was most sorely afflicted by *stasis*.

We have as yet seen Rome only in the days of her growth and her prosperity, overcoming perils of faction and perils of war by her political good sense and her tenacity of purpose, and working up to a certain perfection of government,—not the best form of government (for oligarchy can never be the best), but one well adapted, when used in a moderate spirit, to carry out those ends for which Rome seemed destined. We left her towards the end of the sixth century of her existence, at the time when Polybius was describing her political

[1] *Politics*, 1337 A : cf. 1332 A.

system with admiration and awe, little dreaming of the troubles that were to come upon her, and apparently blind to the social rottenness lying beneath the imposing structure of her constitution. Within a few years after Polybius recorded his observations, Rome was torn asunder by *stasis*, which under varying phases lasted for a whole century, and brought with it evils as terrible and as weakening as those described by Thucydides.

The revolution begun by Tiberius Gracchus in 133 B.C. cannot indeed be aptly compared to the little storms, furious as they sometimes were, which raged in the small City-States of the Greeks. No sooner do we try to probe to the bottom this great *stasis* of Rome, than we find it complicated by so many side-issues, and by problems so vast in their reach and complexity, that we instinctively feel ourselves passing into a new region of politics, in which, if we are to judge fairly, we must adjust our judgment by some other standard than that of the πόλις.

But it is true indeed that this *stasis* sprang, as Aristotle says all such quarrels will, from inequality and from inequality in the distribution of wealth; in its first beginning it can be treated as the *stasis* of a City-State. The oligarchy which had been so long in power, and had steered Rome through so many perils, had also slowly absorbed the land of the State; to inequality in power they added inequality of wealth, and the "people," accustomed to have their affairs managed by trustees in whom they placed implicit confidence, tacitly

acquiesced in this state of things, and let the
dangerous process go on unheeded. When at last
the counter-claim is made by Tiberius Gracchus,—the
claim of the many for equality in wealth,—*stasis* at
once sprang up. The oligarchy found their material
interests assailed, and naturally used their constitutional advantages to defend them; Gracchus, in
attacking their possessions, found it necessary also
to attack their political fortress. He tried to put
the oligarchical Senate aside, and to call to life
again the dormant sovereignty of the people: and
if he had stopped there, no serious harm need have
been done. But he was tempted to break other
sacred traditions of a revered constitution, and in
his hurry and enthusiasm he put himself in the
position of a tyrant; and he paid for his rashness
with his life. " Ubi semel recto deerratum est, in
præceps pervenitur."

So far we seem to see no more than the
phenomena which Aristotle described. But trace
the revolution a little further, and we find ourselves
getting beyond the limits of the City-State, and of
the political reasoning of its philosophers. The
interests involved are not merely those of Rome
and her citizens—the whole population of Italy has
a claim to make; a claim to share in the advantages of Roman citizenship, analogous to that of the
plebeians in days gone by, but infinitely more far-
reaching in its importance to Rome and to the
world. The dependencies which Rome has subdued
have also their claim; not yet a claim for citizenship, but a claim to be governed equitably, to

retain the material means of development and
prosperity, and to be adequately protected against
the threatening attacks of barbarian enemies. Such
claims created problems for the Roman statesman
such as no πολίτης had ever yet had to solve, and
such as had never yet been dreamed of in the philosophy of the πόλις. And we must leave them for
the present, for they have no direct connection with
those internal causes of decay which are the subject
of this chapter. I shall return to them in the
next, and show how they arose as the result mainly
of another set of disintegrating agencies, which we
may call external; and in my last chapter I shall
endeavour to explain how they were finally solved.

But if Aristotle's philosophy of political life did
not embrace such problems as those of the Roman
Empire, we may still ask how far the preventives
which he prescribes for *stasis* had been adopted or
could have been acted on at Rome. Did the
senatorial government, that focus of all Roman experience and wisdom, seek to maintain a vigorous
and comfortable middle class; and did they pay
any attention to the problem of education, or endeavour to have the sons of Rome brought up in
harmony with the best traditions and the growing
needs of the State?

We saw that Rome won her position as a leading
city in Italy by the steady obedience and devotion
of her army of freeholders. The Servian census
reveals beyond doubt a middle class such as
Aristotle thought the best for a healthy state—a
middle class of agriculturists; and this class

continued to exist, if not always to flourish, in the
first two centuries of the Republic, and was also
largely recruited from populations conquered and
absorbed. But during those same centuries we
find a process at work which is incompatible with
the permanent maintenance of that middle class,
and which no legislation seemed capable of effectually checking. The land of Italy is in this period
slowly and surely passing into the hands of wealthy
Romans, plebeian as much as patrician; and as
cattle-breeding pays better than tillage, and winter
pasture is needed for the vast herds which occupy
the higher lands in summer, the small freeholder of
the valleys is gradually got rid of by fair means or
foul, and his land absorbed into the great man's
estate. Nor is he even maintained as a day-
labourer, or allowed, like the Lacedæmonian
Helot, to till the land in return for a proportion
of its fruits; for all that was needed could be done
by slaves at a much smaller expense; and slaves
were cheap, owing to the vast number of prisoners
taken in the endless wars. Nothing was left for
the freeholders of the middle class, who had once
been the very marrow of the State, but to take
refuge in Rome itself. There they could not be
suffered actually to starve, for they were still
wanted for the wars; and there, too, they enjoyed
the privilege of exercising their rights as Roman
citizens. But they no longer represented Aristotle's
τὸ μέσον, and they had no longer the virtues
of the agricultural class which he would have encouraged. They were idle and poverty-stricken,

like the "mean whites" of the Southern States of
America before the emancipation of the negroes;
and they came at last to have all the vices of an
idle proletariat in a great city. Thus the middle
class of the Roman State disappeared, and with its
disappearance came in due time the inevitable
stasis. Efforts were made from time to time to
stay the growing evil, but it could not be effectually
stayed except by interfering with the property of
the ruling class, or by doing away with their system
of slave-labour. It was to the oligarchy that the
disease was due, and it could not be cured so long
as the oligarchy was in power.

And lastly, how far were the Romans conscious
of Aristotle's other safeguard? Did they bring up
their children on any system suited to maintain the
character of their State, or capable of growing with
it as it grew?

In the youth of Rome there had been an
education of unquestionable value, through which
all citizens passed; not an education of the mind,
but an education of the will and of the body, well
suited, like that of Sparta, to preserve the ἦθος of
the State, and adequate to carry it through all its
early perils. This was the education of the *patria
potestas*, supplemented by the discipline of military
training and service. Every Roman son, whatever his age might be, was under the strictest
control of his father; his very life was always in
the hands of him to whom he originally owed it.
When called to arms, he was equally under discipline; for the dread *imperium* of the consul was

unlimited in the field, and the refractory soldier could be punished with instant death.

Such an education of obedience, stern and rude as it seems to us, was of infinite value to the Romans in the career for which they were marked out, for, as Mr. Bagehot has so emphatically put it, the people that can obey is the fittest to survive. And it would still have been of value, though alone it could not have been wholly adequate, even when Rome had passed beyond the limits of the City-State, and entered on new duties and responsibilities; just as our own public school education, though not highly intellectual for the majority of boys who pass through it, is yet a discipline excellently well suited to the needs of a great empire. For a people whose lot is to conquer and to rule, an education of the will and of the body is indispensable, though it is not all that is needed.

But by the time when *stasis* first began to be formidable at Rome, even this excellent training was no longer what it had been. Like so many other Roman institutions, the *patria potestas* survived, but had lost its old virtue; the form of it remained, but the spirit had vanished. The discipline of military life was also fast becoming weaker: the best generals of this age, such as Scipio the Younger, Metellus, and Marius, had as much trouble with their troops as with the enemy. And with the old education thus breaking down, Rome had to meet an entirely new set of responsibilities. The whole end of her existence had changed by the close of the sixth century,—to keep to Aristotelian language, the ἔργον of the State was no longer the same as in her youth. She had resisted enemies and conquered them; but she had now to organise and rule them, to develop their resources and to Romanise them, and to do this work with justice as well as force. What education had she now, to fit her to cope with such a task as this?

A new education had indeed come into fashion, and one of a more intellectual type; but it was wholly inadequate to meet the demands which the world was now making on the Roman. The young man now learnt rhetoric, chiefly from Greeks, and from Greeks of a degenerate age; he learnt the art of making black look like white, and of reconciling consciences to what they inwardly feel to be wrong. Rhetoric might be supplemented by philosophy, but even this was not of a character to train the mind and will to just and generous action. The teachers of childhood were for the most part slaves, and the tutors of youth were Greek rhetoricians; from neither was it to be expected that the Roman could be trained in virtue and self-restraint. And as the temptations of the age were manifold, the Roman character utterly gave way; the characteristics of the period of the revolution are want of principle, unbridled selfishness, recklessness, and cruelty, in all classes. We need not be surprised that *stasis*, when it came, raged with such bitterness and for so long, for the State was left without any safeguard to avert it or to modify it.

I cannot forbear from concluding this chapter

with a passage from Plutarch's life of Cato the
Elder, in which he describes the education given to
his son by a man who was enlightened as well as
austere. It was an exception to the general rule,
and had it been generally imitated, the history of
the later Republic might have been very different.

> " As soon as the dawn of understanding appeared, Cato
> took upon himself the office of schoolmaster to his son,
> though he had a slave named Chilo, who was a respectable
> grammarian and taught several other children. But he did
> not choose (he tells us) that his son should be reprimanded
> by a slave, or pulled by the ears if he happened to be slow
> in learning ; or that he should be indebted to so mean a
> person for his education. *He was therefore himself his*
> *preceptor in grammar, in law, and in the necessary exercises.*
> For he taught him not only how to throw a dart, to fight
> hand to hand, and to ride ; but to box, to endure heat and
> cold, and to swim in the roughest and most rapid parts of
> the river. He wrote histories for him, he further ac-
> quaints us, with his own hand in large characters ; so that,
> without stirring out of his father's house, he *might gain a*
> *knowledge of the illustrious actions of the ancient Romans,*
> *and of the customs of his country.* And he was as careful not
> to utter an indecent word before his son, as he would have
> been in the presence of the Vestal virgins." [1]

This is the older Roman education at its very
best, fulfilling entirely the Aristotelian condition
that the object of education should be to make the
best of every individual in order to preserve the
ἦθος of the State. Nothing is said in it of learning
Greek ; and we know from this same biography
how bitterly Cato distrusted the growing influence
of ˙Greek rhetoric on the young Roman. But Rome

[1] Plutarch, *Cato major*, ch. xx.

was now ceasing to be a true City-State, and to
have an ἦθος of her own in which she could train
up her sons; and Cato was hardly in his grave
when the new education began to gain ground, a
mixture of Roman and Greek culture, less valid for
public and private morality, but more in harmony
with the life of a State which had absorbed all
other States into one far-reaching dominion.   We
might almost say that Cato's life and precepts are
the last, and not the meanest, fruit ever produced
by the ancient form of polity.

CHAPTER X

In the last chapter we made a rapid survey of the operation of *stasis*, as the most striking agent of disintegration in the life of the City-State. We saw that under the influence of this disease, which may be described as internal, organic, and natural to this form of State, unity of feeling and of action tended to disappear, and that with it vanished also much of that youthful health and beauty which we associate with all that is Greek in the best days of Greece.

But there were other causes of decay at work, which for want of a better word we may call *external*; causes, that is, which did not spring so directly from the inner life and the true nature of the City-State as such. These were influences acting from without upon that inner being of the πόλις, modifying it and even distorting it, and often combining with *stasis* to destroy it altogether. In order to make it plain what these external influences were, I must revert for a moment to the distinction between the ancient and the modern form of State which was explained in the first chapter.

The ancient form of State was there described as a city with an adjunct of territory; the citizens being really members of a City-Community, not merely inhabitants of a territory which happens to have a convenient capital town. From this definition it follows that the true City-State should not have too large a territory; for the larger the territory, the less truly would the inhabitants realise their membership of the City-Community. Men living at a great distance from the city, which was the heart and life of the State, could not share adequately in that life, or feel the pulse-beat of the organism to which they belonged. They would be apt to develop interests of their own apart from their interests as members of the State; and thus the essential fact of the true life of the πόλις, the identification of the individual with the State, would be less completely realised in their case. It follows, too, that there must be a limit to the population of a City-State; for a large territory is necessary as a rule to a large population, and if the one is unsuited for the realisation of perfect unity, so also will the other be.

The size of its territory and population was thus a very important question for every City-State, and as we should naturally expect, Aristotle was well aware of this. When he is considering the external features of his ideal State, *e.g.* its geographical position, and the conditions under which it will be and remain free and self-sufficing, and adequate in every respect for its population, he also discusses the question of its size and the proper limits of its increase.   The gist of what he says is as follows : [1]—

There is a certain limit of size, he tells us beyond which the πόλις ceases to be at its best; though many Greeks erroneously believe that the greater the population and territory, the greater will the State be.   Experience shows that the best governed States are not the largest ; in a very large State, for example, we shall not find *law* working with the best result.   Law is a kind of order, and good law is good order ; but a very great multitude cannot be orderly, at least without the aid of some divine power such as that which orders the whole universe.   States are like animals and plants, and even like products of human art, such as tools or ships, in that they cannot exceed a certain size without either losing their true nature, or at least without being spoilt for use.   Where, then, is this limit of size to be found ?   What test can we apply to a State in order to discover whether it has grown beyond its proper and natural size ?

The answer which Aristotle makes to these questions is at first sight a most singular one ; but it is all the more significant of the true nature of the πόλις.   "The true limit of the population of a State is the largest number which suffices for the [higher] purposes of life, and which *can be taken in at a single view*." [2]   Just as the πόλις begins

---

[1] *Politics*, 1326 A and B.

[2] " δῆλον τοίνυν ὡς οὗτός ἐστι πόλεως ὅρος ἄριστος, ἡ μεγίστη τοῦ

truly to exist when it is sufficiently large to realise the good life,—when it rises beyond the mere life of the village to the higher life of the State,—so it ceases to be a useful and beautiful State when it is too large to be easily taken in by the eye and mind of its members. And Aristotle is not writing vaguely or loosely here; he means something definite, as he invariably does. He tells us in the same passage that the citizens ought *to know each other's characters*, if they are to decide suits and to elect magistrates wisely; and also that they ought to be able to recognise foreign visitors and residents readily, so as to keep them outside of their own citizen-body, and to maintain their pure State character undeteriorated.

Aristotle is here, as usual in the *Politics*, only reflecting the normal phenomena of Greek political life; he is discarding the exceptional and (as he would call them) the unnatural tendencies of many States, and especially of the great commercial cities, such as the Athens of his day, and many of the great Greek colonies. He is picturing an ideal State, but he is copying its features from those of the Greek πόλις in its most typical form, indulging its most natural instincts. The true πόλις was, as we have seen, an independent and self-sufficing organism; it had its own tone and character, which its system of education was to keep up; and for

---

πλήθους ὑπερβολὴ πρὸς αὐτάρκειαν ζωῆς εὐσύνοπτος." *Politics,* iv. (vii.) 4 *fin.* I have ventured to insert the word "higher" in quoting Professor Jowett's translation; see Mr. Newman's remarks on this chapter, in his first volume, pp. 313, 314.

this to be realised at its best, the citizen body must be maintained of pure descent, and should be always ready to appear on the scene of State action in the market-place of the city itself. The best example of such a State was perhaps to be found in Sparta. Though Sparta violated some of the best Greek instincts, though her "good life" was not of the finest quality, yet in outward form and in the steady maintenance of her peculiar character, Sparta is a genuine City-State; and for this reason she often attracted the attention and admiration of reflecting Greeks. The same may also be said of Rome in the earlier stages of her history.

Now it is essential to notice the two principal ways in which Aristotle's limit of size could be exceeded, in order to understand how the City-State gradually came to suffer and to decay from external causes as well as internal. In the first place, it is obvious that if a State grew too large and powerful, and came to subordinate other States to itself, a twofold result would follow. The dominant State would be liable to lose its old State character, having to face new duties and responsibilities outside its natural sphere of action. And the conquered States would lose their true existence as πόλεις, being no longer self-sufficing and self-governing, and having in fact no longer any definite State character to maintain. They would resemble a fading photograph, whose colour changes, and whose outlines lose their sharpness. Thus imperial States, in which one city rules a number of others, were clearly not contemplated in Aristotle's political

reasonings; they could not, in his view, realise the
best life, and might do permanent harm to States in
which that best life flourished.

There is also another kind of State which Aristotle does not take into account; this is the *federation* or union of States with each other on equal
terms under a common central government.[1]   In a
true federation this common central government has
some definite controlling influence over the gover-
ments of the several States composing the union;
each of these therefore will have given up some
part of its own independence in order to obtain the
benefits of union, confessing, as it were, that it is not
strong enough to stand and flourish by itself.[2]   Now
it will be at once obvious that a union of this
kind, sufficiently centralised to be called a State in
itself as distinct from its component units, like
the United States of America, or the present Swiss
federation, must have been wholly out of harmony
with the instincts of the free and self-sufficing City-
State; and in fact it is not probable that such a
federation ever existed in Greece until the best
days of Greek life were over.   In Greece the City-
State seems to have had a peculiar repugnance to
this form of union.   The Greeks felt instinctively
that by entering into such federations each πόλις
would lose its own peculiar tone and character, its

[1] The only passage which can be construed into an allusion to
such a federation is in *Politics*, iv. (vii.) 7, 3, 1327 B; and here
it is only spoken of as a necessary condition of Hellenic rule over
barbarians, not as desirable for Hellas itself.

[2] See the most recent discussion of this question in Sidgwick's
Elements of Politics, ch. xxvi.

lively interest in its own political affairs, or even
the efficacy and importance of its own religious
worships ; a feeling inherited from the time when
international relations, as we call them, hardly
existed, and when the citizen of each State was a
total stranger and practically an enemy to the
citizen of every other.

Yet it is most interesting to notice, as we pursue
the history of the City-State century by century,
that our attention is drawn more and more to the
appearance both of imperial and federative States.
The two forms were in Greece very closely connected together ; for federations either came into
existence to resist encroaching cities, or they themselves were slowly but surely converted into imperial States. In these tendencies we cannot fail
to see evidence of the fading individuality of the
true City-State ; we see it passing under new
conditions of life, which in Aristotle's view and in
that of the ordinary Greek of the best age were
incompatible with its existence in perfection, and
with the " good life " of its individual members.

In order, then, to gain some idea of the external
causes, as I have called them, which enfeebled and
finally destroyed the City-State, our plan will be to
take a rapid survey of the growth of federative and
imperial States from the sixth century B.C. onwards ;
and this is what I propose to do in the remainder
of this chapter. Such a sketch must necessarily be
very cursory and imperfect, but it may be sufficient
to mark out the ground for more elaborate studies,
and to give them a definite meaning and object. It

will be convenient to divide the history of Greece for this purpose into three periods—

1. Before the Persian wars.
2. From the Persian wars to the rise of Macedon.
3. From the rise of Macedon to the final conquest by Rome.

1. Down to the time of the Persian wars it may be said that though we find here and there a league or alliance, the πόλεις composing them remained politically independent. There were ancient alliances, for example, for the protection of a temple and its worship. Of these the most famous is the Amphictionic League for the protection of the temples of Apollo at Thermopylæ and Delphi, and for the carrying out of Apollo's precepts for the conduct of the several members towards each other. But this was in no true sense a union of πόλεις; it was one of races,—Dorians, Achæans, Malians, etc., and probably dates from an age before the full development of the City-State. On the politics of a later age it has only an incidental influence, and does not call for further consideration here. It was a civilising and a unifying influence, but not a union in any true political sense. Other leagues, originating probably after the development of the πόλις, are also found among the Achæan cities in the north of the Peloponnese, in the Ionic colonies of Asia Minor, in Arcadia, and elsewhere; but these also were far from being permanent political federations, so far as our knowledge enables us to judge. They are only found in districts inhabited by the

same stock, and they indicate "no inward organic development of the πόλις."[1] They are simply groups of independent πόλεις without real political cohesion. There was indeed one league, that of the Bœotian cities, which even in the sixth century may have approached to the nature of a federation; but our knowledge of it in that period is extremely scanty, and I shall have an opportunity of adverting to it later on.

There were, however, certain centralising forces at work in Greece in the sixth century, one at least of which must be taken into account. Apart from the influence of the Delphic oracle, and the Olympic and other games, which brought the Greeks into more intimate relations with each other, and accentuated the feeling that they all belonged to a common race as distinct from the "barbarian," we have to notice the tendency of one City-State to assert a political predominance over others in the direction at once of empire and federation. This State was Sparta; the very one, it is curious to note, which in the following century assumed the position of champion of the free and self-sufficing πόλις against another far more dangerous centralising power.

By the middle of the sixth century, says Herodotus, Sparta had *subdued* the greater part of the Peloponnese; that is, she was already mistress of a

---

[1] See Holm, *Gesch. Griech.* vol. iii. p. 511. Such unions may have come into play only from time to time, as was the case with the "συγκρητισμός" of the Cretan cities; G. Gilbert, *Handbuch*, ii. 218. and reff.

small empire (ἀρχή).[1] But this empire, if indeed the word can be applied to it, extended only over the south of the peninsula, and it was Messenia alone whose State life was wholly destroyed by it. Over the Peloponnese generally Sparta claimed only a leadership (ἡγεμονία), and this meant no more than the first place in a military alliance of all the cities with the exception of the Achæans in the north, and Argos, Epidaurus, and Trœzen in the east. This alliance, it is true, shows a certain tendency towards centralisation, and we have some evidence that Sparta even interfered in the internal affairs of the cities so far as to put down the tyrannies prevalent at this time.[2] She also put forward claims to a leadership of all Hellas, and tried, though with little success, to meddle with the constitutions of States beyond the Peloponnese, and especially of Athens. But this was under a king of remarkable talent and great energy, Cleomenes I.; and even he failed to secure the adherence of the allies to his schemes for bringing a tyrant back to Athens. The story of this attempt, as told by Herodotus, shows plainly enough how loose the alliance was, and how firmly the idea of independence held its ground even among the Peloponnesian cities.[3]

Besides Sparta there was in Greece at this time

[1] Herod. i. 68, 69. Busolt, *Lakedaimonien*, p. 245 foll. It is difficult to explain this early aggressiveness of the Spartans, which ceased to be characteristic of them later on.

[2] Herod. v. 92, 2 ; Thucyd. i. 18.

[3] Herod. v. 92. 93.

but one other influence which made for political centralisation, namely, the influence of the great tyrants. I have already pointed out the tendency of these to open up relations with other States, and also to conquer or maltreat them for their own private ends. I illustrated this tendency by the example of Polycrates, the mighty master of Samos ; and this Polycrates did actually for a short time acquire something in the nature of a naval empire over the islands of the Ægean.[1] But tyrannies were short-lived, and Polycrates' dominion fell with him. Neither tyranny nor hegemony could force the Greeks out of their chosen path of autonomy, out of the inherited instincts—the εἰωθότα νοήματα of the race as a whole. We may fairly conclude that the whole weight of Greek feeling was at this period entirely at variance with all genuine attempts to blurr the sharp outlines of the individual life of the City-State.

2. With the Persian invasions a new era begins in the external history of the City-State. Their immediate result was to force upon Greece a temporary and imperfect union, and for the first and almost the only time, a general congress of Greeks met together to discuss how the common danger could best be met.[2] No sooner had this danger passed away than the unifying forces ceased to work ; but the Persian power has henceforward a marked influence on the political relations of the Greeks. The cities had been taught that they could not resist such an enemy without some kind

[1] Herod. iii. 39.　　　　[2] Ib. vii. 145.

of cohesion ; but they had learnt the lesson imperfectly and reluctantly.   From this time onward
we have two forces at work side by side in conflict
with each other, and combining to wear out the
vitality of the individual States.   One of these is
the desire of leading States to organise confederacies
under pretext of successive dangers from Persia, or
from some Greek city which had grown too powerful ;
the other is the reluctance of the πόλεις to coalesce
into such unions.   These two forces act and react
on each other throughout the whole of this period.

The familiar story need not be here repeated
how Athens and Sparta gradually fell apart after
Salamis, and how Athens formed a great naval
league for the defence of the Ægean, Sparta retaining her old leadership of the Peloponnesian States
and a few others.   Thus Greece came to be split
into two great alliances ; the one an old and well-
tried institution under the foremost military and
aristocratic State, representing the conditions of
Hellenic development before the Persian wars ; the
other an entirely new organisation under the newly
risen naval leader, representing that spirit of popular
intelligence and political progress which we have
seen ripening into the democracy of Pericles.
Neither of these alliances, however, was a real federal
union ; neither had a common central government
sufficiently strong to constitute a State power in
itself apart from the governments of its component
units.   The keen edge of true city life was not at
first seriously blunted either by the confederacy of
Delos or by the Peloponnesian League.   It might

have been as well if the former at least could have
been established on a true federal basis, even at some
small expense of autonomy to the cities; for the
direction taken by the league was towards empire,
not federation, and the Spartan alliance eventually
followed suit. But the cities would not readily
unite in any really useful or permanent federation,
and their unwillingness gave the leading State the
chance and the excuse to use force to compel them
to do it. Now both force and a leading State are
elements unnatural to a federation, and the ultimate
result was in this case not federation but an
Athenian empire.

The transformation of the Delian confederacy
into the empire of Athens is thus of the utmost
importance in the history of the City-State. We
do not know exactly by what successive steps the
change was brought about, but we have sufficient
material to estimate its nature and its influence on
the life of the πόλεις. To begin with, we can gain
a tolerably clear idea of the character of the confederacy of Delos from Thucydides' own words :[1]—

"Thus the Athenians by the good-will of the allies, who
detested Pausanias, obtained the leadership. They immediately fixed which of the cities should supply money and
which of them ships for the war against the barbarians, the
avowed object being to compensate themselves and the allies
for their losses by devastating the king's country. Then
was first instituted at Athens the office of Hellenic treasurers
(*Hellenotamiai*), who received the tribute, for so the impost
was termed. The amount was originally fixed at 460 talents.
The island of Delos was the treasury, and the meetings of

---

[1] Thucyd. i. 96 ; I quote Jowett's translation.

the allies were held in the temple. At first the allies were independent and deliberated in a common assembly under the leadership of Athens."

It is obvious from these words that every member of the league was as free in all essentials as before the league was formed. All agreed to follow a common foreign policy, and to support that policy by a common fund; but the treasury was at the neutral and sacred island of Delos, and though administered by Athenian officials, was so administered by the general consent of all. At Delos also the representatives of the cities met periodically, not to meddle with each other's affairs, but to deliberate on the policy of the whole league. This was certainly no more than a very loose form of federal union, though Athenian quickness and vigour supplied it with a centralising tendency far stronger than that of any league which had yet appeared in Greece.

But it was this very Athenian energy which constituted the weak point in it as a federation. The superior strength of one member of a league is, as I have already said, a serious difficulty in the way of a true federal union; and in this case the ever-increasing strength of Athens had its natural consequence. The league had been established in 475 B.C.; in little more than twenty years it had begun to pass into an Athenian empire. From 454 onwards we have sure evidence of this in inscribed documents, apart from the literary evidence of Thucydides.[1] It is important for our present pur-

---

[1] For the nature and contents of these documents, see Mr.

pose to see how the true freedom of the πόλεις was thus interfered with by the growing power of Athens.

A perfectly independent State must be able to take its own way without hindrance in at least four several departments of government; in finance, in judicial matters, in the form of its constitution, and in its foreign policy. If Ireland, for example, were wholly independent of Great Britain in these four points, she would constitute a separate State. Now, after 454 it may fairly be said that none of the members of the league were independent of Athens in all these particulars, and that some of them, at least, were subject to her in all. Let us take these points one by one.

1. The common fund had been transferred to Athens. A portion of the contributions was paid into the Athenian treasury; the assessment and administration were alike in Athenian hands. These contributions have therefore practically become a tribute paid to Athens. 2. In the case of some cities, at least, and perhaps of most, the most important lawsuits had to be taken to Athens for trial; and we know from an inscription that in criminal cases involving death, exile, or disfranchisement there was an appeal from one city (Chalcis) to the Athenian popular courts.[1] 3. Though Athens did not usually interfere with the constitution of the

Abbott's *History of Greece*, vol. ii. pp. 370 foll., and Appendix iii. ; Hicks, *Greek Historical Inscriptions*, pp. 29 foll. ; G. Gilbert, *Handbuch*, i. 402.

[1] Hicks, *op. cit.* No. 28 *fin.* p. 35.

cities if they were obedient and gave no trouble, she did not hesitate to do so if she deemed it advisable. She seems to have made separate treaties with individual cities, by which constitutions were set up in them under her own supervision ; and these were naturally of a democratic type.[1]   4. As is evident to every reader of Thucydides, the foreign policy of the "allies" was entirely controlled by Athens ; and, so far as we know, the synod of members which had originally been used to meet at Delos either ceased to exist or fell into utter insignificance.

It is plain, then, that the members of the league, some 200 in number, have ceased to be City-States in the true sense of the word ; that they are no longer free and self-sufficing.[2]   This will be made still more apparent from the following clause in the extant treaty with Chalcis containing an oath to be taken by all adult Chalcidians on pain of disfranchisement.

" I will not revolt from the people of the Athenians, in any way or shape, in word or deed, or be an accomplice in revolt. If any one revolts I will inform the Athenians.   I will pay the Athenians the tribute, which I can persuade them (to accept), and I will be a faithful and true ally to the utmost of my power.   I will help and assist the Athenian people if any one injures them, and I will obey their commands." [3]

---

[1] Treaties with Erythræ, Miletus, Colophon, and Chalcis are in part extant.   *Corp. Inscr. Att.* i. 9, 10, 11, and 13 ; iv. 22*a* and 27*a* = Hicks, No. 28.

[2] Read, for example, the speech of Euphemus, the Athenian envoy at Syracuse, in Thucyd. vi. 82 foll.

[3] This most telling document is translated in full by Mr. Abbott, vol. ii. p. 345 ; Hicks, *Greek Historical Inscriptions*, p. 34.

This Athenian empire is the leading fact in the period we are dealing with. Though it made Athens great and fruitful, it was the first serious blow dealt at the life of the true πόλις. And it had other results, more dangerous because more lasting. It had the natural effect of drawing the members of the other great union closer together, and of putting Sparta, after the downfall of Athens, into the position of their mistress instead of their leader. We saw that this Peloponnesian league was formerly a mere alliance, and that the cities were really autonomous ; even in foreign policy they could successfully press their views against Sparta. But the same change occurred here as in the case of the Delian League ; one State of overwhelming military strength made a fair and equal alliance impracticable, when once that State had been roused into full activity. Sparta began the Peloponnesian war by demanding autonomy for all Greek cities, and she ended it by reducing most of them to subjection ; she forced oligarchies upon them under the superintendence of Spartan " harmosts," and by the aid of Persian satraps compelled them to follow her foreign policy. She was too rough-handed, too ignorant of organisation, to elaborate such an empire as the Athenian ; but in most respects the cities were worse off under this champion of liberty than under the intellectual supremacy of Athens.[1]

The remainder of this period is occupied with

[1] Our knowledge of the Spartan Empire is, however, far less complete than of the Athenian ; see a discussion of the evidence in Holm. *Gesch. Griech.* iii. 15 foll.

the formation or concentration of other leagues, whose
object was to put an end to Spartan tyranny ;[1] and
throughout it we have the melancholy spectacle o
constant appeal on all sides to the Persian power
for aid.   The cities are not only getting accustomed
to the loss of autonomy at home, but also to the loss
of that common feeling of Hellenic freedom which
had sprung independently from the same root.   A
new Athenian league arose in 378 B.C., sheltered
at first under the power of Persia ; the object was
opposition to the tyranny of Sparta, so that the position and policy of the two leading States is now
exactly reversed.   In this union, which only comprised some seventy cities, and did not last long, the
autonomy of each State was guaranteed by Athens.
She was leader, but the contributions of the allies
were not called or considered tribute, and there was
little or no interference with their internal affairs.
The significance of this league is not great for our
present purpose ; but there is one feature in it
which is of real interest.   We know, not only from
historians, but from inscriptions, that the allies
were represented by commissioners (σύνεδροι) at
Athens.   This is clearly an attempt to reproduce
the most significant feature in the early constitution
of the confederacy of Delos,—that feature which
indicates most plainly an approach to a real federation.[2]

[1] Of one of these, which seems to have been the result of the
battle of Cnidus in 394, we know only from the evidence of coins ;
see a valuable note in Holm, iii. 54 foll.

[2] Hicks, *Historical Inscriptions*, No. 81 (C. I. A. ii. 17) ;
Diodorus, xv. 28.

But the Spartan Empire was also the cause of
the rise of another power, much stronger than the
new Athenian alliance, and more strikingly illustra-
tive of the growing weakness of the individual πόλις.
In Bœotia there had always been a league of cities,
and the physical conditions of the district seemed to
make a real federal union more possible here than
elsewhere in Greece proper. Bœotia was full of
cities, which were not separated from each other by
great mountain chains ; but one of these cities,
Thebes, was larger, stronger, and more renowned
than the rest. A true federation of equals was
therefore here again impossible ; and as Professor
Freeman has suggested, a συνοικισμός with Thebes,
like that of the Attic communities with Athens,
would have been a more practicable form of union.[1]
But the other Bœotian towns were probably much
stronger than the village communities of Attica, and
a loose federal union was the utmost they would
bear. Of the constitution of this union we know
very little ; but the one indisputable fact in it is
that Thebes constituted a centralising tendency
which was apt to irritate the other cities, and drove
Platæa and Thespiæ into the arms of Athens.[2]

It is obvious that under pressure of a common
danger this centralising tendency of Thebes would
rapidly gain ground. Thebes had missed her chance
in the Persian wars by ignobly taking the side of

[1] *History of Federal Government*, vol. i. 155 foll. The evidence
for this league is succinctly brought together by Gilbert, *Handbuch*, ii. 52 foll. Read Herod. vi. 108 ; Thucyd. iii. 53 ; iv. 76,
91, 92.

[2] Herod. v. 79 ; vi. 108 ; Thucyd. iv. 133.

the enemies of Greece. But against Athenian
aggression she only too gladly took the lead, and at
Delium in 424 was at the head of an army of an
almost united Bœotia. Thus the Athenian Empire
had its natural result in strengthening this league as
well as the Peloponnesian ; but it was the Spartan
Empire that completed the work by occupying the
Theban fortress with a garrison, and treating Thebes
as a dependency. The rise of Thebes to supremacy
in Bœotia was the result of a sudden revolt against
this Spartan tyranny. Only eight years after that
revolt (371 B.C.) Theban envoys could claim at Sparta
to be enrolled in the peace of that year, not as
Theban but as Bœotian. The policy of Thebes must
be the policy of Bœotia, and any rebellious city
must pay the penalty.[1] Orchomenus, the ancient
rival of Thebes, was utterly destroyed by Epaminondas himself. It would seem as though no City-
State could rise to power as the champion of Hellenic
autonomy without using that power to take her share
in destroying it. Athens, Sparta, Thebes, all in
turn yield to the temptation ; they deal successive
blows at the πόλις, and they all negotiate with
Persia for help in gaining their ends. Even such
a man as Epaminondas, a Greek man of action of
the noblest type, is not free from the prevailing

[1] So, too, with the coinage ; from 374 to 338 B.C. the other
Bœotian cities have no independent coinage ; see the Brit. Mus.
Catalogue of Greek Coins, *Central Greece*, introduction, p. xlii.
At this time there was a real federal currency, and the coins bear
the name not of any city, but of the federal magistrate. Orchomenus alone, the ancient rival of Thebes, issued a few "separatist"
coins of her own.

weakness. But as the determined enemy of the narrow Spartan spirit, he worked mainly in the right direction ; and his death at Mantinea in 362 B.C. deprived the Greeks of the only leader capable of dealing successfully with the dangerous man of genius who three years later ascended the throne of Macedon.

To sum up: in this period we find the Greek States much more ready than in the previous one to coalesce into leagues of real political importance. They combine, it is true, only under pressure from without ; at first against the Persian enemy, and later against the leading cities which successively convert their own leagues into powerful empires. Leagues, imperial States, and Persian arms and diplomacy, all have their share in wearing out the vitality of the individual cities ; the free and self-sufficing πόλις seems to be fading away, and it is hard to see what new political combination can be found to take its place.

3. A new period opens with the growth of the Macedonian power under Philip (359-336 B.C.). We are here chiefly concerned to notice the effect on the City-State, not only of the strength and policy of this new power, but also of the efforts of the Greeks themselves to counteract it.

At the time of Philip's accession the so-called Theban supremacy had just practically ended with the death of Epaminondas. There was now a kind of balance of power between the three leading States, Sparta, Athens, and Thebes, no one of which was greatly stronger than the others ; and such a balance could easily be worked upon by any great power from without. Thus when Macedon came into the range of Greek politics, under a man of great diplomatic as well as military capacity, who, like a Czar of to-day, wished to secure a firm footing on the sea-board of the Ægean, she found her work comparatively easy.

The strong imperial policy of Philip found no real antagonist except at Athens. Weak as she was, and straitened by the break-up of her new confederacy, Athens could still produce men of great talent and energy ; but she was hampered by divided counsels. Two Athenians of this period seem to represent the currents of Greek political thought, now running in two different directions. Demosthenes represents the cause of the City-State in this age, of a union, that is, of perfectly free Hellenic cities against the common enemy. Phocion represents the feeling, which seems to have been long growing up among thinking men at Athens, that the City-State was no longer what it had been, and could no longer stand by itself ; that what was needed was a general Hellenic peace, and possibly even an arbiter from without,[1] an arbiter not wholly un-Hellenic like the Persian, yet one who might succeed in stilling the fatal jealousies of the leading States. We may do well to compare the views of these two statesmen somewhat more closely.

---

[1] The connection between a general peace and a strong arbiter is curiously expressed by Dante in his *De Monarchia*, ch. iv. foll. The relation of the Greek cities to Macedon is not unlike that of the Italian States to the Empire in Dante's time : See Bryce's *Holy Roman Empire*, pp. 76 foll.

The Policy of Demosthenes.

Let us note, in the first place, that the efforts of Demosthenes to check Philip fall into two periods divided by the peace of Philocrates in 346 B.C. In the first of these he is acting chiefly with Athens alone ; Philip is to him not so much the common enemy of Greece as the dangerous rival of Athens in the north. His whole mind was given to the internal reform of Athens so as to strengthen her against Philip. In her relation to other Greek States he perhaps hardly saw beyond a balance of power ; and as Athens alone was far too weak to resist Macedon, this policy in which Demosthenes represents the old patriotism of the πόλις was doomed to certain failure.

It is true that after 346 his Athenian feeling seems to become more distinctly Hellenic.[1] But what could even such a man as Demosthenes do with the Hellas of that day ? He could not force on the Greeks a real and permanent union ; he could but urge new alliances. His strength was spent in embassies with this object, embassies too often futile. No such alliance could save Greece from the Macedonian power, as subsequent events plainly showed. What was needed was a real federal union between the leading States, with

[1] Traces of such a feeling are certainly to be found at an earlier date, *e.g.* in the speech for the Megalopolitans (352 B.C.) ; but I believe I am representing rightly the general change in the character of Demosthenes' public orations.· See Curtius, *Hist. of Greece.* vol. v. 251.

a strong central controlling force ; and Demosthenes' policy was hopeless just because Athens could never be the centre of such a union, nor could any other city.

Demosthenes is thus the last, and in some respects the most heroic champion of the old Greek instinct for autonomy. He is the true child of the City-State, but the child of its old age and decrepitude. He still believes in Athens, and it is on Athens that all his hopes are based. He looks on Philip as one who must inevitably be the foe alike of Athens and of Greece. He seems to think that he can be beaten off as Xerxes was, and to forget that even Xerxes almost triumphed over the divisions of the Greek States, and that Philip is a nearer, a more permanent, and a far less barbarian foe. Splendid figure as he is, the failure of Demosthenes shows clearly that the vitality of the πόλις has been greatly weakened since the Persian wars, and at the same time that the old instinct still has force enough to make a real and life-giving union impracticable.

The Policy of Phocion

This remarkable Athenian figure was the somewhat odd exponent of the practical side of a school of thought which had been gaining strength in Greece for some time past. This school was now brought into prominence by the rise of Macedon, and came to have a marked influence on the history of the City-State.

It began with the philosophers, and with the

idea that the philosopher may belong to the world as
well as to a particular city. When Socrates described
himself as κόσμιος, *i.e.* a citizen of the world, he
meant that the State did not bind him in everything,
that there was a world of duty and of thought
beyond and transcending the State.[1] We can recognise this feeling also in the Republic of Plato,
and connect it with a philosophical reaction against
the political life of the Athenian citizen. Athens
was far more open to criticism now than in the
days of Pericles; and a cynical dislike betrays itself
in the Republic for the politicians of the day and
their tricks, and a longing for a strong government
of reason, which Plato could find in no existing
Greek πόλις.[2] Not indeed that Plato really gave up
the πόλις as hopeless, or sought for a new form of
State to take its place. His object, as seen more
especially in his later work, the Laws, is rather " to
re-adapt it to the promotion of virtue and noble
living." [3] And it is true that the most practical
of all the thinking men of Greece, one who lived in
this age and was intimately connected with Macedon and her two great kings, has nothing to tell us
of the insufficiency of the πόλις as such; in his
eyes it was Nature's gift to man to enable him to
perfect himself in the " good life." Aristotle took
the facts of city life as they were and showed how
they might be made the most of. " Not a par-

---

[1] Bernays, *Phokion*, 31 ; Cic. *Tusc.* v. 108 ; Plutarch, *de
exilio*, 5. Cf. Butcher, *Demosthenes*, pp. 25, 26.

[2] See *e.g. Republic*, vi. 496 B.

[3] Newman, *Politics of Aristotle*, vol. i. 478.

ticle of his attention," says a great authority, " is
diverted from the πόλις to the ἔθνος.[1] But to him
Macedon was assuredly not wholly barbarian ; and
war to the death with her kings could not have
been to him as natural or desirable as it seemed to
Demosthenes. And though he has nothing to tell
us of Macedon, we can hardly avoid the conclusion
that his desire was for peace and internal reform,
even if it were under the guarantee of the northern
power, for the sake of the πόλις itself rather than
for the sake of gaining military strength to oppose
that power as an enemy.

Of this philosophical view of Greek politics
Phocion was in a manner the political exponent.
But his policy was too much a negative one ; it
might almost be called one of indifferentism, like the
feeling of Lessing and Goethe in Germany's most
momentous period. So far as we know, Phocion
never proposed an alliance of a durable kind, either
Athenian or Hellenic, with Macedon ; he was content to be a purely restraining influence.[2] Athens
had been constantly at war since 432 ; her own
resources were of the weakest ; there was little
military skill to be found in her, no reserve force,
much talk, but little solid courage. Athens was
vulnerable at various points, and could not possibly
defend more than one at a time, therefore Phocion

---

[1] Newman, *ib.* p. 479. Read also the valuable discussion of
the connection of Aristotle with Macedon, pp. 469 foll. Bernays,
Phokion, pp. 40 foll.

[2] Plutarch's *Life of Phocion*, ch. viii. ; " ἐπολιτεύετο μὲν ἀεὶ πρὸς
εἰρήνην καὶ ἡσυχίαν," etc. Cf. ch. xvi.

despaired of war, and the event proved him right. The faithfulness of the Athenians towards him is a proof that they also instinctively felt that he was right. But he was wanting on the practical and creative side, and never really dominated either Athens, Greece, or Philip.

There seems then to have been no way of saving the πόλις from the threatening power of Macedon, either by united resistance or by the acceptance of Macedonian leadership. A policy of resistance found the City-State too weak to defend itself; a policy of inaction would land it in a Macedonian empire which would still further weaken its remaining vitality. The first policy, that of Demosthenes, did actually result in disaster and the presence of Macedonian garrisons in Greek cities. The second policy then took its place, and initiated a new era for Greece. After the fatal battle of Chæronea (338 B.C.) Philip assumed the position of leader of the Greek cities. Inspired by his Greek education, by the memory of the Persian wars, by the career of the Spartan Agesilaus, and by the writings of Isocrates, he determined to lead a united Greece against Persia, and summoned representatives of the cities to meet him at the Isthmus as the first step. Assassination cut short his designs; but in his son Greece found a still mightier exponent of this idea of her true relation to Macedon. Under Alexander it was not Macedon that conquered the East, but Greece. And at home it was not only Alexander's generals who kept Greece under the influence of Macedon but Greeks and even Athenians,— Phocion

and Demetrius of Phalerum.¹ Thus the policy of
union and reorganisation for the πόλεις under the
strong guardianship of Macedon was the one which
was eventually successful; but it cost them the
loss of much of their remaining vitality as free and
self-sufficing political organisms. True, neither
Philip nor Alexander dealt hardly with the cities,
Thebes alone excepted; they left them nominally
free,² and they identified the interest of the Greeks
with their own. But they could and did interfere
with them whenever they chose, and without meeting with any successful resistance. Their forcible
supervision cast a great shadow upon the City-State,
dimming and almost obliterating the clear outlines
of its political life.

A great future was still before the Greek race,
which was yet to set its mark upon the world's
history, with a force it never could have exerted
under the older political system. But the πόλις,
the peculiar product of the political genius of the
Greeks, their true *home* in which all their choicest
work had been done, was now no longer their own.
They were like the freeholder of an ancient family,
who has mortgaged and lost his inheritance, but is
still allowed to live on in the old home as tenant.

¹ Of this philosopher-statesman, who was ἐπιμελήτης of Athens
under Cassander, and altered her constitution perhaps on the
model of Aristotle's ideal State, we should be glad to know more.
What little we do know will be found succinctly put together in
Thirlwall, *Hist. of Greece*, vol. vii. 355 foll.

² Alexander, for example, made proclamation of their autonomy
after the battle of Issus. See Plutarch's life of him, ch. xxxiv., and
cf. xvi. *fin.*

The essential charm of ownership was gone for them, and with it all the joy and intensity of social life; and though this very calamity might widen their mental horizon, and find them new interests and fresh work to do, the stream of their intellectual effort would never again run so clear and strong as in the days of the perfect freedom of the individual City-State.

Of the ultimate fate of the Greek cities I shall give some account in the next chapter. But it may be as well to follow out the story we have been pursuing by referring at once to the last attempt of the Greeks to recover political independence; especially as that attempt was for a time successful, and successful just because the old instinct of autonomy had steadily become feebler, and the cities were more willing than in the earlier periods to unite into real federal unions.

After Alexander's empire had been broken up, his successors on the throne of Macedon continued to press more or less heavily on the Greek cities. Though for the most part left nominally independent, they were not really so; more than one of them was a Macedonian fortress, and in others the old disease of tyranny, aided now by the Macedonian power, begins once more to appear. About 280 B.C. four cities of the old Achæan League, which had been dissolved by Alexander, united afresh in a more solid union than their former one. These were quickly joined by others, and in 251 Aratus of Sicyon compelled his native city to join the league. From this latter year we may date the

beginning of the first real federation which Greece
had ever known. This federation, of which Aratus
at once became the leading spirit, was beyond all
doubt what the Germans happily term a Bundes-
staat, as distinguished from a Staatenbund ;[1] that
is, it constituted a State in itself, and was not
merely an alliance of perfectly independent cities.
Plutarch, who had studied it carefully, in order to
write his life of Aratus, thus briefly sketches it in
his later biography of Philopœmen (ch. viii.) :—

"Aratus was the first who raised the commonwealth of
the Achæans to dignity and power. For whereas before
they were in a low condition, scattered in unconnected cities,
he combined them in one body, and gave them a moderate
civil government worthy of Greece. And as it happens in
running waters that when a few small bodies stop others
stick to them, and one part strengthening another the whole
becomes one firm and solid mass, so it was with Greece. At
a time when she was weak and easily broken, dispersed in
a variety of independent cities, the Achæans first united
themselves : and then attaching some of the neighbouring
cities by assisting them to expel their tyrants, while others
voluntarily joined them for the sake of that unanimity
which they beheld in so well constituted a government, they
conceived the design of incorporating Peloponnesus into one
great power."

The general idea of the character of the League
which is here indicated is borne out by the valuable
evidence of Polybius, whose connection with it in
its later days was an important though a melancholy
one. Chiefly from him we learn the following
significant facts.[2] Unlike the older Greek leagues,

---

[1] Freeman, *Comparative Politics*, p. 387.
[2] Polyb. ii. 37. The evidence from coins is here interesting, as

in which some dominant city was almost always an
element of insecurity, the Achæan federation was
composed of cities among which no single one was
decidedly preponderant; each of these had one vote
only in the common assembly, which was held in
the later period of the League at least turn by turn
in all of them. And further, the central government
was a strong one, consisting of a single στρατηγός or
general, assisted by a council of ten, and having for
the year of his office complete administrative and
executive power. The central government thus
constituted exercised control over the foreign policy
of the League, over its military resources, its
finance, coinage, and weights and measures. What
was the judicial and constraining power which supported the central government we do not clearly
know; but we can hardly doubt that there was a
judicial tribunal of some kind common to the whole
League.[1]

These facts show beyond question that the
Achæan federation formed a State in itself as
distinct from the States composing it; and in this

showing that some important cities, *e.g.* Argos and Sicyon, issued
their own coinage independently of that of the League. Hence we
learn (1) that the spirit of autonomy was still alive in them, and
(2) that though no one city was preponderant, a few were far
more powerful than the rest,—many in fact being still mere
villages. See Brit. Mus. Catalogue, *Peloponnesus*, p. 24 foll.

[1] The evidence for this constitution is to be found discussed in
Freeman's *History of Federal Government* (unfortunately a difficult
book to procure), vol. i. 236 foll.; or in a more concentrated form
in Gilbert, *Handbuch*, ii. 110 foll. The authorities are chiefly
Polybius, Livy's later books, Plutarch's Lives of Aratus, Cleomenes
and Philopœmen, and a few passages in Pausanias, etc.

consists at once its peculiarity and its significance in Greek history. As in all true federations, the members were quite free to manage their own local affairs, but by uniting into one great State they now at last made confession that those local affairs were no longer of absorbing interest. Even now it is curious to notice that the more famous cities, Athens, Sparta, Corinth, which had once drawn their health and strength from the older system, were always reluctant to come into the League; but among the lesser ones at least the old passion for autonomy has fretted itself away, and they are now able to unite without misgivings or jealousies.

But this new form of State proved hardly more capable of defending or uniting Greece than the one which had gone before it. To increase its strength the Achæan League sought to compel other cities to join it, and to attain this object it allied itself with the very enemy whose encroachments had called it into existence. The rivalry and hatred between the League and Sparta is the saddest fact in the last pages of Greek history; and when we find Achæans under such a Greek as Philopœmen united with Macedon in crushing the noblest of all Spartan kings on the heights of Sellasia, we feel that the City-State and Pan-Hellenic feeling are vanishing away together, and that with them passes also all that is best and noblest in the most gifted of all races.

CHAPTER XI

IT has often been said that the history of Greece
starts afresh with the conquests of Alexander. True
as this is in many ways, it is not really true of the
political life of the Greeks. The Greek City-State
makes no fresh start at this point, but languishes on
in gradual decay for nearly three centuries.

Yet Greece, through Alexander, her foster-child
and pupil, came herself very near to the discovery
of a new political system. For the few short years
of Alexander's manhood it must have seemed as
though the City-State were to escape further linger-
ing decay, and to pass at once into a new existence
as the organised material of a great empire. Just
as the Greeks were now to turn their intellectual
gifts in new directions, so it seemed as if they were
about to put their peculiar political creation to a
new use. In the marvellous career of Alexander,
it is easy to forget that he was at heart a Greek,
and that he identified himself and his aims with
Greece and her ancient aspirations ; but this must

be clearly understood, as well as the ideas of empire which were fermenting in his mind, if we would see how the Greeks had once the chance of anticipating the work of Rome, and how it came about that they lost it.

Even in Philip, as we saw in the last chapter, the desire for empire was combined with the conviction that such empire must be founded on a basis of Greek civilisation. Philip is, as has often been said, one of those men of whose inner history we would fain know more. His respect for Greek culture, combined with his strife for empire, make him one of the most singular figures in history. He dealt gently with Greece; he respected the Greek religion; he called on the Greeks to unite with him in freeing their Asiatic brethren from Persian domination. But in his son, whose character has come down to us as clearly as the features on his coins, we see the Greek influence most unmistakably. It is just this Greek side of Alexander's nature, or at least the result of a thoroughly Greek training on his mind, which gives Plutarch's biography its special value as distinct from other accounts of him; and it may be as well to dwell on this for a moment if we would appreciate the bearing of his brief and wonderful life on the history of the City-State.

Plutarch's portrait of Alexander is that of a man whose power of self-restraint (σωφροσύνη) makes him even more Greek than most Greeks of his day, in spite of an occasional outbreak of passion.[1]   It is

---

[1] Plutarch, Alex. 21-23 ; cf. 40.   "τοῦ νικᾶν τοὺς πολεμίους τὸ κρατεῖν ἑαυτοῦ βασιλικώτερον ἡγούμενος."

a portrait also of one in whom can be discerned a
humanity and sensibility which are perhaps not
essentially Greek, but might well be the result of a
Greek education on a fine semi-Hellenic mind.[1] And
Plutarch also depicts him as feeling his permanent
source of strength to be Hellenic, and looking upon
his Macedonians as little more than necessary tools.
Allowing something for Plutarch's Hellenism, we
find that the facts bear out these statements. " The
Greeks are demigods among Macedonian brutes,"
Alexander cried in one of his fits of passion. The
Greek Eumenes was his secretary ; with Aristotle,
his former tutor, and Phocion, who understood his
aspirations, he is said to have kept up correspondence.[2] The boys in Babylon were educated in Greek fashion, though they were taught
the Macedonian drill. After the battle of Issus
he sent a portion of the spoils to Greek cities as far
distant as Croton, and at the same time made
proclamation of their autonomy. He told the
Athenians, after the destruction of Thebes, " to
attend to affairs, as they would have to rule Greece
if anything happened to him ; " and even if this
last story be only an Athenian invention, the fact
that it could be invented is itself significant.[3]

It seems, then, that whether we look at his
character, or at his conduct towards the Greeks,
and his respect for their culture, Alexander had
advanced a long way beyond his father in his
acknowledgment of the claims of the Hellenic

[1] Plutarch, *Alex.* 27 *sub fin.*, 29, 39 *sub fin.*
[2] *Ibid.* 39 ; cf. 17 *sub fin.*   [3] *Ibid.* 13.

genius. But we have also to consider what he did, or meant to do, as a military Statesman representing Greece. English writers, with the exception perhaps of Thirlwall, have not taken a high view of Alexander's schemes of empire; but the following facts seem to have been sufficiently proved by the one great modern historian of this and the following age.[1] *First,* he projected the foundation of cities throughout his conquests, to be peopled as far as possible by Greeks, and governed under Greek constitutional forms; and it is matter of history that he himself actually began this work. Not only the new foundations of Tyre and Gaza, and the still more famous Alexandria, attest his intention of carrying the Greek πόλις into his new dominions, but also many cities in the far east, even in Afghanistan and India, in which we now know that there was a Greek element, though they were largely made up of the native populations. Alexander indeed himself was cut short at the outset of his work; but it was carried on by the successors among whom his empire was divided, and especially by Seleucus, who left a great name behind him as a founder of cities. *Secondly,* it is beyond question that Alexander had in his mind the establishment of a great system of world-commerce, which should draw together Greece and Egypt and the East, and of which the Nile, the Tigris, and the Indus were to be the principal channels.

Combining these facts with what we have

---

[1] Droysen, *Hellenismus,* vol. iii. The same view is taken by Professor Gardner in his *New Chapters of Greek History,* ch. xiv.

already seen of Alexander's Hellenic feeling, we can hardly avoid the inference that the idea was present to his mind of Hellenising the world by means of cities and communications, and that he looked upon Hellenic civilisation as the only existing cement capable of holding together the structure of a universal empire.

It is hardly necessary to point out what would have been the result for the City-State of such an empire as this, had it been possible for Alexander or his successors to realise it. The Greek race as a whole might have gained much, but the πόλις would have sunk into the position of a municipal town. Each State would have lost at once and for ever those very conditions of life in which had been nurtured all that was most brilliant in the Greek character; that absolute freedom and independence of all others, which brought thought and action into such perfect harmony, and gave to the life of every citizen a unique value in relation both to himself and his State. This at least would have been the loss of a people who had proved that they could bring their form of State very near to perfection. But the last two chapters will have shown in some degree that this form of State was very far from being any longer perfect; and from such an empire as that which Alexander's imagination suggested, something at least might have been gained for the Greeks, if not for their πόλις. Had he lived to carry out his great schemes, a new prospect of life, social, political, intellectual, might have opened before the Greek race : the whole stream of their infinite capacity might have been turned into a new channel. Even as it was, they left the mark of Hellenic genius in every land to which Alexander led them; and who shall say that such a people might not have developed also a system of law and government adequate to the needs of the human race from the Indus to the Adriatic?

But the idea and the possibility of such a system perished for the time with Alexander. At the moment of his death two problems called imperatively for solution, if the project of universal empire were to be carried out; and these two problems were equally insoluble. First, the Persians had to be combined with the Macedonians; secondly, the Macedonians had to be combined with the Greeks. The hopelessness of the first of these combinations made itself felt at once. The Macedonians would not accept as king the child of Alexander by an Oriental; and as they were the real instruments of conquest, with them lay the fatal decision. The Persians were ready, not the Macedonians. No union was possible save through a personality such as Alexander's had been, for there was no idea to ground it on, or none that was sufficiently clear and comprehensible. For the union of Macedonians and Greeks there might indeed have been some faint hope. There was one striking character, a Greek of culture, ability, and feeling, the subject of one of Plutarch's most interesting biographies, who continued to represent the union of Greece and Macedon for some time after Alexander's death. But Eumenes struggled in vain against a combination of uncultured rivals, and was finally betrayed by the Macedonians whom he had taught, as Plutarch tells us, to love and obey him.[1]

Alexander's empire was soon broken up into Macedonian satrapies or kingdoms. Greece was the continual prey of one of these, and the scene of struggle between others ; and the difficulty of maintaining these kingdoms, together with the rude character of their Macedonian rulers, led to continual wars between individual kings at the head of mercenary armies,—wars which seem for a time to deprive history of all its value. Meanwhile the Greeks, instead of finding new life and hope in a mighty political combination of which they, like their πόλις in its surrounding territory, were to have been the brain and life, were left to continue half-heartedly, weary and worn-out, in their City-States, under the ominous shadow of Macedonian kings, until some new power should appear with a political genius adequate to the organising of the world afresh.

Such a power at last appeared, after an interval of a century and a half, in that great City-State of the West whose political development has been already sketched. In tracing this development I intentionally dwelt upon those points which seemed to indicate that of all City-States Rome was the best equipped for the task of governing the world.

---

[1] It is possible that Plutarch's life of Eumenes may be too favourable, as based on the evidence of his fellow - townsman Hieronymus ; but it is not contradicted by other writers. Cf. Ranke, *Weltgeschichte*, vol. i. pt. ii. 221 foll.

We saw that from the beginning she was not a
wholly isolated community, but the member of a
Latin league, of which she made herself successively
the leader and the mistress. We have noticed the
strength of her early realisation of the meaning of
magisterial power and the ready faculty she displayed in the conception, and later in the extended
application, of legal ideas. We have seen in passing
how the habits and temperament of her people fitted
them for war and conquest, and how as early as the
age of kingship her military resources were fully
organised. And we traced in outline the steady
development of her institutions in the direction of
popular sovereignty, and the course of the counter-
current that brought her under the rule of an
oligarchy of wonderful aptitude for the detailed
business of government. It remains to explain
how Rome, herself a City-State, ceased at last to
be one; how in the vast reach of her endeavour
to deprive all others of their autonomous life, she
too lost the genius of the πόλις. And we must
take also a glance, however rapid and superficial,
at the system of universal empire which Romans,
rather than Rome, succeeded at last in creating
out of the old materials.

Almost before her history can be truly said to
begin, the Roman territory had already exceeded
the limits which Aristotle regarded as sufficient for
the perfect City-State. When Alexander died at
Babylon in 323 B.C. she had reduced her own
kindred, the Latins, together with other peoples in
her vicinity, and was engaged in a deadly struggle

with the hardy stocks of the interior of the peninsula. While his successors were fighting amongst
themselves, and wasting the strength of Greece by
the loss of one mercenary army after another, Rome
was conquering and organising all Italy, and wrest-
ing from Carthage the empire of the Western Mediterranean. During the age of the struggles and
intrigues of the Achæan League, she was going
through her mortal conflict with Hannibal, in the
course of which she acquired a Spanish dominion,
and from which she rose more formidable than ever,
to attack and ruin the Macedonian power itself.
Greece then passed under her protection, and before
long was united with Macedonia as a Roman province. The Greek king of Pergamus bequeathed
his kingdom to her; the one Greek City-State
which still retained a real independence and prosperity, the city and island of Rhodes, was her firm
friend and ally. Greek historians, and especially
the cosmopolitan Polybius, began to recognise a new
order of things in the world, and like Virgil
a century later, and Dante in the Middle Ages,
looked upon Rome, as destined from her foundation
to be the mistress of a mighty empire. By the
end of the second century B.C. that empire included
every valuable region of the Mediterranean except
Egypt, and a century later it stretched from the
Euphrates to the Atlantic.

And yet, during almost the whole of this period,
Rome continued to be in some sense a City-State,
and what is more, for some time at least believed
herself to be maintaining the free city-life of her

Greek subjects wherever it still existed. Civic life
and civic government are terms which perfectly
well express the nature of the Roman polity even
after all these conquests. The government which
conquered Spain and Africa, Syria and Gaul, was
essentially the same in form as that which had
ruled Rome when she had yet to conquer Italy.
The magistrates continued to convene the Senate
in Roman temples, to transact there the business of
the world; in the ancient Forum of Romulus the
" Roman people" still passed laws and ratified
treaties. Even after Rome had become the world's
emporium, and the resort of men of business and
learning from every quarter of the Empire, her
social life was still, as it was for Cicero,[1] that of a
City-State, and it was as a City-State that she still
ruled the world. And wherever she found the
City-State in existence among the cities she conquered, she retained it, if only as a matter of policy,
at least in its outward form and features.

We may best realise the truth of all this, and
the nature of the change which finally came over
the world, if we turn our attention for a moment to
the way in which the Roman oligarchy of the
Republic dealt with the conquered peoples. To
meet the needs of government as they successively
arose, the Roman Senate invented no new system;

---

[1] Cicero stands in this respect to Rome as Demosthenes to
Athens; he was the last-born legitimate son of the Roman City-
State. Perhaps this may be best seen illustrated in the second and
third books of his treatise, "De Legibus"; but it is obvious
throughout his writings, and is the real clue to the right appreciation of his political career.

adaptation rather than invention was what they chiefly excelled in. In dealing with their conquests they turned to account their faculty of adaptation in two distinct ways. First, they used their city-magistracy for the government of their new acquisitions; that dread *imperium*, which their fathers had handed down to them as the greatest political treasure of their State, they now simply extended in its full force over the vast territories they conquered. We saw (p. 108) that the consul in the field retained undiminished the *imperium* of the Rex. Now as fresh wars or rebellions might always be expected in the conquered lands, this undiminished *imperium*, *i.e.* supreme military and judicial power in combination, was utilised to do the required work. The consul, holding this power, presided over Italy as the sphere of his government (*provincia*). Even when the islands of Sicily and Sardinia were annexed, no new office was created; four prætors were elected, instead of two, and among these four the *provinciæ* were allotted, two of jurisdiction at home, two of government beyond the sea. Those who undertook these last held an *imperium* precisely equal in all essentials to that of the consul in the field; and like him they were in the eye of the law simply magistrates of the City-State of Rome. With a slight extension this simple system was maintained during more than two centuries. In course of time the *imperium* of consul or prætor came to be prorogued, as it was called, so that he might discharge the growing business of the home government during one year, and proceed

in the second to his provincial command; but
viewed constitutionally his magistracy was precisely
the same during both years. Thus the ancient
imperium of the City-State was found to be sufficient for all purposes of government, whether in
Rome, Italy, or beyond the sea.[1]

Secondly, wherever the Romans found City-
States in the countries they subdued, they retained
them together with their local institutions; modifying these so far as they deemed it advisable, but
rarely putting fresh ones in their place. This was
their policy in Italy, in Sicily, in Greece, in Asia,
wherever in fact the city-community had flourished
in any form. Occasionally indeed they destroyed
a city, as they wantonly destroyed Corinth; and
sometimes they might deprive it of all real self-
government, as they degraded Capua after the
Hannibalic war. But for the most part, both as
matter of convenience and policy, they let the local
magistrates and councils continue to administer the
local laws. Even in those provinces where the
City-State had never really existed, as in North
Italy and in Spain, they did all that could be done
to initiate city-life on the model of their own. Like
Alexander, they began the foundation of cities by
drawing the native population together into new
centres; and as time went on, colonies of the full
Roman, as well as of the inferior Latin franchise,
each a miniature Rome, with its own magistrates
and Senate, began to appear even in the transmarine

[1] Mommsen, *Staatsrecht*, vol. ii. pt. i. (ed. 2) 229 foll. Willems,
Droit public Romain, pp. 249 foll., 274 foll.

provinces. Neither Romans nor Greeks could think of civilised life apart from the city as a centre of business, government, and pleasure; and the Roman oligarchy, true to its practical instincts, saw also in the city a most convenient machinery for raising the taxes they imposed.[1]

It need hardly be said that it was the city, rather than the City-State, which they thus turned to account. Here is exactly the point at which we can best see how the older form of State slowly passed into an imperial one, forming, as it were, out of its old and well-worn material a fresh cellular tissue for a new political system. It will be by this time sufficiently obvious that the real life of the πόλις was now everywhere already extinct, or rapidly passing away. The bodily appearance was there, but the spirit had departed. Yet the material which remained could be turned to new purposes; the cities could become, by an easy transition, the municipal towns of an empire. Some few indeed were still nominally the allies of Rome, had their freedom guaranteed by treaty, and paid no taxes to the Roman Government; but all the rest were now to be treated as convenient centres of administration, and to pass under the control, more or less direct in various degrees, of the magistrates of the mistress of the world. And this mistress, though

---

[1] A useful account of Roman policy in regard to town-life will be found in the last chapter of W. T. Arnold's *Roman Provincial Administration*, based chiefly on the *Staatsverwaltung* of Marquardt. See also articles "Colonia" and "Fœderatæ civitates" in the last edition of Smith's *Dict. of Classical Antiquities*.

herself still in outward form a City-State, had also long ago passed beyond the limits within which it was possible to realise at its best the life of this ancient form of polity.

It will thus appear that there were two leading principles in the treatment of their conquests by the Roman oligarchy of the Republic: first, government by the Roman city magistrate, under supervision, of course, by the great oligarchical council; and secondly, local self-government within certain limits, as yet not clearly defined, by the magistrates and councils of the subject cities. For a time these two principles worked fairly well in combination; so long, that is, as the Roman oligarchy maintained its old vigour and integrity, and so long as any healthy life was left in the cities, such as might fit them for their new duties as the municipal towns of a great empire. During the greater part of the period of its growth the dominion of the Republic was so far a success that it astonished and overawed the world; it seemed as though the universal empire were at last about to be realised, spreading from the west instead of from the east. But time showed that in this case the Roman policy of adaptation was in all essential respects a failure. A City-State had been called on to undertake the government of an empire as great as Alexander's; and the machinery and the morality which it could bring to bear upon the work were alike found wanting. The machinery, — magistrates, senate, and people, — might possibly have been adequate to the task; but for the good government of

dependencies you must have more than machinery,
— you must have also conscience and self - re-
straint. The Romans might extend their civic
government and law, but they could not extend
their ancient civic virtues, to the government of
an empire.

The story of this failure of the Republican
Empire is familiar enough; I can only here allude
to the more obvious causes of it.[1] The governors
of provinces began to enrich themselves by using
their *imperium* to rob their subjects; and there
was no way found of keeping them under proper
control. The Senate, admirable in the management
of the details of war and diplomacy, could discover
no effective check on the rapacity of the governors,
and after a time they ceased to have any real
desire to do so. There was no real guarantee that
the local institutions, or even the lives and the
property, of the subject peoples would be respected
by the Roman governor; and as a matter of fact
they were often treated with the utmost contempt.
And in all cases, whether the governor were just or
unjust, whether or no he adhered to the terms on
which local government had been granted to the
cities of his province, the life of the City-State,
which had been so long decaying, was now finally
crushed out under the pressure of the Roman
imperium. True loyalty towards that *imperium*
could not grow up under such a system. There
was no solid and well-meaning government to which

[1] Read the chapter on " The Government and the Governed " in
the second vol. of Mommsen's *Hist. of Rome*.

to be loyal. There was therefore little apparent hope that a great imperial State could be constituted on a solid and permanent basis, which might embrace and protect the innumerable City-States which it had absorbed. There was no principle of unity in this great dominion,—such unity as springs from the vigorous action of a strong central power, aided by responsible subordinates in the various parts, as well as by the healthy local action of the smaller centres of which it was composed.

There were other causes too at work which made it almost impossible for this vast dominion to progress successfully towards the realisation of true political unity. There was the startling difference between the peoples of the east and the peoples of the west; between the Greeks, including all who had felt the magic of Greek civilisation, and the inhabitants of Spain and Gaul, who had as yet developed no State, no law, no art, and no literature. There was the no less startling distinction between the status of the Roman citizen, whose life and property were everywhere sacred, and the status of the citizen of a subject community, which might look in vain to the Roman governor for protection. There was again, during the whole of the last century of the Republic, constant danger from the enemies of the Roman power on its frontiers; from powerful kings like Jugurtha, Mithridates, or Ariovistus, with whom the Senate could only cope by allowing ambitious generals to continue for years in command of large armies, thus straining the machinery of the City-State far beyond its

Y

natural capacity of endurance. And lastly, there was that fatal *stasis* within the State itself of which I have already spoken, paralysing the energies of men whose attention should have been given to the work of union and defence, narrowing their views, embittering their hatreds, and making all honest discussion in the great council ever more hopeless and impossible.

If in fact we test the Roman dominion in the last century of the Republic by our definition of the State as given in chapter i., it is difficult to see in what sense it could be called a State at all. Of the natural ties it had none; neither community of race or religion, nor of common feeling and history. The common government which constitutes the chief artificial bond in a State it was indeed supposed to possess; but this government had grown to be so weakened and discredited, so beset by enemies within and without, that it could hardly be said to exist except in name. The oligarchical Senate could no longer keep its magistrates under control, and save in this Senate, to which the whole world had once looked up with reverence, there was no central unifying influence to be found. From the City-State, whether in Rome or her dependencies, there was no longer any regenerating influence to be looked for; its part in the history of the world had been played to the end. It is clear that we have come at last to the end of our story; that one City-State has sucked the life out of all the rest, and has herself lost her ancient Statehood in the gigantic effort. From this last century of the

Republic the City-State may truly be said to have ceased to exist.

Yet it was found possible to build up out of the ruins left by the older civilisation a new State of sufficient strength and unity to supply almost all the needs which in this melancholy age were most keenly felt. When the Roman Republic came to an end, leaving the whole dominion in conflict and disorder, what was most urgently needed was a great central unifying force, competent to protect against invasion from without, and against injustice and dissension from within; something to which to be loyal; something to constitute a clear visible impersonation of the majesty of the Roman government. Nor was this all. Within the State so constituted there was need for uniformly organised municipal life, in which the rights and duties of every man should be clearly laid down for him, even in the parts most distant from the centre. There was need, in short, for an order and a civilisation which, far from breaking wholly with the past, should be capable of retaining and handing on all the treasures which the City-State had accumulated,— treasures of government and legal knowledge, treasures of literature and art, of science and of philosophy.

For a few brief months before the assassination of the Dictator Cæsar an outward imperial unity was actually realised. There was a general peace, and an almost universal recognition of the pre-eminent power of a single determined ruler, who, wherever he might be in the Empire, was a centre of government far more effectual than the City-Senate of the last few generations. This extraordinary man did not live to organise the new State-unity which his military genius had forced upon the world. There is indeed sufficient proof that he was ready as well as able to put his hand to that work.[1] But assassination put an end to his endeavours, and his death was followed by a new period of confusion.

Then at last upon his foundation the mighty fabric began slowly to arise. In its first form it was almost complete at the close of the long life of Augustus. That skilful architect, with the true Roman instinct to pull down nothing that had once been erected, and with the just feeling that the Senate of the Republic could not be degraded or rudely set aside, perceived that the ruins of the great City-State of Rome might be embodied in the new structure. Later on, as men's eyes grew accustomed to the fabric that was being reared, the old fragments became more and more obscured, though they were never entirely hidden; and by the second century A.D. it may be said that the Roman Empire was an entirely new form of State, such as the world had never yet seen, and had hardly as yet hoped for.

It was not unlike that which had presented itself to the mind of Alexander, for the intellectual forces

[1] In the Lex Julia Municipalis and the Lex Rubria, regulating the municipal towns of Italy and Cisalpine Gaul. Of the former a large portion is extant; of the latter only a small but valuable fragment. Bruns, *Fontes juris Romani*, p. 91 foll. (ed. 4).

at work in it were in the main Greek, and in the
system of its construction his two leading ideas of
city-life and commercial communications were
elaborately carried out. It resembled his transient
dominion also in the fact that its centre of gravity
was no longer a City-State, but a personality,—
the personality of the Cæsar wherever he might be
in the Empire. And it had one advantage which
Alexander's empire could never have realised. It
drew its chief material strength, not from worn-out
Greece, or from an effeminate East, but from the
youth and vigour of those western peoples, the fruits
of whose civilisation have been in modern times the
most complete justification of Roman conquest.

It was not indeed a perfect system; there were
weak points inherent in it, some of which, already
indicated in this chapter, were handed on to it from
that wholly inadequate system with which the
Roman Republic had sought to govern the world.
Yet it was a real State, united together by artificial
ties of great power of endurance; and what has
proved for us even more valuable, it remained for
more than three centuries a loyal trustee of the
treasure which the City-State had bequeathed to it.
The literature, the art, the philosophy, the law,
and in great part even the religion of the
πόλις, were valued and preserved under the Roman
Empire, which thus became an indestructible bridge
uniting ancient and modern civilisation.

It is beyond the scope of this little book to
attempt to explain, even in outline, the details
of this great structure, or to point out how it

supplied the demands for unity and local organisation, which had arisen with the dissolution of the
City-State. But the Roman Empire is now attract-
ing the attention of scholars more perhaps than any
other period of history, owing to the vast accumulation of valuable evidence which the collection of inscriptions has supplied in recent years, and is still
steadily increasing; and as the work to be done is
of immense extent, and of infinite human interest,
it may be as well to conclude by indicating the
several lines on which that work must necessarily
be carried on.

First, there is the study of the new Imperial
Constitution. Here the special interest lies in
tracing the process by which the authority of the
Cæsar, based on the old *imperium*, and called by
the same name, came in time to penetrate every
department of government; and it is here more
particularly fruitful to examine the methods of provincial government, because it is in the provinces
that the unifying force of the whole system may
best be observed at work. Augustus had left the
quieter provinces in the care of the Senate, which
continued to send out its proconsuls,—relics of the
old city-magistracy,—as it had so long done under
the Republic ; while he himself, like Julius, governed
the others and watched the enemies of the State
beyond their frontiers by the agency of his own
delegates. But the student of the Empire has also
to learn how even the Senate and its executive
came to be controlled indirectly by the supreme
ruler, and how by slow degrees one senatorial pro-

vince after another passed under his immediate
authority. If we open the correspondence, most
fortunately preserved to us, between Trajan and his
friend Pliny the younger, whom he had sent out to
regulate the province of Bithynia, we get a wonder-
fully vivid picture of the working of the new
centralised government. This province had been
badly administered under senatorial rule, and was
now to be reorganised by a delegate of the emperor.
The lesson we learn from these letters is that to be
governed by the delegate was equivalent to being
governed by Trajan himself. Even at a distance
of 1000 miles Pliny writes to consult his master
on matters of the minutest detail, and invariably
receives an answer sufficiently definite to guide him.
These answers of Trajan are very brief and business-
like ; they show that he had found time to attend
to the question addressed to him, and that he had
made up his mind upon it ; while at the same time
they often leave the delegate to act on his own
discretion without needlessly hampering his freedom
of action. Nowhere can we get a better idea of
the way in which government was actually carried
on in this new form of State by an intelligent and
industrious ruler.[1]

Secondly, there is the study of the various forms
of local government within each province. We are
still learning how city-life was everywhere encouraged and organised ; how towns were formed

These letters may conveniently be consulted in Mr. E. G.
Hardy's edition ; a good example, taken at random, is letter 65,
with Trajan's reply, which follows it.

where there had been none before, whether as
Roman or Latin colonies, or as accretions round the
military stations of the legions, or by the gathering
together of smaller communities round a newly
founded centre. We are still learning how the local
institutions of all towns were regulated on the
Roman model with tolerable uniformity; how the
central authority slowly gained an increasing influence
over them; how the cities were grouped together
for purposes of administration, with the worship of
the Cæsars as a unifying factor; and how the
enjoyment of life was made possible for the inhabitants by the erection of baths, theatres, and porticoes.
All these and many others are matters of which
we have only recently come to know much or fully
to appreciate the value. To take the question of
municipal government alone, we have now several
valuable documents relating to this subject, which
have either recently been discovered, or have only
of late years been adequately interpreted,[1] besides
innumerable inscriptions of less value individually,
yet each making its contribution to our knowledge
of the whole. At any moment we may be put in
possession of something even more valuable than
any of these. The territory of the Roman Empire
is full of monuments which still lie buried beneath

---

[1] Besides the Lex Julia Municipalis already referred to we have
parts of the "Lex Coloniæ Genetivæ" (a Spanish foundation of
Cæsar's), and of the laws regulating two Spanish non-Roman towns,
Salpensa and Malaca. Bruns, *Fontes*, etc., p. 110 foll., 130 foll.
Cf. Mommsen, *Provinces of the Roman Empire*, p. 285 foll. The
whole of Mommsen's chapter vii., to which reference is here
made, may well be carefully studied in this connection.

its ruins; and it is not too much to say that if we had the whole number of inscriptions set up in any Roman town during a single century, we should have an almost perfect picture of its life and government.

Thirdly, in order fully to understand the nature of the new State and the progress towards a substantial unity of all its parts, it is necessary to have some acquaintance with the history of Roman law under the Empire, and of what is closely connected with it, the history of the incorporation of all free inhabitants into the Roman citizenship. We have seen how upon the law of the City-State (*jus civile*) was engrafted a new body of legal rules (*jus gentium*), through the agency of the prætor peregrinus, destined in time to cover all the difficulties that might arise between man and man, whether Roman or non-Roman. Strictly speaking, this new law had been administered in Rome only; in the provinces either the local communities administered their own law, or the provincial governor decided cases after his own method,—that method being often arbitrary, and not necessarily brought into harmony with the principles on which the prætor was acting at home. Only in communities of Roman or Latin citizens was the Roman law alone supreme. But even before the Republic came to an end it is probable that many non-Roman towns voluntarily adopted the Roman law. And at the same time we find the process of extending the citizenship to such towns already beginning; so that, just as Roman law had become the general law of Italy after the citizenship had been extended to all the Italians, so it now sets out on its course of extension over the whole civilised world. The process was complete in the year 212 A.D. when Caracalla gave the Roman franchise to all free inhabitants of the Empire, so that one uniform legal system was henceforward in use from Syria to Britain. And meanwhile that system was being perfected by the most illustrious series of lawyers that the world has ever seen; men from all parts of the Empire, some of whom brought the acute intelligence of the Greek to the aid of the practical good sense of the Roman legal mind.[1]

Without going further, it will be possible to gain from such studies as these some idea of the nature of the new imperial State which arose out of the scattered ruins of the older one. There are indeed other lines of research in the history of the Empire, in themselves of the deepest interest, which bear less directly on the political aspect of the age, yet reveal to us more of that life and thought of the people which is to the State itself as the circulating blood to the living animal. There is the study of the economical conditions of life in the various parts of the Empire; of the way in which land was held and cultivated, of the methods of commerce and credit, of the distribution of wealth among the various classes of society, the incidence of taxation, and the prices of the necessaries of life. Again there is the whole range of the litera-

[1] See Sohm's *Institutes of Roman Law* (translated by Ledlie), ch. ii.

ture of the Empire; a literature quite distinct from that of the vigorous youth of the City-State, when thought and action were more completely in harmony, and creative power more natural and spontaneous. The literature of the Empire is neither civic nor national; it has not the freshness and originality which civic or national life alone can give. But it reflects the life and thought of a Græco-Roman age, and whether it be Greek or Roman, the traces of ancient nationality are now merged in the consciousness of a new and cosmopolitan era. Lastly, the religious history of the Empire offers a vast field of study which has as yet been only half explored. Here, more clearly perhaps than elsewhere, we may be able to trace the gradual dissolution of the older forms of thought and life. The intensely local character of the religion of the City-State now gives place to a new religion of the world. The old city-worships,—the divine inhabitants of each individual city,—die out slowly but surely; at first, under the influence of the all-pervading worship of the Cæsars, and later, under the irresistible spell of a new religion, of which the inspiring principle was the brotherhood of all men.

The Roman Empire was at last broken up; it had its own inherent weaknesses, which increased as time went on, and rendered it incapable of further resistance to the flood of barbarism which had long been surging on its frontiers. But it had accomplished its work. Had the northern peoples swept over the Empire in the last century of the Republic, it is not impossible that the world might have lost for ever all or most of what mankind had learnt in the age of the City-State. As it was, the Roman Empire of the Cæsars held the barbarians at bay long enough to inspire them with such reverence for its own greatness, that the rich legacy which it had inherited from its forefathers of the πόλις could not be entirely dissipated in the general confusion which followed its downfall.

THE END.

Printed in the United Kingdom
by Lightning Source UK Ltd.
113410UKS00001B/4